FROM GENERATION TO GENERATION

The Health and Well-Being of Children in Immigrant Families

Donald J. Hernandez and Evan Charney, *Editors*

Committee on the Health and Adjustment of Immigrant
Children and Families

Board on Children, Youth, and Families

National Research Council
Institute of Medicine

NATIONAL ACADEMY PRESS
Washington, D.C. 1998

National Academy Press • 2101 Constitution Avenue, N.W. • Washington, D.C. 20418

NOTICE: The project that is the subject of this report was approved by the Governing Board of the National Research Council, whose members are drawn from the councils of the National Academy of Sciences, the National Academy of Engineering, and the Institute of Medicine. The members of the committee responsible for the report were chosen for their special competences and with regard for appropriate balance.

This study was supported by the U.S. Department of Health and Human Services through the Office of the Assistant Secretary for Planning and Evaluation (OASPE) under contract number 282-95-0020 and the National Institute of Child Health and Human Development (NICHD) under cooperative agreement number NO1-HD-6-3253, by the Office of Educational Research and Improvement (OERI) in the National Institute on Early Childhood Development and Education of the U.S. Department of Education, the Carnegie Corporation of New York under grant number B6347, the W.T. Grant Foundation under grant number 94160394, the Rockefeller Foundation under grant number SI9522, and the California Wellness Foundation under grant number 9700139. Any opinions, findings, conclusions, or recommendations expressed in this publication are those of the author(s) and do not necessarily reflect the view of the organizations or agencies that provided support for this project.

Library of Congress Cataloging-in-Publication Data

From generation to generation : the health and well-being of
children in immigrant families / Donald J. Hernandez and Evan
Charney, editors ; Committee on the Health and Adjustment of
Immigrant Children and Families, Board on Children, Youth, and
Families, National Research Council and Institute of Medicine.
    p. cm.
  Includes bibliographical references and index.
  ISBN 0-309-06561-5 (cloth)
  1. Children of immigrants—United States. 2. Children of
immigrants—Health and hygiene—United States. 3. Children of
immigrants—Services for—United States. 4. Child welfare—United
States. I. Hernandez, Donald J. II. Charney, Evan. III. Committee
on the Health and Adjustment of Immigrant Children and Families
(U.S.)
  HV741 .F845 1998
  305.23′086′910973—ddc21

                           98-25472
                              CIP

Additional copies of this report are available from:
National Academy Press
2101 Constitution Avenue, N.W.
Washington, D.C. 20418
Call 800-624-6242 or 202-334-3313 (in the Washington Metropolitan Area).

This report is also available on line at http://www.nap.edu

DONALD J. HERNANDEZ, *Study Director*
KATHERINE DARKE, *Research Assistant*
NANCY GEYELIN, *Research Assistant*
KAREN AUTREY, *Senior Project Assistant*

The National Academy of Sciences is a private, nonprofit, self-perpetuating society of distinguished scholars engaged in scientific and engineering research, dedicated to the furtherance of science and technology and to their use for the general welfare. Upon the authority of the charter granted to it by the Congress in 1863, the Academy has a mandate that requires it to advise the federal government on scientific and technical matters. Dr. Bruce M. Alberts is president of the National Academy of Sciences.

The National Academy of Engineering was established in 1964, under the charter of the National Academy of Sciences, as a parallel organization of outstanding engineers. It is autonomous in its administration and in the selection of its members, sharing with the National Academy of Sciences the responsibility for advising the federal government. The National Academy of Engineering also sponsors engineering programs aimed at meeting national needs, encourages education and research, and recognizes the superior achievements of engineers. Dr. William A. Wulf is president of the National Academy of Engineering.

The Institute of Medicine was established in 1970 by the National Academy of Sciences to secure the services of eminent members of appropriate professions in the examination of policy matters pertaining to the health of the public. The Institute acts under the responsibility given to the National Academy of Sciences by its congressional charter to be an adviser to the federal government and, upon its own initiative, to identify issues of medical care, research, and education. Dr. Kenneth I. Shine is president of the Institute of Medicine.

The National Research Council was organized by the National Academy of Sciences in 1916 to associate the broad community of science and technology with the Academy's purposes of furthering knowledge and advising the federal government. Functioning in accordance with general policies determined by the Academy, the Council has become the principal operating agency of both the National Academy of Sciences and the National Academy of Engineering in providing services to the government, the public, and the scientific and engineering communities. The Council is administered jointly by both Academies and the Institute of Medicine. Dr. Bruce M. Alberts and Dr. William A. Wulf are chairman and vice chairman, respectively, of the National Research Council.

Acknowledgments

The committee and staff were assisted, during the course of this study, by many researchers and other individuals who willingly shared their expertise and insights. Without their generous assistance, the committee would not have been able to complete its work.

Nearly two dozen researchers participated in the work group convened by the committee to develop new analyses of more than a dozen data sets, preparing papers that characterize the circumstances of children in immigrant and in U.S.-born families along a wide variety of dimensions. These papers are by Donald J. Hernandez and Katherine Darke (National Research Council) on socioeconomic and demographic risk factors and resources; by Nancy S. Landale, R.S. Oropesa, and Bridget K. Gorman (Pennsylvania State University) on infant health; by Fernando S. Mendoza and Lori Beth Dixon (Stanford University) on health and nutritional status; by Kathleen Mullan Harris (University of North Carolina at Chapel Hill) on the health status and risk behaviors of adolescents; by Grace Kao (University of Pennsylvania) on psychological well-being and educational achievement; by Rubén G. Rumbaut (Michigan State University) on the adaptation of children of immigrants in Southern California; by Christine Winquist Nord (Westat) and James A. Griffin (National Institute on Early Childhood Development and Education) on the educational profile of 3- to 8-year-old children; by Sandra L.

Hofferth (University of Michigan) on public assistance receipt among Mexican- and Cuban-origin children; by Peter D. Brandon (University of Massachusetts) on public assistance receipt of immigrant children and families; by E. Richard Brown, Roberta Wyn, Hogjian Yu, Abel Valenzuela, and Lianne Don (University of California at Los Angeles) on access to health insurance and health care; and by Richard Mines (U.S. Department of Labor) on children of immigrant farmworkers.

Katherine Darke planned and coordinated the committee's December 1996 workshop in Irvine, California, regarding ethnographic research on the health and well-being of immigrant children and families. A dozen presentations were made by David Hayes-Bautista (University of California at Los Angeles) on children's access to care in Los Angeles; by Ruth E. Zambrana (George Mason University) on access and use of care; by Roberta D. Baer (University of South Florida) on "folk" illnesses of children in migrant worker families; by Sylvia Guendelman (University of California at Berkeley) on prenatal care, nutrition, maternal health, and birth outcomes; by Judy Wingerd (Center for Haitian Studies) on health practices and well-being of Haitian infant-mother pairs; by Katherine M. Donato (Louisiana State University) and Shawn Malia Kanaiaupuni (University of Wisconsin at Madison) on health in Mexican-American communities in Texas; by William Arroyo (University of Southern California) on mental health and adjustment among children in refugee families from Central America; by Nestor Rodriquez (University of Houston) on trauma and stress among Central American adolescents attempting to cross the U.S. border unaccompanied by adults; by Andrea S. Moskowitz (University of California at Los Angeles) on mental health, emotional stress, and family functioning; by Keith T. Kernan (University of California at Los Angeles) on family functioning and resilience among adolescent native blacks, Belizean Creoles, and Garifuna immigrants; by Arturo Cervantes (Harvard University) on social adjustment of Mexican adolescents in Chicago; and by Ellen B. Gold (University of California at Davis) on effects of organophosphate exposure on children of migrant farmworkers.

Nearly three dozen people assisted the committee in its deliberations by providing commissioned papers and/or new data analyses in specific areas: Richard Alba (State University of New York at Albany) on assimilation in multicultural America; Ronald J. Angel (University of Texas at Austin) on health practices and beliefs; Katherine Baisden (Stanford University) on cigarettes and substance and alcohol use and abuse; David Battille (Texas Tech University) on health and adjustment of immigrant Hispanic children in Texas; Peter D. Brandon (University of Massachusetts) on public program use across generations; Claire Brindis (University of California at San Francisco) on teen pregnancy; Glorisa Canino (University of Puerto Rico) on mental health, health-seeking behavior, and culture; Cynthia Garcia Coll (Brown University) on immigration and developmental processes; Elena Fuetes-Afflick (University of California at San Francisco) on chronic and disabling conditions and a family-community model of health; Noel Chrisman (University of Washington at Seattle) on the health care seeking process; Noreen Goldman (Princeton University) on the effects of treatments on health outcomes; Peter Guarnaccia (Rutgers University) on mental health and adjustment, health care-seeking behavior, and culture; Robert Gunn (San Diego County Department of Health and Human Services Office of Community Disease Control) on sexually transmitted diseases among adolescents; Sharon Hernandez (Texas Tech University) on the health and adjustment of immigrant Hispanic children in Texas; Ray Hutchison (University of Wisconsin at Green Bay) on marriage, fertility, and education among Hmong adolescents; Grace Kao (University of Pennsylvania) on educational aspirations by generation; Frank Kessell (Social Science Research Council) on culture, health, and human development; Jonathan D. Klein (University of Rochester) on adolescent mortality; Jill E. Korbin (Case Western Reserve University) on child maltreatment among immigrant and refugee children; Peter Kunstadter (University of California at San Francisco) on health and health services among ethnic Hmong children; Maria Elena Lara (University of California at Los Angeles) on chronic and disabling conditions and a family-community model of health; Yvonne A. Maldonado (Stanford University) on the epidemiology of pediatric HIV infection and other infectious diseases; Elizabeth R. McAnarney (University of Rochester) on adolescent mortality; Michael McGinnis (scholar in residence, National Research Council) on the effects of treatments on health outcomes; Lisandro Perez (Florida International University) on health care institutions of Cuban immigrants; James M. Perrin (Harvard University) on asthma; Francisco J. Ramos-Gomez (University of California at San Francisco) on oral health; Melissa Ream (Texas Tech University) on the health and adjustment of immigrant Hispanic children in Texas; Frederick P. Rivara (University of Washington at Seattle) on unintentional injuries; Rubén G. Rumbaut (Michigan State University) on current numbers of children in immigrant families; James Sargent (Dartmouth Hitchcock Medical Center) on iron deficiency and lead poisoning; Linda M. Whiteford (University of South Florida) on health care-seeking behavior; and Min Zhou (University of California at Los Angeles) on the context of reception for the second generation.

This report has been reviewed by individuals chosen for their diverse perspectives and technical expertise, in accordance with procedures approved by the NRC's Report Review Committee. The purpose of this independent review is to provide candid and critical comments that will assist the authors and the NRC in making the published report as sound as possible and to ensure that the report meets institutional standards for objectivity, evidence, and responsiveness to the study charge. The content of the review comments and draft manuscript remain confidential to protect the integrity of the deliberative process.

We wish to thank the following individuals for their participation in the review of this report: Shirley Brice-Heath, Department of Linguistics, Stanford University, and Carnegie Foundation for the Advancement of Teaching, Menlo Park, California; Catherine R. Cooper, Departments of Psychology and Education, University of California, Santa Cruz; Ronald Feldman, School of Social Work, Columbia University; David Hayes-Bautista, Center for the Study of Latino Health, School of Medicine, University of California, Los Angeles; Eleanor E. Maccoby, Department of Psychology, Stanford University; Marcelo Suarez-Orozco, Harvard Immigration Projects, Harvard University; Rainer K. Silbereisen, College of Behavioral and Social Sciences, Jena, Germany; Ciro Sumaya, School of Rural Public Health, Texas A&M University; David Takeuchi, Department of Psychology, University of California, Los Angeles; Michael Teitelbaum, Alfred P. Sloan Foundation, New York; George Vernez, Center for Research on Immigration Policy, RAND, Santa Monica, California; Mary Waters, Department of Sociology, Harvard University; and Virginia V. Weldon, Monsanto Company, St. Louis. Although the individuals listed above have provided many constructive comments and suggestions, responsibility for the final content of this report rests solely with the authoring committee and the NRC.

The committee would like to thank Reynolds Farley and Marta Tienda for their contributions in the early stages of the committee's deliberations. The Institute for Social Research at the University of Michigan, with the leadership of its director, David L. Featherman, provided necessary resources for the work group convened by the committee to conduct new data analyses. The Population Studies Center at the University of Michigan provided access to computing facilities and to census data that were essential to the work of the committee, and Lisa Neidert of the Population Studies Center provided invaluable technical assistance in conducting analyses for this study. The National Center for Health Statistics generously assisted with data from the National Health and Nutrition Examination Survey (NHANES III); both Clifford Johnson and Susan Schober provided critical technical assistance, and Margaret Carroll conducted important special data analyses.

Funding for this study was provided by the Office of the Assistant Secretary for Planning and Evaluation (OASPE) and the National Institute of Child Health and Human Development (NICHD) in the U.S. Department of Health and Human Services. Our project officers were especially helpful; David Nielsen in OASPE and Rose Li in NICHD provided guidance and technical support, and they contributed to the development of ideas for the special analyses work group. Support was also provided by the Office of Educational Research and Improvement (OERI) in the National Institute on Early Childhood Development and Education of the U.S. Department of Education, the Carnegie Corporation of New York, the W.T. Grant Foundation, and the Rockefeller Foundation. The California Wellness Foundation is providing partial support for the dissemination of this report.

The committee also benefited from the support of many individuals at the Board on Children, Youth, and Families and the

Commission on Behavioral and Social Sciences and Education. For her prescience in conceiving the need and obtaining funding for this study long before the recent welfare reforms, for her extensive contributions to drafts of the report, and for her support and encouragement, we are indebted to Deborah A. Phillips, director of the Board on Children, Youth, and Families. Elena O. Nightingale, scholar in residence with the board, generously contributed insights and draft materials on the needs and rights of the immigrant children who may face the most severe difficulties and those who are undocumented and unaccompanied by an adult, and her enthusiasm for the study was much appreciated. Faith Mitchell drafted important materials on health status and adjustment, as did Michelle Kipke on the culturally competent provision of health care. Katherine Darke conducted literature searches that identified relevant materials throughout the study and performed numerous computer analyses of contemporary and historical census data concerning socioeconomic and demographic risk factors. Adrienne Davis, Tanya Elaine Hamilton, Jim Igoe, and Raymond W. Lemons of the National Research Council library provided essential assistance in identifying and collecting research materials. Special thanks are due to senior project assistant Karen Autrey, who provided administrative support, including meeting arrangements and preparation of several drafts of the report, to Nancy Geyelin for research assistance, and to Carole Spalding for project assistance. Thanks go to Anne Bridgman for careful readings of draft chapters and for critical guidance and planning of report dissemination, and to Nancy Geyelin for supporting the dissemination effort. The committee is indebted to our editor, Christine McShane, whose superb editorial skills contributed substantially to the organization and presentation of the committee's views. Eugenia Grohman provided invaluable guidance and assistance throughout the report review process. Most of all, we want to thank the members of the committee for their dedication and many contributions.

Evan Charney, *Chair*
Donald J. Hernandez, *Study Director*
Committee on the Health and Adjustment
of Immigrant Children and Families

Contents

Preface

Children in immigrant families figured prominently in the board's earliest discussions about critical, but neglected, areas of research and policy. They were the subject of a workshop, in September 1994, on the Invisible Immigrant Population: Young Children and Their Families, supported by The David and Lucile Packard Foundation and the National Research Council's internal funds. Appendix A provides a list of the workshop participants. The workshop participants strongly urged the board to undertake a comprehensive study of these children, in part to bring them to the forefront of attention of those who fund research and make policy on behalf of children, youth, and families.

The Board on Children, Youth, and Families of the Commission on Behavioral and Social Sciences and Education (CBASSE) of the National Research Council (NRC) and the Institute of Medicine (IOM) established the Committee on the Health and Adjustment of Immigrant Children and Families in March 1996. The committee was composed of 19 members with expertise from public health, pediatrics, child psychiatry, developmental psychology, population studies, anthropology, sociology, economics, public policy, law, and history. The committee's charge was to synthesize the relevant research literature and provide demographic descriptions of immigrant children and families; clarify what is known about the varying trajectories that now characterize the families and development of immigrant children, about the risk and protective factors associated with differential health and well-being of different immigrant groups, and about the delivery of health and social services to these groups; and assess the adequacy of existing data and make recommendations for new data collection and research needed to inform and improve public policy and programs.

In order to address the various elements of the study charge, the committee and study staff engaged in a range of information collection activities. It invited presentations and written submissions from many experts involved in immigrant policy and research. A workshop on ethnographic research on the health and well-being of immigrant children and families was held to further expand the knowledge base of the committee.

The committee also commissioned new, detailed analyses of more than a dozen existing data sets that constitute a large share of the national system for monitoring the health and well-being of the U.S. population. Because, prior to these new analyses, few of these data sets had been used to assess the circumstances of children in immigrant families, the analyses enormously expand the available knowledge about the physical and mental health status and risk behaviors, educational experiences and outcomes, and socioeconomic and demographic circumstances of first- and second-generation children, compared with those with U.S.-born parents. The results from these analyses will be published in a separate volume tentatively titled *Children of Immigrants: Health, Adjustment, and Public Assistance.*

The committee's early deliberations coincided with congressional actions that made far-reaching changes in immigrants' eligibility for public benefits, effectively reversing years' of precedent by which immigrants residing legally in the United States received most benefits on the same terms as U.S. citizens. These changes, enacted as part of welfare reform, emerged from highly contentious debates about the role of working-age immigrants in today's society—their impact on labor markets, dependence on public assistance, and contributions to the changing ethnic composition of our citizenry. Immigrant children, who will be profoundly affected, were essentially invisible in those debates. As a result, policies for children in immigrant families are being forged by default, without the benefit of an informed discussion about potential impacts on their development and future prospects.

This salient policy context lent added urgency to the work of the committee. Although we could not draw any conclusions about the recent policy changes, our work offers a critical "baseline" portrait of immigrant children prior to welfare reform against which their status can be compared in the coming years. Equally important, the committee has high hopes that this study will ensure that immigrant children will be centrally featured in future discussions of policies that shape their lives.

The well-being and development of children are a priority for all America, because they are our future and because the rapid growth in the number of children who live in immigrant families gives them special prominence. The study makes specific recommendations concerning research, data collection, and information dissemination that are intended to expand scientific knowledge about children in immigrant families and to help inform future public policy deliberations. It is the collective product of the entire committee, and it could not have been produced without the generous contributions of time, thought, and hard work of all members.

Evan Charney, *Chair*
Donald J. Hernandez, *Study Director*
Committee on the Health and Adjustment
of Immigrant Children and Families

FROM GENERATION
TO GENERATION

Executive Summary

The children of today offer a preview of the nation's future citizens, workers, and parents. One of every five children under age 18 living in the United States—that is, 14 million—is an immigrant or has immigrant parents. Available evidence suggests that, on many measures of health and well-being, they perform as well as or better than U.S.-born children with U.S.-born parents. Over time and across generations, however, as immigrant children become part of American society, many of these advantages do not appear to be sustained.

The vast majority of children in immigrant families are admitted legally or are citizens by dint of birth in the United States to parents who are immigrants. Family reunification is a cornerstone of U.S. immigration policy, and many immigrants enter as family members of U.S. residents or as spouses or children of persons who enter legally under various immigration statuses. Three-fourths of all children in immigrant families have been U.S. citizens all their lives because they were born in this country, and one-fourth immigrated to the United States from elsewhere. Since 1990, the number of children and youth in immigrant families has expanded almost seven times faster than the number in U.S.-born families.

The majority of these children are of Hispanic or Asian origin and, as such, are contributing to the growing racial and ethnic

1

diversity of the U.S. child and youth population. As the predominantly white baby-boom generation reaches retirement age, it will depend increasingly for its economic support on the productivity, health, and civic participation of adults who grew up in minority immigrant families. Indeed, the *long-term* consequences of contemporary immigration for the American economy and society will hinge more on the future prospects of children in immigrant families than on the fate of their parents.

Because of the burgeoning importance of children and youth in immigrant families to the vitality of the nation, the Committee on the Health and Adjustment of Immigrant Children and Families was appointed to conduct a study to:

• synthesize and supplement the relevant research literature and provide a demographic description of children in immigrant families,
• clarify what is known about the development of children in immigrant families regarding the risk and protective factors associated with differential health and well-being of different immigrant groups and the delivery of health and social services to these groups, and
• assess the adequacy of existing data and make recommendations for new data collection and research needed to inform and improve public policy and programs.

The committee was keenly aware throughout its deliberations that children who live in poverty—many of them racial and ethnic minorities—often experience restricted access to many of the resources, programs, and benefits that it considered specifically with respect to immigrant children and children with immigrant parents. African-American children, in particular, whose historical legacy arises from one of this nation's earliest immigration policies and from the abiding significance of race in American culture, face life chances that are often characterized by the same risks and foreclosed opportunities that are thought to apply to many immigrant children. In its calls for new research, the committee is explicit about the importance of making comparisons between today's children in immigrant families and U.S.-born black children whose immigrant ancestry is many generations removed (as well as to other children in "at risk" groups) in order to better understand the successes and failures of our nation's child and family policies and to understand fully the forces that shape successful adaptation and incorporation.

POTENTIAL INFLUENCES ON HEALTH AND ADJUSTMENT

All children share the same basic needs. Children in immigrant families are no different from others in the United States in their need for food, clothing, shelter, physical safety, psychological nurturing, health care, and education. They also share a dependence on adults in their families, communities, and governments to ensure their healthy development. And many of the factors that affect children's future opportunities for employment, stable families, and constructive roles as citizens undoubtedly affect all children similarly.

Beyond shared needs, however, the conditions associated with immigrant status have important and distinct consequences. The extent to which children in immigrant families experience healthy development and successful adjustment depends on: (1) the assets and resources they bring from their country of origin, (2) how they are officially categorized and treated by federal, state, and local governments, (3) the social and economic circumstances and cultural environment in which they reside in the United States, and (4) the treatment they receive from other individuals and from health and social institutions in the receiving community.

Most immigrant children and youth have origins in Latin America or Asia, regions with dozens of languages and enormous diversity in cultural beliefs and practices. Those who speak English or acquire English quickly—and who have parents who speak English—are likely to have an advantage as they adjust to school, attempt to fit into peer groups, and, in general, navigate within American culture. Immigrants who live in a U.S. community with a large network of family members and other people from their home country may receive substantial personal, social, and economic support, including information about medical and health services, schools, jobs, and other resources, that ease the adaptation process. Immigrants who are more isolated may face greater difficulties, although, depending on where they settle, they may avoid some of the deleterious aspects of living in the large U.S. cities where many immigrant families reside.

Immigrants also differ greatly in their reasons for migrating and in the socioeconomic resources they bring to the United States. Some arrive with limited education, seeking work as manual laborers in unskilled jobs; others may be characterized by high educational accomplishments and come in search of skilled, technical, or professional positions. Immigrants motivated by family ties may wish to join family members already in the United States or to accompany family members who are emigrating. Refugees arrive in the United States having fled war-torn or politically repressive or unstable countries and sometimes to avoid persecution or death.

Prior to passage of the Personal Responsibility and Work Opportunity Reconciliation Act of 1996 (PRWORA, hereafter referred to as welfare reform), eligibility rules for most health and welfare programs were nearly identical for legal immigrants, refugees, and native-born citizens. Under welfare reform, the extremely restrictive eligibility rules for many programs that applied historically only to illegal immigrants are now also applied to legal immigrants who arrived after August 22, 1996 (when the law was enacted), unless they become citizens, and to refugees beginning five to seven years after their arrival in the United States. In addition, the locus of many decisions affecting the eligibility of immigrant children and families for many benefits has shifted from the federal government to the states—a situation that is likely to lead to more variability in their access to benefits.

The law's impact on immigrant children will derive in large part from the programmatic reach of the new restrictions on immigrants' eligibility for public benefits, which go beyond welfare as conventionally known to encompass Medicaid, Supplemental Security Income (SSI), the Food Stamps Program, and noncash services. And yet these policy changes were made with virtually no explicit debate about their potential effects on children and without consideration of the need for new scientific evidence on these effects.

Low income is a well-documented negative risk factor for the healthy development of children generally. The income level of children in immigrant families is determined largely by the employment opportunities of their parents, although publicly funded health and social programs have historically provided a safety net for very low-income families. Since 1980, employment and real wages have declined for men with less than a college education, which includes many immigrants, and the earnings gap separating Hispanics and blacks from whites has expanded among both men and women. Children and parents in immigrant families belonging to these racial and ethnic minorities may assimilate to native minority groups and thus find their opportunities restricted in ways similar to these nonimmigrant minorities.

Children in immigrant families who belong to racial and ethnic minorities may face more or less discrimination depending on where they live, which can also affect their access not only to economic opportunities, but also to medical, health, educational, and housing resources. Access to valuable or necessary services can be facilitated for those who do not speak English well if those services are provided in the native language of immigrants or in a culturally competent fashion.

HEALTH, ADJUSTMENT, AND PROTECTIVE FACTORS

The physical and mental health of children and youth in immigrant families and the extent to which they adjust successfully to U.S. society is a very broad topic for which available evidence is sparse. Along a number of important dimensions, children in immigrant families appear to experience better health and adjustment than do children in U.S.-born families. There are important exceptions, however.

Parental reports suggest that, compared with children in U.S.-born families, children in immigrant families have fewer specific acute and chronic health problems and have lower prevalences of accidents and injuries. Rates of low birthweight and infant mortality also are lower among children born to immigrant women than to U.S.-born women. In fact, the substantial positive differential in neonatal outcomes for foreign-born women has been called an epidemiological paradox because it would be expected, based on their lower socioeconomic status and sometimes lower utilization of prenatal care, that they would have worse birth outcomes than U.S.-born women.

There may also be increased risk for some adverse health conditions: children in immigrant families from specific countries of origin may experience elevated risks from malaria, helminthic infections, congenital syphilis, hepatitis B, and drug-resistant tuberculosis. Children of migrant farmworkers may be exposed to damaging environmental toxins. And Mexican-origin children in immigrant families are considerably more likely to be reported by their parents as having poor health and dental problems, and they have been found to exhibit elevated blood lead levels.

Among adolescents overall and for most specific countries of origin studied, immigrants are less likely than U.S.-born adolescents with immigrant and U.S.-born parents to consider themselves in poor health or to have school absences due to health or emotional problems. First-generation immigrant adolescents are also less likely to report that they engage in risky behaviors, such as first sexual intercourse at an early age, delinquent or violent behaviors, and use of cigarettes and substance abuse. Yet immigrant adolescents living in the United States for longer periods of time tend to be less healthy and to report increases in risk behaviors. By the third and later generations, rates of most of these behaviors approach or exceed those of U.S.-born white adolescents. Adolescents in immigrant families also appear to experience overall levels of psychological well-being and self-esteem that are similar to, if not better than, adolescents in U.S.-born families. At the same time, however, immigrant adolescents report feeling less control over the outcomes in their own lives and less popular with their classmates.

For young children generally, success in school is fostered by family members who teach their children letters and numbers, read to them, and work on projects with them; take them on a variety of educational outings; and become involved at their children's schools. Three- to 8-year-old children in immigrant families are as likely, or only slightly less likely, as children in U.S.-born families to have parents that contribute to their educational adjustment and success in these ways. However, children in immigrant families, compared with their U.S.-born peers, are much less likely to experience the benefits of attending a prekindergarten program.

Several studies have reported that educational aspirations, grade point averages, and math test scores for adolescents in immigrant families are comparable to or higher than those for adolescents in U.S.-born families. However, Mexican-origin adolescents of all generations have grade point averages and math test scores that are substantially lower than those of white adolescents in U.S.-born families. The positive achievements of immigrant Chinese students appear to deteriorate, such that by the third generation they reach levels about the same as white adolescents in U.S.-born families.

Thus, along several important dimensions, immigrant children and youth appear to be protected from negative risks, but this advantage tends to decline with length of time in the United States and from one generation to the next. The social, economic, or cultural factors that may be responsible for providing this protection are largely unexplored and unknown. Care must be taken not to overgeneralize these findings, in light of the diversity that characterizes children from different countries of origin with different histories of migration, family circumstances, and experiences at school and in their neighborhoods.

SOCIOECONOMIC RISK FACTORS

One of the best-documented relationships in epidemiology and child development is that children who have family incomes below the poverty threshold, parents with low educational attainments, one parent or many siblings in the home, or overcrowded housing conditions are at risk of negative health, developmental, and educational outcomes. Children in immigrant families in 1990 experienced, on average, a somewhat higher poverty rate—largely attributable to the high poverty rate for first-generation immigrant children—but were less likely than children and youth in U.S.-born families to have only one parent at home and, for most countries of origin, had fathers with high rates of labor force participation. They were also, however, more likely to have many siblings, much more likely to have parents with very low educational attainments, and to live in overcrowded housing. Along each dimension, second-generation children (those born in the United States with at least one immigrant parent) experienced substantially less risk than did first-generation children (the foreign-born).

Socioeconomic risk levels differed enormously among children in immigrant families with different countries of origin. Of particular concern are children with origins in 12 specific countries that account for close to half of all children in immigrant families; their average poverty rates exceed 25 percent; their parents tend to have very little formal education; and they are at high risk of living in overcrowded housing. Interestingly, poverty within this subgroup of countries was not consistently related to low rates of labor force participation by fathers or to living in a single-parent family or a family with many siblings. Many officially recognized refugees come from five of these countries (the former Soviet Union, Cambodia, Laos, Thailand, and Vietnam) and immigrants from four of these countries have fled countries experiencing war or political instability (El Salvador, Guatemala, Nicaragua, and Haiti). Two are small countries sending many migrants seeking unskilled work (Honduras and the Dominican Republic). The 12th country is Mexico, which currently sends the largest number of both legal and illegal immigrants and which has been a major source of unskilled labor for the U.S. economy throughout the twentieth century.

RISK FACTORS SPECIFIC TO IMMIGRANTS

Lack of English fluency and other cultural differences may not pose enormous difficulties for immigrants in communities with a large number of individuals from the same country of origin, but they can limit their effective functioning in the broader society in health facilities, schools, and other settings that provide essential resources to children in immigrant families. Children from the 12 countries noted above with especially high socioeconomic risks are highly likely to live in linguistically isolated households in which no one age 14 and over speaks English very well. Overall, the proportion of children with non-English-speaking parents today is similar to the level at the turn of the century. Nevertheless, there is considerable documentation of the very rapid rate at which immigrant children and youth acquire English proficiency.

Access to needed services may be further complicated by cultural beliefs that differ from Western concepts, most notably with regard to perceptions of illness, health care-seeking behavior, and response to treatment. In recognition of these facts, the medical community through its major professional arms has repeatedly called for the provision of services that are provided in a culturally competent and sensitive manner and that take language barriers into account. Implementation of these ideals, however, remains limited and data regarding the health consequences of culturally sensitive practices remain largely anecdotal or based on small, nonrepresentative samples.

PUBLIC ASSISTANCE AND HEALTH SERVICES: PARTICIPATION AND USE

Benefits and services provided by health and social programs, whether from public or private sources, represent important investments in and critical resources for all children and youth, including but not restricted to those in immigrant families. Prior to welfare reform, children in immigrant families were about as likely as, or only slightly more likely than, children in U.S.-born families to live in families receiving public assistance, particularly noncash assistance. Most of the differences that existed reflected higher participation for first-generation children.

The comparatively high rates of reliance on public assistance among first-generation families are largely attributable to their disadvantaged socioeconomic and demographic characteristics, not to their immigrant status per se. When comparisons are made between children in immigrant and U.S.-born families at the same socioeconomic levels, either the differences disappear, or children in immigrant families, including those of Mexican origin, are found to rely less on many public assistance programs than children in U.S.-born families. In addition, the special refugee status of many immigrants from Southeast Asia and the former Soviet Union appears to involve comparatively high participation rates for the first generation.

Access to health services, particularly for children, is essential to ensure that preventive services are provided as recommended, acute and chronic conditions are diagnosed and treated in a timely manner, and health and development are adequately monitored so that minor health problems do not escalate into serious and costly medical emergencies. Access, in turn, is facilitated by health insurance coverage and having a usual source of care.

Immigrant children and youth are three times as likely and second-generation children and youth are twice as likely, compared with the third and later generation, to lack health insurance coverage, mainly because of its high cost and lack of employer coverage. Even among children whose parents work full-time, year-round, those in immigrant families are less likely to be insured than those in U.S.-born families. Hispanic children are the most likely of all immigrant groups studied to lack health insurance.

Medicaid has played an important role in reducing the risk of uninsurance among children and youth in immigrant families, with about one in four receiving their coverage through this source. Moreover, in large part due to the automatic eligibility of refugees for Medicaid, Southeast Asian children exhibit very low rates of uninsurance despite their very low socioeconomic status.

Immigrant children—regardless of whether they are Hispanic, Asian, or white—are considerably less likely than U.S.-born children with either immigrant or U.S.-born parents to have had at least one doctor's visit during the previous 12 months. They are also less likely to have a usual health care provider or source of health care. Children in immigrant families who are uninsured are less likely to have a connection to the health care system than those with Medicaid or private or other coverage. Those who are uninsured and who have no usual source of care have the lowest probability of having seen a doctor.

These associations replicate those found in the pediatric health services literature for children in general, suggesting that the health of children in immigrant and U.S-born families depends on the same factors and benefits from the same supports. It is thus of particular concern that, unlike any other group of children in the United States, those in immigrant families have been barred from eligibility for Medicaid, Supplemental Security

Income, and, in all likelihood, the new State Child Health Insurance Program (SCHIP) that is designed to extend coverage to children not presently eligible for existing health benefits.

THE LIMITS TO CURRENT KNOWLEDGE

Valid conclusions about differences across generations for children from diverse countries of origin require that they be identified according to their own and their parents' countries of birth and their immigrant and citizenship status. Such inferences also require sample sizes by generation, immigrant status, and country of origin that are large enough to support statistically reliable estimates.

Meaningful conclusions about the circumstances and causal processes affecting children in immigrant families require, in addition, the identification and measurement of those aspects of the immigrant experience, context, and culture that are unique to immigrants, as well as those factors that are relevant to the healthy development of all children living in the United States. Few national information systems currently collect the full array of data needed on country of origin and immigrant status, few have samples large enough to support conclusions for more than three or four specific countries of origin, and none has progressed significantly in collecting information on aspects of healthy development and adjustment that may be unique to children in immigrant families. Thus, most conclusions regarding children in immigrant families in the United States must be viewed as first steps toward acquiring more definitive knowledge.

In this context, our recommendations for new research and data collection are intended to lead to increased knowledge in a wide range of areas, including the extent to which and the reasons that (1) high poverty and other socioeconomic and demographic risk factors among children in immigrant families do or do not lead to negative outcomes, compared with children in U.S.-born families, (2) beneficial circumstances and outcomes for children in immigrant families appear to deteriorate over the life course and across generations, and (3) recent and continuing changes in welfare and health care policy have positive or negative consequences for children in immigrant families.

RECOMMENDATIONS FOR RESEARCH

Recommendation 1. The federal government should fund a longitudinal survey of children and youth in immigrant families, measuring physical and psychosocial development and the range of contextual factors influencing the development of these children.

The healthy development, assimilation, and adjustment of children in immigrant families involves developmental issues and processes that are in some ways different from the experience of children in U.S.-born families. Yet many commonalities exist, and the assimilation and adaptation experience occurs within the same broad social, economic, and cultural context for children in both immigrant and U.S.-born families.

Trajectories of healthy development, assimilation, and adjustment occur across periods of years or decades for individuals, and the nature of individual outcomes depends on the timing and sequencing of specific personal, family, neighborhood, and historical events in the child's life. These are best measured and analyzed through longitudinal data collection and research that follows the same individuals over extended periods. No existing research effort provides an adequate basis for a national assessment of these issues. Moreover, several of the most intriguing findings in the current literature on immigrant children—notably those pertaining to unexpected positive outcomes and deteriorating outcomes over time—require longitudinal data and substantial contextual information if their causes and pathways are to be clarified.

In addition, it is critical that the sampling strategy of the survey allows for explicit comparisons not only among the various immigrant groups, but also to U.S.-born black, Hispanic, and white children with U.S.-born parents so that lessons can be learned about policies and practices that either have worked or failed for different groups of children in the United States. Only with appropriate comparison groups will knowledge about the development of children in immigrant families be placed in the context of the range of experiences and outcomes experienced by native groups and, particularly by minority children whose immigrant origins are generations removed.

Recommendation 2. A series of ethnographic studies on the physical and mental health of children and youth in diverse immigrant families should, insofar as possible, be embedded in the proposed longitudinal survey of children in immigrant families or in other national surveys.

The proposed longitudinal survey of children in immigrant families can provide statistically reliable estimates of major outcomes and processes for children in immigrant families as a whole, and for important social and cultural subgroups. But survey methodology is limited in its ability to study the meaning and interpretation that individuals give to their situations.

Ethnographic studies have small samples that may not statistically represent the larger population, but they can provide rich interpretations of the processes that can only be highlighted, not probed in depth, with survey methodology. The origins and effects of health-promoting behaviors; individual, family, and community coping strategies; and the role of biculturalism in child development are examples of issues that lend themselves to this methodology.

Recommendation 3. Both quantitative and qualitative research should be conducted on the effects of welfare and health care reform for children and youth in immigrant families, and on how access to and effectiveness of health care and other services are affected by the provision of culturally competent care.

The consequences of recent and continuing changes in welfare and health policies may be more immediate and profound for children in immigrant families than for others because eligibility has been cut most drastically, or made a state option, for noncitizen legal immigrants. Yet none of the major evaluations of welfare and health reform is focused particularly on consequences for children in immigrant families, nor have these children been identified as a major subgroup for study. At a minimum, efforts to assess the consequences of health and welfare reforms need to include substantial subsamples of children in immigrant families. They should also pay attention to factors uniquely relevant to outcomes for these children, such as their circumstances of migration, the duration of child and parental residence in the United States, and the immigrant status of siblings and parents.

The need for care to be provided in a culturally competent manner, including immigrant involvement in programs for their own care, has being widely recognized by numerous federal and international health agencies and professional associations of physicians, nurses, and social workers. Efforts supported by federal and state governments, professional organizations, and health care institutions should be systematically assessed to provide the basis for implementing and evaluating community intervention programs that are also culturally sensitive.

RECOMMENDATIONS FOR DATA COLLECTION AND INFORMATION DISSEMINATION

Recommendation 4. The federal government should collect and code information on country of birth, citizenship status, and parents' country of birth in key national data collection systems. This information should be made available through public use microdata samples and other vehicles for public distribution of data.

Federal agencies currently conduct or fund major data collection and research efforts that constitute the core of the national information system for monitoring and understanding changes in the physical and mental health of the U.S. population, as well as the circumstances and risk factors related to the family, education, employment, income, participation in public benefit programs, housing, and crime. Despite the growing importance of children in immigrant families to the well-being of the nation, few of these information-gathering efforts provide a sound basis for monitoring changes in the conditions and needs of children in immigrant families, as distinct from children in U.S.-born families, because immigration and citizenship status and country of origin are not collected or are not made available for research purposes.

Recommendation 5. As the federal government develops new surveys or draws new samples to supplement or extend existing surveys, it should select and include subsamples that are large enough to reliably monitor the circumstances of children and youth in immigrant families as a whole and, where feasible, for specific countries of origin.

New samples are drawn periodically for continuing surveys and will be drawn for new national surveys in the future. Despite growth of the immigrant population, samples in most national surveys are too small to sustain statistically reliable estimates for the foreign-born population as a whole. This difficulty can be resolved by drawing samples in which the foreign-born and their families represent a larger proportion than they are in the general population.

Recommendation 6. Key indicators of child well-being published in the annual report of the Federal Interagency Forum on Child and Family Statistics should, insofar as possible, distinguish among foreign-born immigrant children (first generation), U.S.-born children in immigrant families (second generation), and U.S.-born children in U.S.-born families (third and later generations).

Children in immigrant families are the fastest-growing component of the child population, and often their language and culture make them a distinguishable minority group. Although a recent presidential executive order mandates the Federal Interagency Forum on Child and Family Statistics to publish an annual report on children (U.S. Department of Health and Human Services, 1996, 1997), as yet there is virtually no public dissemination of information on even the most basic indicators of the conditions and well-being of children in immigrant families. We recommend that key indicators of child well-being published in this report should distinguish insofar as possible between immigrant children, U.S.-born children in immigrant families, and U.S.-born children in U.S.-born families.

CHAPTER 1

Children in
Immigrant Families

N o group of children in America is expanding more rapidly than those in immigrant families. During the seven years from 1990 to 1997, the number of children in immigrant families grew by 47 percent, compared with only 7 percent for U.S.-born children with U.S.-born parents. By 1997, nearly one of every five (14 million) children was an immigrant or had immigrant parents. More than three-fourths of children in immigrant families have been U.S. citizens all their lives because they were born in this country, and fewer than one-fourth immigrated to the United States from another country.

The physical and mental health of children in immigrant families is consequential for their civic participation, labor force productivity, and quality of parenting in the coming years and decades. Whether they experience healthy development and successful adaptation to life in 21st-century America will profoundly affect their roles as future citizens, workers, and parents.

CHARGE AND SCOPE OF THE STUDY

Despite the importance of children in immigrant families to the social and economic future of the United States, existing scientific research on them is disturbingly sparse. For this reason, the Committee on the Health and Adjustment of Immigrant Children and Families was charged with three tasks:

- To synthesize the relevant research literature and present results from secondary analyses of existing data sets (see National Research Council and Institute of Medicine, 1998) to provide demographic descriptions of children in immigrant families;
- To clarify what is known about the varying trajectories that now characterize the families and the development of immigrant children, about the risk and protective factors associated with the differential health and well-being of different immigrant groups, and about the delivery of health and social services to these groups; and
- To assess the adequacy of existing data and make recommendations for new data collection and research to inform and improve public policy and programs.

A large and complex array of conditions can influence the physical and mental health of children, and factors associated with immigration expand the range and complexity of these conditions. Their health and adjustment cannot be addressed without attending to the factors relevant to all children generally; insofar as possible, this report discusses ways in which these factors are similar or different for children in immigrant families and U.S.-born children in U.S.-born families. But we are especially interested in the circumstances that may be particularly relevant to these children, as well as those that may vary greatly across children whose families hail from different continents or countries.

This report does not address many important issues of immigration processes and policies that are not directly linked to the health and adjustment of children in immigrant families, nor does it explore in detail the processes influencing the physical and mental health of children and adolescents generally. For example, the report does not assess the economic, demographic, or fiscal effects of immigration (see National Research Council, 1997). It does not provide an analysis of why the recent changes in welfare policy for immigrants came about, or of their possible effects on future immigrant streams, return migration, or trends in the number of immigrants seeking citizenship. The report does not provide a detailed assessment of the causes or reasons for immigration to the United States. It also does not address issues related to foreign adoption.

Similarly, although poverty and violence impose major burdens on health—burdens shared by people in developing and developed countries alike (Institute of Medicine, 1997)—this report does not review or analyze in detail the mechanisms by which poverty or violence foster physical, psychological, or social difficulties among children and youth. Because many children in immigrant families live in poverty or may be exposed to violence, however, and because poverty and exposure to violence can profoundly affect health, this report does discuss experience with such conditions among children in immigrant families.

Although the movement of people across national borders, not only through migration but also through tourism and international commerce, is inevitably associated with transfers of health risks, such as infectious diseases, contaminated foods, terrorism, and legal or banned toxic substances, the primary focus of this report on children precludes discussion of these issues. A recent report by the Institute of Medicine (1997) discusses the critical need for major research efforts devoted to identifying the relationships linking international movements, poverty, and health.

Finally, the history and major sources of support for this study led to a focus on health care and social welfare policies for children in immigrant families. As a result, the report does not address the many critical issues facing education policy for them. The report also does not provide a thorough analysis of their educational progress. It does, however, include some discussion of achievement outcomes in the context of assessing their adjustment (see Chapter 3). In the committee's judgment, these issues warrant a thorough analysis in light of relevant emerging new research and proposed major shifts in state education policy for children in immigrant families.

THE POLICY CONTEXT

In this context, children in immigrant families are an important focus of attention for a number of interrelated reasons, discussed below.

Future Population Growth

Children in immigrant families now have a dominant role in future U.S. population growth. Today, the fertility rate in the United States is near or below the level required to replace the population, and the baby-boom generation is moving beyond childbearing ages. Therefore, most future growth in the population of the United States will occur primarily through immigration and through births to immigrants and their descendants (Rumbaut, 1998b).

In fact, largely because most immigrants belong to Hispanic or nonwhite racial and ethnic minorities, Census Bureau projections indicate that the proportion of children under age 18 who are white and non-Hispanic[1] will decline steadily and rapidly, from about 69 percent in 1990 to 50 percent in 2030 (Day, 1993). Conversely, by 2030, children who are Hispanic, black, or some other racial minority will constitute the other half of the childhood population of the United States, growing from 30 percent in 1990. As the white majority becomes the numerical minority, America's well-being will increasingly depend on the children

---

[1]In its data collection activities, the U.S. Bureau of the Census uses a race question that distinguishes whites, blacks, American Indians, Asian and Pacific Islanders, and various subgroups, as well as a Hispanic-origin question that distinguishes Mexicans, Puerto Ricans, Cubans, and other Spanish/Hispanic origin from non-Hispanic origin. Non-Hispanic whites are persons categorized as both white and not of Hispanic origin. Throughout this report, the term "white" is used to refer to persons who are non-Hispanic white.

Population projections for ethnic groups are not necessarily accurate predictions of the future population, but are based on reasonable assumptions at the time they are made. For a discussion of the limitations of standard projection procedures, including the issues of intermarriage and the attribution of race and ethnicity to persons with multiple ancestries, as well as an alternative procedure and projections, see National Research Council (1997).

who today live in immigrant families and on the children they will bear as adults.

Geography

The U.S. immigrant population is concentrated in a handful of states and in less than a dozen major metropolitan areas. In 1990, 76 percent of immigrants arriving in the United States in the 1980s resided in only six states: California, New York, Texas, Florida, New Jersey, and Illinois (National Research Council, 1997).

Accordingly, children in immigrant families show pronounced geographic concentrations. In 1990, California accounted for 35 percent of all children in immigrant families, followed by New York, Texas, Florida, Illinois, and New Jersey, at 12, 11, 7, 5, and 4 percent, respectively, for a total of 74 percent in six states. An additional seven states had at least 2 percent of all children in immigrant families: Arizona, Massachusetts, Michigan, Ohio, Pennsylvania, Virginia, and Washington. Three less populous states also had comparatively high proportions (higher than the national average) of children in immigrant families: Hawaii, Rhode Island, and Nevada. These 16 states accounted for 84 percent of all children in immigrant families (Hernandez and Darke, 1998).

Demographic Context

The increasing racial and ethnic diversity of the U.S. population due to immigration and differential birth rates among immigrants will occur in the context of an aging population. Between 1990 and 2040, as the population of children is becoming more racially and ethnically diverse, the proportion of children in the total population is projected to decline from 26 to 23 percent. Although increased racial and ethnic diversity will occur at all ages, greater increases will occur at younger ages. Projections indicate that, by 2040, 75 percent of the elderly will be white, compared with 59 percent of working-age adults and 50 percent for children. As a result, the growing elderly population will depend increasingly for its economic support on the productive activities of working-age adults who are members of racial or ethnic minorities.

Welfare Reform

Welfare reform is another major reason for the importance of an increasing focus on immigrant children and families. The Personal Responsibility and Work Opportunity Reconciliation Act (PRWORA) of 1996 fundamentally altered the nature of the safety net for people in need. The ramifications of the new law are particularly far-reaching for legal resident immigrants, including children, who arrived in the United States after August 1996, eliminating their eligibility for many programs until and unless they become U.S. citizens.

As discussed in Chapter 4, the law's impact on children in immigrant families derives in large part from new restrictions on a wide range of benefits, including income assistance, Medicaid, Supplemental Security Income (SSI), the Food Stamp Program, and noncash services. Moreover, the devolution of responsibilities from the federal to state governments implies that eligibility for and access to publicly funded health, medical, and social services by children in immigrant families will depend increasingly on decisions and investments of state and local governments. States now have discretion in determining eligibility for many programs for immigrants residing in the United States prior to August 1996. Because children in immigrant families are concentrated in a few states, and a small number of states have comparatively high proportions of children living in immigrant families, the eligibility rules in these states will be critical both to these children and to state expenditures. Major public policy research is needed to focus on the consequences of this significant departure from prior policy.

THE SCIENTIFIC CONTEXT

The health and development of children in immigrant families are severely understudied issues. Little attention has been paid to them in studies of immigrants and their assimilation, and they have been virtually invisible in the developmental research literature (Booth et al., 1997; Buriel, 1994; Garcia Coll and Magnuson, 1997; Laosa, 1990, 1997; Rumbaut, 1997a). The absence of a research literature specifically on children in immigrant families posed a major challenge to the committee's inquiry into their circumstances, well-being, and life prospects.

In our efforts to develop recommendations to fill this large gap, the committee examined key concepts and recent advances in four research traditions that have the potential to inform the development of a knowledge base on children in immigrant families: (1) immigration and assimilation, (2) the development of minority children, (3) life-course development, and (4) risk and protective factors in development. This research extends across the disciplinary boundaries of the behavioral and social sciences and embraces cross-national networks of investigators. It provides a bridge to the long-standing research on immigration and suggests the structure of an emerging research enterprise focused on children in immigrant families. We briefly describe key developments in these research traditions that the committee views as relevant to understanding the development of these children.

Immigration and Assimilation

The concept of assimilation has been at the center of research on U.S. immigration since the turn of the century (Gordon, 1964; Park and Burgess, 1924; Warner and Srole, 1945). Both the terminology of assimilation and research in this area have been controversial, in part due to their close ties to the politics of race. Studies of assimilation have traditionally focused on the experiences of adults and, accordingly, have not been influenced by nor have exerted influence on theory in child development. Research on children in immigrant families has the potential to bring theory and research on assimilation and development into closer alignment and thereby enhance research on immigrants of all ages.

Historically, study of the assimilation of immigrants to the United States involved the study of European ethnic groups in American society. This literature conceived of assimilation not only as taking place within a single immigrant generation, but also as a process occurring over the course of successive generations (Alba and Nee, 1997; Gans, 1992; Lieberson, 1973). Assimilation was operationalized primarily by examining educational and economic attainments, as well as intermarriage and child-bearing behavior (Chiswick, 1977, 1978, 1986; Lieberson and Waters, 1988; Neidert and Farley, 1985; Warner and Srole, 1945).

Early literature also pointed to the persistence of diverse outcomes and distinct ethnic subcultures (Gordon, 1964; Lieberson and Waters, 1988; Lind, 1995), cautioning that assimilation does not occur at the same pace or even in the same direction for all immigrants. Accordingly, research in this area employed a comparative historical approach that examined differing contexts of ethnic contact, competition, conflict, and assimilation (Shibutani and Kwan, 1965).

Following in this tradition, the literature on more recent immigrants examines ways in which the outcomes of the assimilation process are affected by the changing opportunities for upward mobility and social integration that different immigrants confront (Alba and Nee, 1997; Borjas, 1995; Gans, 1992; Nee et al., 1994; Lalonde and Topel, 1991; Rumbaut, 1997b). Recent evidence linking declining health and mental health outcomes among immigrants to length of time in the United States (Guendelman and Abrams, 1995; Marks et al., 1990; Rumbaut and Weeks, 1996) has, in particular, spurred research that considers the adaptation process as one of "segmented" assimilation to the cultural practices, health behaviors, and economic fortunes that characterize different sectors of American society (Alba and Nee, 1996; Lalonde and Topel, 1991; Portes, 1996; Rumbaut, 1997a).

This contemporary literature suggests that society's incorporation of the children of immigrants today is likely to take different pathways, depending on a variety of conditions and contexts, vulnerabilities, and resources. The new immigration is characterized by enormous variation in ethnic and socioeconomic background, neighborhood contexts, and the opportunities for work experience and education. At the turn of the century, most jobs required low levels of skill, but the expanding urban-industrial economy provided opportunities for upward economic mobility, and high levels of intergenerational assimilation may have been related to the subsequent low levels of immigration. For recent immigrants with limited education and skills who are entering an economy with many jobs that require high educational attainments, their opportunities for upward economic mobility may be more limited, and continuing immigration may slow assimilation.

As a result, rather than being a homogenizing experience, assimilation may produce highly divergent trajectories among different immigrant groups, with some experiencing upward mobility and others experiencing persistent poverty and other detrimental outcomes (Portes and Rumbaut, 1996; Portes and Zhou, 1993; Rumbaut, 1994b). Moreover, the assimilation process may not be uniform in terms of variations in health and nutrition, acquisition of English, educational and economic attainments, and cultural experiences.

Points of intersection between research on assimilation and models of development can be readily identified. Certainly, the economic, linguistic, and social assimilation of immigrant parents will influence the well-being of their children and the likelihood that they will successfully adapt to American society. Immigrant parents who experience economic assimilation are more able to provide the material, social, and cultural resources that facilitate the successful adaptation of their children. However, in the absence of economic assimilation, the harsher material circumstances and sociocultural isolation of immigrants locked into low-paying jobs may impede successful adaptation by their children. It is clearly important to study separately the well-being and adaptation of children of more highly educated immigrants who experience more rapid economic assimilation and that of children whose parents enter the United States with less education and fewer skills.

Knowledge about the actual adaptation patterns of the children of immigrants and how they relate to the assets, circumstances, and fortunes of their parents is quite fragmentary. Studies of the children, more so than of their parents, raise important issues about how development and adaptation to American society are affected by the process of migration (Laosa, 1984). For example, how does age at entry and level of schooling affect assimilation? Research on children in immigrant families has identified their responses to acculturative stress as central to their adaptation in other arenas, ranging from school engagement and achievement to mental health (Chud, 1982; Cooper et al., 1994; Laosa, 1989, 1997). Yet little is known about subjective aspects of their experiences (for example, modes of ethnic self-identification, aspirations for the future, intergenerational cohesion or conflict within families) and how these may be related to more objective indices of adaptation, such as school performance and English acquisition (Rumbaut, 1994b).

Finally, Buriel and De Ment (1997) have proposed that the family acculturates as a unit and conditions the acculturation of individual members, suggesting the need for family-level and longitudinal studies of children's assimilation and the effects on their health and well-being. As noted by Rumbaut (1997a:498), "Becoming American . . . may well turn out to be a lifelong occupation [suggesting] the importance of applying a life-course perspective to the analysis of social change and individual identity."

Racial and Ethnic Stratification and the Development of Minority Children

The integration of immigrants into American society is not only a matter of education and economics. It is also profoundly affected by processes of racial and ethnic stratification. At the beginning of the 20th century, most immigrants came from Europe. Despite the enormous racial differences perceived at the turn of the century to separate northwest and southeast Europeans (U.S. Immigration [Dillingham] Commission, 1911), this earlier wave of immigrants has been characterized by high levels of intergenerational assimilation. Today, most immigrants come from Latin America, the Caribbean, and Asia and are racially classified as Asians, blacks, Hispanics, or whites, using American norms that may be quite different from the racial and ethnic stratification systems in their homelands (Alba, 1990; McDaniel, 1995).

The processes through which race and ethnicity affect the assimilation of today's immigrants are poorly understood. Research has been based largely on models developed for U.S.-born minority populations, which focus on understanding the lingering effects of the "failed assimilation" of Africans brought to the United States through practices of slave trading or immigrating voluntarily but becoming absorbed into the category of "black American." This literature has focused on the role of discrimination, residential segregation, and racial differences in educational attainment, labor force attachment, and marital, childbearing, and criminal behavior, which are viewed as both fostering and resulting from racial stratification. But it is increasingly accepted that immigrants, as well as U.S.-born minorities, assimilate as members of different racial and ethnic groups and that this has vast implications for their life chances in the context of racially and ethnically based social hierarchies in the United States (Alba and Nee, 1997; Borjas, 1995; Gans, 1992; Keith and Herring, 1991; Lalonde and Topel, 1991; McDaniel, 1995; Nee et al., 1994; Rumbaut, 1997b; Telles and Murguia, 1990).

Critical to understanding the role of racial and ethnic stratification in the adjustment of immigrants to American culture and society is the issue of identity formation. Recent research on ethnic identity formation has focused on social learning experiences, through which children learn about their race and ethnicity starting at very young ages. These experiences may involve exposure to discrimination and, in turn, shape children's understanding of their racial and ethnic identity and its implications for self-appraisals over the life course (Garcia Coll et al., 1996; Rumbaut, 1994b; 1997a, 1997b; Spencer and Markstrom-Adams, 1990). The work of Rumbaut and his colleagues has called attention to the complexity of identity development among immigrant children and youth (Rumbaut, 1994b, 1998b). The ethnic identities of these children range from a plain "American" identity to national-origin (e.g., "Cuban") and pan-ethnic (e.g., "Asian") identities and often evolve over the course of development. Moreover, these more detailed categories of ethnic identity have been found to predict patterns of school achievement and aspirations. The roles of bilingualism and second-language acquisition are also critical issues, not only in identity formation, but also in understanding family processes, adaptation to and performance in school, and peer relations (National Research Council and Institute of Medicine, 1997).

Although this research highlights strengths as well as signs of trouble and deprivation in multicultural and minority populations, it has not focused on the development of children in immigrant families. One notable exception is the emerging literature on biculturalism and multiculturalism (Buriel, 1984, 1994; Buriel and De Ment, 1997; Chud, 1982; Gutierrez and Sameroff, 1990;

Ogbu, 1994; Szapocznik and Kurtines, 1980). This literature poses the intriguing question of when does the ability to function effectively in two or more cultures act to enhance or impede development. For example, does it lead to an expanded repertoire of coping strategies? Or, in contrast, does it produce identity confusion and conflicts within families? To date, research on biculturalism suggests that children in immigrant families who are able to accept both their own and the new host cultures are more likely to be well-adjusted and to achieve in school (Buriel, 1994). But this very new literature focuses primarily on limited samples of Mexican-origin immigrants, with few replicated findings. Other evidence suggests that bilingualism has a positive effect on child school achievement only until the immigrant parents themselves achieve a moderate level of English language proficiency (Mouw and Xie, 1997).

The recent resurgence of research on minority children may provide insights into the development of today's children in immigrant families, who are primarily of Hispanic and Asian origins. This literature similarly faces the triple challenge of distinguishing developmental mechanisms that are unique or more prominent for racial and ethnic minority children from those that characterize development for all children, understanding diversity within minority populations, and disentangling the consequences of minority status from those of its strong association with poverty.

Research on minority children also provides a compelling illustration of the importance of understanding the factors that contribute to widely varying outcomes within groups (McLoyd, 1990; McLoyd and Randolph, 1984). Variables that best explain differences in achievement *within* certain minority groups, for example, are sometimes different from those that best explain differences *between* groups (Howard and Scott, 1981). However, because research to date has been limited mainly to a single minority group—blacks—information about the extent to which processes are similar or different for other minority groups or immigrant populations awaits future research.

Life-Course and Ecological Models of Development

The field of developmental psychology, with its legacy of longitudinal research (see Block, 1971; Eichorn et al., 1981; Elder, 1974; Holahan et al., 1995; Kagan and Moss, 1962) and closely aligned theories of social ecology (Bronfenbrenner, 1979, 1992; Bronfenbrenner and Ceci, 1994) and life-course and life-span development (Baltes et al., 1997; Elder, 1997; Featherman and Lerner, 1985), has brought concepts of time and place to the forefront of how development is now understood to unfold—concepts that have obvious significance and perhaps special meaning for the study of children in immigrant families. These literatures have highlighted the critical importance of studying children as they develop over years or decades and across the changing social contexts of families, neighborhoods, local institutions, government policies, and social, economic, and cultural systems. They have also identified the need to pay special attention to the order and timing of events and social roles as they are experienced over the course of individual and intergenerational development, and to focus on transitional events and periods as windows for gaining insights into successful or unsuccessful responses to changing life circumstances.

The ecological approach highlights the embedded nature of both individuals and institutions that affect children's development. Family members, friends, caregivers, and teachers, as well as the nature of relationships among these individuals in the immediate, everyday environment, affect children's development and well-being. More broadly, the policies and practices of local social institutions, such as town or state governments, schools, places of worship, and the local media, can affect child development directly or by influencing activities and relationships among people in the child's immediate environment. Finally, at the broadest level, the national government, international organizations, transnational processes, and economic, religious, and cultural systems can influence child outcomes by affecting the nature and availability of resources and by shaping processes at the local, family, and individual level.

Life-course theory, which emerged in the 1960s in part from the increasing recognition that children who grow up in different historical times and places experience distinct contexts for development (Elder, 1997), has brought to the study of human development a temporal view of individual development across *historical* time and changing environments. These time- and place-bound contexts, in turn, shape the particular adversities and opportunities that impinge on and influence children's development.

As the research of Elder and his colleagues illustrates, children growing up in families affected by the Great Depression (Elder, 1974) or the farm crisis of the 1980s (Conger and Elder, 1994) show patterns of development that can be explained only when traced back to their age, family circumstances, and surrounding social relationships at the time these socioeconomic events occurred. The life-span perspective (Baltes and Brim, 1979; Baltes et al., 1997; Featherman, 1983) has demonstrated that individuals change and adapt not only during childhood but also into the middle and elderly years, thereby extending the time lines for longitudinal research and explicitly linking research on children in immigrant families to more prominent concerns about the economic fortunes and assimilation of adult immigrants.

By linking societal and historical changes to individual lives and providing conceptual models and strategies for studying these links as they shape family dynamics, social roles, and child development over time, contemporary theories of development bear directly on the lives of children in immigrant families. Their lives are inextricably tied to particular historical and political events in both their countries of origin and in the United States; to immigration and resettlement transitions experienced by them, their parents, or their grandparents; and to the context of their receiving communities and the roles they assume within these communities.

Researchers who have studied children in immigrant families agree that more explicit attention is needed to their migration histories, social norms and cultural traditions in both sending and receiving communities, and the changing social-familial roles that often accompany the migration experience (Garcia Coll and Magnuson, 1997; Laosa, 1997). Unfortunately, the focus of study in this fledgling area of research has been on negative outcomes and obvious stresses associated with the transitions of migration and resettlement, rather than on normative experiences or processes that lead to differential outcomes (Laosa, 1997). As a consequence, research has largely overlooked the children who successfully adapt—presumably the majority of them—despite the presence of challenging circumstances.

Little disagreement exists that migration from one country to another is stressful (Desjarlais et al., 1995; Laosa, 1990, 1997). However, the conditions surrounding the decision to migrate as well as the migration process itself—including who (if anyone) accompanies the child, family resources, and the response of the receiving community—are likely to produce varying outcomes for both children and their families. Changes that reverberate from the migration experience, such as the dissolution of and need to reestablish supportive interpersonal bonds, and cultural differences across family members in gender and generational role expectations that can produce marital and parent-child tensions, also warrant study over time (Garcia Coll and Magnuson, 1997).

The wide range of policies that flow from conditions of entry (for example, refugee or not, legal or illegal) are a critical component of these transitions, given their direct implications for the access of children to public benefits and services. Each of these issues, in turn, requires a developmental approach that considers how the role and importance of various factors involved in the processes of migration and adaptation are mediated and differentiated by the age of the child (Garcia Coll and Magnuson, 1997; Hirschman, 1994; Laosa, 1989; de Leon Siantz, 1997).

Risk and Protection in Child Development

Many studies have identified a wide range of conditions that can compromise or impair children's development, including poverty, low levels of parental education, living in a one-parent family or in large families with many siblings, exposure to racial or ethnic discrimination, residential mobility, and depleted neighborhood resources (Bradley and Whiteside-Mansell, 1997; Brooks-Gunn et al., 1997; Duncan and Brooks-Gunn, 1997; Huston et al.,

1994). More recently, recognition that some children and adults transcend these difficult life circumstances and vulnerabilities to lead successful lives, whereas others are susceptible to negative life outcomes, has given rise to an extensive knowledge base on risk and protective mechanisms in development (Garmezy, 1991, 1993; Hauser and Bowlds, 1990; Rutter, 1985, 1987; Rutter et al., 1995; Werner, 1989, 1995; Werner and Smith, 1992).

Risk factors are conditions or circumstances that are associated with a greater likelihood of negative or undesirable outcomes. Protective factors, in contrast, are associated with a reduced likelihood of negative outcomes, because of their own direct effects, or because they moderate the relationship between risk factors and negative outcomes. Protective factors may be conceived in two ways: as the opposing end of a risk-factor continuum—high parental education, for example—or as separate dimensions that act independently of or interactively with risk factors (Jessor et al., 1995; Rutter, 1987). This may be the case, for example, with beneficial cultural influences on development.

Circumstances that foster successful adaptation despite high-risk status are: (1) individual/dispositional features, such as self-efficacy, optimism and perception of opportunity, cognitive competence, active coping strategies, strong interpersonal skills, and good health; (2) family characteristics, such as cohesion, shared values, warmth and acceptance, absence of conflict, consistent rules and responsibilities, financial security, appropriate monitoring, high parental expectations and support for learning, and religiosity; and (3) features of the communities in which the child and family live, such as availability of external supports, access to constructive out-of-school activities, strong schools with supportive teachers, positive role models in the community, housing quality, and residential stability.

Interest in community-level influences on development has increased in the mid-1990s, motivated in part by rising concern about the transformation of many urban neighborhoods where most immigrant children are growing up (Brooks-Gunn et al., 1997; Wilson, 1990, 1997). Issues in this area that may influence not only child behavior but also efforts to address social problems in urban settings include social organization, consensus on values, and "collective efficacy," defined as social cohesion among neighbors combined with their willingness to intervene on behalf of the common good (Elliott et al., 1996; Sampson et al., 1997). This area of inquiry is unique in drawing together ethnographic, epidemiological, and quantitative data and, as such, offers a promising model for integrating the range of methods that have been used to study immigrant children.

Other promising developments in this area of research include: (1) efforts to understand how risk and protective mechanisms act in concert to affect development (Garmezy et al., 1984; Sameroff et al., 1993), (2) conceptual models that shift the balance of attention in this literature away from a focus on risk toward examining positive outcomes and the protective or compensatory conditions that enable children to thrive despite adversity (Bradley et al., 1994; Masten et al., 1991; Seifer et al., 1992; Takanishi et al., 1997), and (3) research designs that view development for all individuals as entailing gains and losses that accrue over time to shape development (Bradley and Whiteside-Mansell, 1997). This research has also focused new attention on strategies that children and their families and communities employ to navigate difficult circumstances in their physical and social environments (see, for example, Furstenberg et al., 1998).

Only recently have researchers sought to adapt this literature to children in immigrant families (Buriel, 1994; Buriel and De Ment, 1997; Chud, 1982; de Leon Siantz, 1997; Garcia Coll and Magnuson, 1997; Laosa, 1997; Waters, 1997). Studies have begun to focus on the exposure of some children in immigrant families to a wide range of conditions that have been found to compromise the development of children in U.S.-born families. Potentially protective conditions have also been identified, such as health-promoting behavior during pregnancy, close family ties, religiosity, and high parental expectations and supports for achievement.

But critical questions remain largely unexplored: Do risk factors, which have been identified as sources of vulnerability for U.S.-born children in U.S.-born families, affect children in immigrant families similarly? Are children in immigrant families insulated from risk by the same conditions and coping strategies as have been identified for U.S.-born children in U.S.-born families? Do the dynamics of risk and protective factors operate similarly for both groups? Do different immigrant groups face different risks?

Although subgroups of children in immigrant families who have been the subject of research have been found to vary widely in their coping strategies, adjustment, development, and adaptation (de Leon Siantz, 1997, Laosa, 1990; Rumbaut, 1994a, 1994b, 1997a, 1997b), efforts to disentangle the multiple determinants of this variation and to juxtapose this research with the empirical literature on U.S.-born children in U.S.-born families are in their infancy.

Implications for the Study

Research on the developmental processes in children have helped identify health, nutritional, and family nurturance needs that all children share (Maccoby, 1980). It is not known, however, to what extent these developmental processes differ for children in immigrant families. Among the fundamental questions requiring attention are: Do the conditions that foster or compromise development for U.S.-born children in U.S.-born families also apply to children in immigrant families? Can approaches to understanding the adjustment of adult immigrants be generalized to children? If not, how can research more accurately capture and understand the lives of children in immigrant families?

The committee draws four implications from its review of the pertinent literatures:

1. The early studies of children in immigrant families reviewed above suggest that many of them experience unusual circumstances and special challenges and benefit from some culture-specific strengths that must be incorporated into a theory of development of children in immigrant families. The closest analog is developmental research on minority children, but evidence of within-group and contextual variations suggests caution before generalizing from prior theory and research.

Far greater attention needs to be paid in the developmental literature to issues of (a) bilingualism and biculturalism as they manifest themselves in families and in the broader society; (b) racial or ethnic discrimination and intergroup relations, particularly as they affect the values, adult role models, and peer groups toward which these children gravitate; and (c) the influence of access to income, health, and other benefits as they are legally conditioned by the specific immigrant statuses of family members.

2. The health and adaptation of children in immigrant families unfolds in the context of two inextricably linked processes: the process of development and the process of migration and assimilation. Efforts to understand their development must examine both processes. Unlike other children, those who immigrate to the United States straddle the social contexts of departure from the homeland and of reception and integration in their host community. Indeed, their development incorporates the physical transition from one context to another, and perhaps to multiple places of settlement in the United States. Children born in the United States to immigrant parents also straddle the contexts of sending and receiving communities, albeit more indirectly, through cross-national social networks, family traditions and expectations, and connections to ethnic communities and resources within the United States.

3. Studies of children in immigrant families must pay far greater attention to diversity in the immigrant population than has been the norm in research on minority children. There is no typical immigrant child; indeed, they span the full spectrum of socioeconomic status, economic opportunity, race and ethnicity, family circumstances, and social context. This fledgling area of research affords an opportunity to incorporate the importance of historical circumstances, local place, and within-group variation into research designs.

4. The differing contexts and outcomes of assimilation experienced by different subgroups may be the most important issue for research on children in immigrant families. To what extent are different trajectories shaped by the characteristics and experiences of children at the time of their entry into the United States, their parents' mix of assets and resources, and the particular events and people who shape their experiences in the United States? Although some research on adolescents in immigrant families is beginning to address this issue (see Portes, 1996; Rumbaut, 1994b), no research follows young children in immi-

grant families over time, systematically incorporates samples of children that have immigrated to the United States at different ages and from different countries, or adopts an intergenerational time span that can provide answers to critical questions about the effects of exposure to American culture within a single life-span and across generations.

The issue of appropriate comparison groups is also extremely important. In addition to internal comparisons within the immigrant population, it is essential to compare the development of children in immigrant families with that of their U.S.-born peers and to consider the role of immigration-related factors per se compared with the many other factors known to affect development. Comparisons are also needed between children in U.S.-born families and children in immigrant families both within and across ethnic and racial groups.

The committee was struck by the paucity of research on each of the issues identified and, accordingly, keenly aware of the great extent to which our capacity to draw conclusions about the health and adjustment of children in immigrant families was constrained. Accordingly, we sought to summarize and supplement, through research expressly conducted for this study, what is known about the circumstances and characteristics of children in immigrant families, noting both strengths and potential risk factors; to understand their adaptation over time, albeit in the absence of longitudinal research and research that incorporates information about their countries of origin or about the migration process itself; to remain sensitive to the vast diversity that characterizes them; and to inform the next phase of research on the differing contexts and outcomes of assimilation that characterize children in immigrant families.

Because the unanswered questions far exceed those for which even preliminary answers can be given, perhaps the most significant outcome to emerge from the committee's work will be the impetus it provides for a sizeable increase in research on this rapidly expanding population of children. Not only would such research inform the nation about the development of children in immigrant families, but it would also afford substantial opportunities to reexamine and enrich existing understanding of developmental processes for all children, to render research on both development and immigration more widely generalizable, and to encourage interdisciplinary research and collaboration on issues of extreme national importance.

TERMINOLOGY AND ANALYTICAL DISTINCTIONS

The report discusses children in immigrant families in terms of several dimensions. The most basic distinction is between *first-generation* immigrant children, who are foreign-born children who emigrated from their country of birth to the United States, and *second-generation* immigrant children, who are U.S.-born children who have at least one foreign-born parent. First-generation children are not U.S. citizens at birth but may become citizens through the process of naturalization.[2] First-generation immigrant children are also referred to in this report as immigrant children and foreign-born children of immigrant parents.

Second-generation children, because they were born in the United States, are citizens, regardless of their parents' citizenship or immigrant status. Second-generation immigrant children are also referred to in this report as U.S.-born children of immigrant parents.

Third-generation immigrant children are U.S.-born children of U.S.-born parents. They are distinguished from foreign-born and U.S.-born children of foreign-born parents.

First- and second-generation children are distinguished further according to the country in which they or their parents were born. Populations of different countries vary in the language spoken, socioeconomic circumstances, demographic behavior, customs and culture, and race and ethnic composition. The primary reasons that people immigrate to the United States also vary from country to country. Some, for example, come to avoid persecution or death; others seek an occupational environment that allows them to fully utilize knowledge gained in earning advanced degrees in science or engineering.

---

[2]Children can automatically become naturalized while under the age of 18 if both parents become naturalized; or the child can naturalize himself or herself after reaching the age of 18.

Each of these distinctions has potentially important implications for the physical and mental health of first- and second-generation children in immigrant families. Judgments about whether they are doing well or poorly, and assessments of reasons for differences among foreign-born children or between foreign-born and U.S.-born children, must be based on comparisons with other relevant groups. Because this report focuses on immigration to the United States, the situation of first- and second-generation children is assessed here mainly in comparison to children in the third and later generations—that is, families in which both parents, as well as the children, were born in the United States.

In addition, because race and ethnicity are critical indicators of life chances in the United States, and because the racial and ethnic composition of immigrants has shifted markedly during recent decades toward a larger representation of Hispanic and nonwhite minorities, this report often compares the situation of immigrants and natives who are white, black, Hispanic, or Asian.

In this context, the committee was keenly aware throughout its deliberations that children who live in poverty—many of them U.S.-born minorities—often experience restricted access to many of the resources, programs, and benefits that are discussed in this report specifically with respect to children in immigrant families. U.S.-born black children, in particular, whose historical legacy arises from one of this nation's most profound immigration policies and from the abiding significance of race in American culture, face life chances that are all too often characterized by the risks and foreclosed opportunities that are considered in this report. In its calls for new research, the committee is explicit about the importance of making comparisons between today's children in immigrant families and U.S.-born black children whose immigrant ancestry is many generations removed (as well as to other children in "at risk" groups) in order to better understand the successes and failures of the nation's policies for children and families. Only by placing efforts to understand the life chances of today's children in immigrant families in the context of the range of life chances experienced by children in U.S.-born families can we begin to understand fully the forces that shape successful adaptation.

ORGANIZATION OF THE REPORT

This committee's review and analysis begins with Chapter 2, which portrays socioeconomic and demographic risk factors experienced by children in immigrant families from many countries of origin. Chapter 3 presents information on the health status and adjustment. Chapter 4 discusses public policies and the use of public benefits, as well as information on health insurance and access to health care. Chapter 5 presents the committee's conclusions and recommendations for future research, data collection, and reporting.

CHAPTER 2

Socioeconomic and Demographic Risks

Very little information is available about the effects of either risk or, to an even greater extent, protective factors for children in immigrant families, or indeed about other factors that seem likely to be influential specifically for children in immigrant families (see Chapters 1 and 3 for a discussion of these). In order to expand available information about the incidence of socioeconomic and demographic risk factors among first-, second , and third and later-generation children, new analyses of decennial census data for 1910, 1960, and 1990 were conducted for the committee (Hernandez and Darke, 1998).

These analyses focused especially on information from the 1990 decennial census, because it is the most recent source of information on risk factors for children with origins in a large number of countries. These results were supplemented insofar as possible with comparative data using the 1910, 1960, and 1990 decennial censuses to examine historical changes in key risk factors following the decade of peak immigration to the United States (1901-1910), the subsequent era of very low immigration (1931-1960), and the most recent decades of increasing immigration for which census data are available (1970-1990).

This assessment is the first to use decennial census data with children as the unit of analysis to study long-run historical changes in foreign-born and U.S.-born families. It draws on analytical approaches to identifying first-, second-, and third- and later-generation children developed during the last few years (Hernandez, 1993; Jensen and Chitose, 1997; Landale et al., 1997; Oropesa and Landale, 1995, 1997a, 1997b). These data are the best available for assessing the process of assimilation by comparing the socioeconomic and demographic risk factors of first-, second-, and third- and later-generation children from various countries (see Appendix Tables B-1A through B-1E and B-2A through B-2E).

Nevertheless, conclusions must be treated as preliminary here, as throughout the report. Differences from generation to generation may to some extent result from changes in the characteristics of immigrants from decade to decade or even year to year (Borjas, 1991). In addition, in census data, second-generation children can be identified by the foreign-born status of their parents only if they live in the home; hence some second-generation children may be misclassified as belonging to later generations.[1]

This chapter presents information on the exposure of first-, second-, and third- and later-generation children to risk factors known to affect children generally: poverty, limited parental education and employment, living in a one-parent family or with many siblings, and in overcrowded housing. It then discusses potential risk factors specific to children in immigrant families: English language fluency, living in a linguistically isolated household, and not being a U.S. citizen or having parents who are not U.S. citizens.

GENERAL CHILDHOOD RISK FACTORS

For children generally, negative outcomes have been demonstrated to result not only from poverty, but also independently from low parental educational attainments and from living in families with only one parent or with a large number of siblings

---

[1]In addition, among children not living with a parent, second generation children cannot be distinguished from third- and later-generation children. To ensure that estimates for various risk factors are maximally comparable across generations, children with no parent in the home are excluded from these estimates.

(Alwin, 1984; Blake, 1985; Blau and Duncan, 1967; Featherman and Hauser, 1978; Kohn, 1969; Kohn and Schooler, 1983; Kominski, 1987; McLanahan and Sandefur, 1994; Sewell and Hauser, 1975; Sewell et al., 1980). In addition, overcrowded housing conditions can facilitate the transmission of communicable diseases such as tuberculosis, hepatitis A, and intestinal and respiratory infections (Coggon et al., 1993; Fall et al., 1997; Guberan, 1980; Paul et al., 1993; Rosenberg et al., 1997). We discuss each of these risk factors in turn for children in immigrant families.

Poverty

In 1990, children in immigrant families were somewhat more likely than U.S.-born children in U.S.-born families to live in poverty (22 versus 17 percent).[2] Most of the difference was accounted for by the high poverty rate of first-generation immigrant children (33 percent), whereas the second generation was only slightly more likely (19 percent) to be poor than third- and later-generation U.S.-born children (17 percent). In 1960, in contrast, first- and second-generation children were *less* likely to be poor than third- and later-generation children (23 and 19 percent versus 26 percent), although, as in 1990, the proportion in poverty was greater for the first than for the second generation.

Variations by Country of Origin

Poverty rates differed enormously in both 1960 and 1990 for first- and second-generation children from various countries of origin, and for third- and later-generation children by race and ethnicity. For example, in 1990 the poverty rate for third- and later-generation white children was only 11 percent, and it was 2.5 to 4 times greater for third- and later-generation black, Hispanic, and American Indian children, at 40, 28, and 35 percent, respectively.

---

[2]For limitations of the current official poverty measure for current and historical comparisons see National Research Council (1995) and Hernandez (1993).

Similarly, in 1960 and 1990 poverty rates for first- and second-generation children ranged widely, from a low of about 5 percent to a high of about 50 percent. For children in immigrant families from about two dozen countries in Latin America and the Caribbean, Asia, Europe, the Middle East, and Africa, poverty rates were about equal to, or even substantially less than, the rate of 11 percent for third- and later-generation white children in 1990 (see Appendix Table B-1A). Children with origins in these countries accounted for 28 percent (2.3 million) of all children in immigrant families in 1990 (8.4 million).

At the other end of the spectrum, for children in immigrant families from 12 countries, poverty rates exceeded 25 percent in 1990 (the range for this group was 26 to 51 percent, depending on the country of origin). In view of the negative risks associated with poverty generally, the situation of children from these 12 countries may be particularly serious. Children with origins in these 12 countries accounted for 46 percent (3.9 million) of all children in immigrant families in 1990. Mexico alone accounted for 31 percent of children in immigrant families (2.6 million). Moreover, children from these 12 countries whose family income was below the official poverty threshold in 1990 accounted for about 80 percent of all children in immigrant families who lived in poverty; these estimates may be low, given evidence that the decennial census underestimates the number of Mexican-origin children living in poverty.[3]

Of the 12 countries, 5 are the source of many officially recognized refugees (the former Soviet Union, Cambodia, Laos, Thailand, Vietnam); 3 are war-torn countries in Central America (El

---

[3]Analyses carried out for the committee using the National Agricultural Workers Survey indicate that more than 67 percent of U.S.-based children in migrant farmworker families lived in poverty in each year from 1993 to 1995, that is, more than 590,000 of the 880,000 total (Mines, 1998). Insofar as a substantial portion of migrant farmworker families and their children are of Mexican origin (69 percent of the U.S.-based children in the survey were from Mexico) and are not counted in the decennial census, the total number (and percentage) of children in immigrant families, especially of Mexican origin, who were living in poverty is higher, perhaps by several hundred thousand (and several percentage points), than indicated by the decennial census data.

Salvador, Guatemala, Nicaragua); and 3 are small, impoverished Central American or Caribbean countries (Honduras, Haiti, Dominican Republic) that are sources of unskilled labor. The 12th country is Mexico, which currently sends the largest number of both legal and illegal unskilled immigrants, and which has been a ready source of unskilled labor for the U.S. economy throughout the 20th century (Romo, 1996; Rumbaut, 1996). Within the racial and ethnic stratification system of the United States, most children from these 12 countries, except the former Soviet Union, are classified as minority—Hispanic, Asian, or black.

Variations by Generation

In 1990, poverty rates for children in immigrant families were lower, sometimes much lower, for second-generation children than for first-generation children for nearly all countries of origin, including most of the 12 countries with the highest poverty rates (see Appendix Table B-2A). But for children from Mexico, who account for about two-thirds of the children in immigrant families from these 12 countries, the poverty rates for the second and the later generations were quite similar, at 32 and 28 percent, respectively, which is 2.5 to 3 times greater than for third- and later-generation white children.

For children from the 4 Central American countries in the cluster of 12 high-poverty countries (El Salvador, Guatemala, Nicaragua, Honduras), the decline in poverty from the second to the third and later generations is somewhat larger than for Mexican-origin children. It is significant that the poverty rates for the later generations drop to the range of 14 to 17 percent, only somewhat greater than for third- and later-generation white children. The lower poverty rates among third- and later-generation children from these four countries, compared with those from Mexico, may reflect differences in the socioeconomic status of their parents at the time they entered the United States rather than intergenerational socioeconomic assimilation.

In 1990, children in immigrant families with origins in the Dominican Republic and Haiti had extremely high poverty rates, and they were nearly the same for the first and second generations (41 and 42 percent, respectively, for the Dominican Republic, 30 and 26 percent for Haiti). Available data for the Dominican Republic indicates no change for the third and later generations (40 percent).

The high poverty rates of second- and third- and later-generation children from these Caribbean countries and from Mexico suggest the possibility that racial and ethnic stratification has been restricting socioeconomic opportunities across the generations. In the case of immigrants from Mexico, the pattern has remained the same for many generations—a conclusion that is strikingly similar to that for U.S.-born black children. Since at least 1960, the intergenerational pattern for Mexican-origin children has been quite similar, with poverty rates for the first, second, and third and later generations of 58, 48, and 53 percent, respectively, about 2.5 to 3 times greater than the rate of 19 percent in 1960 for third- and later-generation white children.[4] This persistent pattern of very high poverty rates across generations suggests that ethnic stratification may have continuing power in determining the life chances of children of Mexican origin. Potential additional or alternative explanations that merit attention in future research, particularly for the Mexican-origin population, include their continuing high levels of immigration, the extent of back-and-forth movement between the United States and Mexico, and the large size and residential concentration of the Mexican-origin population, as well as the declining need for very low-skilled entry-level workers in the U.S. economy.

---

[4]Of course, it is possible that a substantial portion of third- and later-generation children with a Mexican parent or grandparent also have a non-Mexican parent or grandparents, and that such children tend not to be reported as being of Mexican origin and tend to have lower poverty rates than children with two Mexican parents who are reported as being of Mexican origin. As of 1990, because only 9 percent of third- and later-generation children who were identified as Mexican or as having at least one Mexican parent had a Mexican parent but were not themselves identified as Mexican, the exclusion of these children from the poverty estimates above could not affect the poverty rates of third- and later-generation Mexican children by more than a percentage point or two. Additional research is required to assess the effect of marriage between Mexican origin and non-Mexican-origin grandparents.

Parents' Education and Employment

The percentage of children whose parents have graduated from college was very similar for those in immigrant and U.S.-born families in 1990. At the same time, however, children in immigrant families were much more likely than children in U.S.-born families to have parents with very low educational attainments. In other words, there is comparability at the top of the spectrum but, below this threshold, children in immigrant families are more likely to be concentrated at the lower end.

Specifically, first- and second-generation children in families with fathers in the home were about as likely in 1990 to have fathers who were college graduates (23 percent) as were third- and later-generation children (26 percent). First-, second-, and third- and later-generation children in families with mothers in the home were also about equally likely to have mothers who were college graduates (14 to 18 percent). In addition, in 1990, among children in immigrant families from about two dozen countries, 35 percent or more had a father in the home who was a college graduate—a rate that is higher than the 28 percent recorded for third- and later-generation white children (see Appendix Tables B-1D and B-2D).

At the other end of the spectrum, in 1990, first- and second-generation children living with fathers were 2 to 3 times more likely than third and later generations to have fathers who had not graduated from high school, at 49, 36, and 15 percent, respectively. Those with fathers in the home who had completed no more than eight years of schooling for the three generations were 34, 23, and 3 percent, respectively. Patterns in mothers' educational attainment were quite similar. Mexican-origin children constitute a large portion of the children in immigrant families with very low parental educational attainments (see Appendix Tables B-1A, B-1D, B-2A, and B-2D).

In 1960, parental educational attainment followed a similar pattern of improvement from the first to the third generation. It is striking, however, that the second and third generations showed substantially higher rates of very low educational attainment in 1960 than in 1990. Among first-, second-, and third- and later-generation children with fathers in the home in 1960, the proportions with fathers in the home who had completed fewer than eight years of schooling were 41, 40, and 31 percent, respectively. The only measure of educational attainment in the 1910 census is the literacy rate. Second and later generations of children were similar in their chances of having a parent in the home who was illiterate, at 9 to 14 percent, but the first generation was substantially more likely to have an illiterate father (22 percent) or mother (34 percent).

Variations by Country of Origin and Generation

Parental educational attainment varied enormously by country of origin for children in immigrant families, and by race and ethnicity among U.S.-born children in U.S.-born families (see Appendix Tables B-1A, B-1D, B-2A, and B-2D), both historically and today. In 1990, with the exception of the former Soviet Union, children in immigrant families from the 12 countries with the highest poverty rates were somewhat to much more likely than third- and later-generation white children to have parents in the home who had not graduated from either high school or elementary school.

For children from 11 of these countries (all but Mexico), parents' educational attainment generally increased substantially from the first to the second to the third generation. Although most third- and later-generation children from these countries have parents who have completed eight years of schooling or more, it is also true that most have parents who have not completed college.

The proportion of third- and later-generation Mexican-origin children with parents not graduating from high school remains in the range of 30 to 34 percent for all generations, similar to the level for third- and later-generation black children (26 to 29 percent), and substantially higher than for third- and later-generation white children (12 percent). Earlier in the century, too, there was a substantial deficit in parental educational attainment (1960) and literacy (1910) among children of Mexican origin of all generations, and among third- and later-generation black children, compared with third- and later-generation white children. Throughout the century, then, these racial and ethnic minorities have been more likely to experience low parental educational attainment than third- and later-generation white children.

Relation Between Parental Education, Employment, and Poverty

Throughout the century, the vast majority of children of all generations had fathers who were in the labor force. The proportions of children with fathers in the home who were in the labor force were essentially identical in 1910 (95 to 96 percent) and 1960 (97 percent), but slightly lower for the first generation in 1990 than for the second and third and later generations, at 88, 94, and 95 percent, respectively.

Children of all generations have also been similar, historically, in their likelihood of having a mother in the labor force, although enormous increases occurred for all generations during the past century. Among first-, second-, and third- and later-generation children with mothers in the home, the proportions with their mother in the labor force were 7, 6, and 12 percent, respectively, in 1910, increasing to 33, 25, and 27 percent, respectively, in 1960. By 1990, 55, 58, and 66 percent, respectively, had mothers in the labor force.

It is not surprising that very low parental educational attainment characterizes children from the 12 countries of origin with very high poverty rates in 1990. Yet among these children, poverty and low parental educational attainment were not usually associated with especially lower rates of labor force participation by fathers and mothers. For example, only for children in immigrant families from Cambodia, Laos, and Thailand was low parental educational attainment accompanied by low parental labor force participation rates. The high proportions of children in immigrant families with parents in the labor force, including those with origins in these 12 countries with especially high poverty and lower parental educational attainments, suggests that immigrants may be more likely to have high levels of ambition and motivation to work than those who do not immigrate. It is the case, however, that low parental educational attainment and poverty in these 12 countries are associated with especially high proportions of children in immigrant families whose fathers do not have full-time, year-round jobs (ranging from 31 to 68 percent) (see Appendix Tables B-1C and B-2C).

Children in immigrant families from an additional and sizeable number of countries (especially Israel, Nigeria, Pakistan, Jamaica, Syria, and Japan) also have very high proportions of fathers who do not work full-time year-round, but they are not characterized by extremely high poverty rates. What appears to distinguish these children with lower poverty rates is that most live with at least one person who speaks English exclusively or very well, and most have parents with more than eight years of education. Thus, despite generally high proportions with fathers and mothers in the home who are in the labor force, very high poverty rates for children in immigrant families tend to occur among children from countries with very low parental educational attainment (no more than eight years of schooling), fathers who cannot find full-time, year-round work, and parents who do not speak English well.

One-Parent Families

First-generation children from most countries of origin, and, to an even greater extent, second-generation children, were less likely to live in a one-parent family in 1990 than were third- and later-generation white children. Important exceptions are children in immigrant families with origins in Cambodia and most Central American and Caribbean countries. First- and second-generation children of Mexican origin were about as likely in 1990 to live in a one-parent family as were third- and later-generation white children (23, 18, and 18 percent, respectively).

The proportion of children living in one-parent families increased, sometimes dramatically, from the second to the third generation. For example, the share of third- and later-generation children with origins in most countries of Central and South America and the Caribbean living in one-parent families was at least twice as great as for third- and later-generation white children.

Relation Between Poverty and One-Parent Families

Among children in immigrant families in 1990, poverty was not necessarily associated with high proportions living in a one-parent family. For example, looking at the 12 countries of origin with very high poverty rates, children in immigrant families from Laos, the former Soviet Union, Mexico, Thailand, and Vietnam showed rates of living in one-parent families that were lower than or approximately the same as the rate for third- and later-generation white children. In contrast, those from the Central American and Caribbean countries and from Cambodia were substantially more likely to live in one-parent families than third- and later-generation white children.

Historical Trends in One-Parent Families

First-, second-, and third- and later-generation children were about equally likely, overall, to live in one-parent families in 1910 and in 1960, at 9 to 10 percent for children who lived with at least one parent.

First-generation children in families from Mexico were, however, much more likely in both 1910 and 1960 (but not in 1990) than third- and later-generation white children to live in one-parent families, although the differences disappeared by the second generation. The same was true for first- and second-generation children from Central America and the Caribbean in 1960. One-fourth of third- and later-generation black children lived in one-parent families in 1960, more than for nearly every country of origin for first-generation children, except perhaps the Dominican Republic. In 1910, third- and later-generation black children were substantially more likely (19 percent) than others to live in a one-parent family, with the exception of first-generation children from Mexico (24 percent).

Families with Many Siblings

The proportion of children living in families with five or more siblings in 1990 declined from 17 percent for the first generation to 9 percent for the second and to 5 percent for the third and later generations. For most specific countries of origin, not only did smaller proportions of second-generation children in 1990 live in large families than first-generation children from the same countries, but also the proportions for the second generation by country of origin were usually similar to third- and later-generation white children, at 5 percent or less. These differences in the number of siblings in the homes of first-, second-, and third- and later-generation children are consistent with changes in fertility measured in the 1990 census (Chiswick and Sullivan, 1995); immigrant women have higher fertility than native-born women, but there is a convergence in fertility to U.S. norms across generations.

In 1910, first-, second-, and third- and later-generation children as a whole were about equally likely to live in families with many siblings; the range was 38 to 43 percent. The proportions in such large families were much smaller in 1960, but they remained similar across the generations, within the range of 17 to 21 percent. But the proportions living in large families in 1960 were much higher for first- and second-generation children of Mexican origin and for third- and later-generation black and Hispanic children, at 40 to 51 percent. These proportions were nearly as high as they had been in 1910, when the range was 47 to 61 percent. By 1990, among first- and second-generation children of Mexican origin and among third- and later-generation black and Hispanic children, the proportions living in large families had fallen to the range of 8 to 19 percent.

Overcrowded Housing

In 1990, only 12 percent of third- and later-generation children lived in overcrowded housing with more than one person per room, compared with 38 percent for the second generation and 62 percent for the first generation. Children in immigrant families from most specific countries of origin in 1990 also had high proportions living in overcrowded housing, and children in immigrant families from the 12 high-poverty countries were much more likely than most to live in such conditions (Appendix Tables B-1B and B-2B). For children from most of these 12 countries, declines in overcrowding are substantial across the first, second, and third and later generations, but the third generation from countries for which data are available continued to experience high levels of overcrowding, especially Mexican-origin children at 31 percent.

Overcrowding cannot be measured in the 1910 census, but overall levels of overcrowding were much higher among children in 1960 than in 1990. In 1960, the proportions living in overcrowded housing were about equal for first-, second-, and third- and later-generation children, at 31 to 36 percent. However, 75 percent of first- and second-generation Mexican-origin children and 69 percent of third- and later-generation black and Hispanic children lived in crowded conditions in 1960.

Summary

Children in immigrant families in 1990 were less likely than U.S.-born children in U.S.-born families to have only one parent in the home, but they were substantially more likely to live in poverty, with many siblings, with parents who had not finished school beyond the eighth grade, and in overcrowded housing. Children in immigrant families were similar to those in U.S.-born families with fathers in the home in having a father who was in the labor force, but substantially more likely to have a father who did not work full-time, year-round.

But the socioeconomic and demographic risk factors experi enced by children in immigrant families from various countries are extremely diverse. Children in immigrant families from about two dozen countries experience socioeconomic and demographic circumstances similar to or better than third- and later-generation children. At the other extreme are the children in immigrant families from 12 other countries with very high poverty rates, who experience socioeconomic and demographic circumstances in the range experienced by third- and later-generation black, Hispanic, and American Indian children.

Children from these 12 countries, or their parents, entered the United States as officially recognized refugees from Southeast Asia or the former Soviet Union in order to leave the dangerous conditions behind, fled warring countries in Central America, or came as unskilled migrant laborers from the Caribbean or Mexico in search of improved economic opportunities. With the exception of the former Soviet Union, children from these countries experience not only very high levels of poverty, but also very low parental educational attainment and a high likelihood of living in overcrowded housing. Low parental educational attainment appears to contribute to poverty not by leading to low rates of labor force participation (Laos, Cambodia, and Thailand are the main exceptions), but instead because fathers with very limited education who do not speak English very well do not have full-time, year-round work.

The proportions of children exposed to important socioeconomic and demographic risk factors declined for most of these factors between the first and second generation for children from most of the 12 countries of origin with high child poverty rates. But data available for selected countries suggest that, for third- and later-generation children from Mexico and the Dominican Republic, and perhaps the Central American countries, the proportions living in poverty with parents who have not graduated from high school, in overcrowded housing conditions, and with only one parent remain quite high.

Children in immigrant families from Mexico account for nearly two-thirds of the children with origins in these 12 countries, and for nearly one-third of all children in immigrant families in 1990. Thus, Mexican-origin children account for a large proportion of children in immigrant families who experience high rates of poverty, low parental educational attainments, and fathers who do not work full-time, year-round. The history of immigration from Mexico is unique, in that Mexico has for many decades been an important source of low-skilled labor for the U.S. economy, and it has also been the most important source of undocumented immigrants. Mexican-origin children of all generations have also, throughout the century, been among those with high proportions exposed to elevated socioeconomic and demographic risks.

RISK FACTORS SPECIFIC TO
CHILDREN IN IMMIGRANT FAMILIES

English Language Fluency

Children in immigrant families from countries in which English is not the native language or is not widely taught may be at special risk, compared with U.S.-born children in U.S.-born families, because they may not speak English well or they may live with parents who do not speak English well. A lack of English fluency can limit effective communication and functioning in health facilities, schools, and other settings that provide essential resources to children and their families.

In 1990, at least 60 percent of children in immigrant families spoke a language other than English at home, regardless of their own proficiency with English. The exceptions were English-speaking countries of origin, as well as Austria, Germany, the Netherlands, Nigeria, and South Africa. In contrast, using as an outcome the percentage of children who do not speak English "exclusively or very well,"[5] only in 13 countries of origin did the proportion of children in immigrant families reach the substantial proportion of 30 percent or more; 11 of these countries are among the 12 high-poverty countries (all but Haiti); the remaining two were China and Hong Kong (see Appendix Tables B-1F and B-2E).

Generational differences are large, however. The proportion of children who speak English "exclusively or very well" is only 54 percent for the first generation but 81 percent for the second generation. For children in immigrant families from the 12 countries with very high poverty rates, the range is only 35 to 53 percent for the first generation, but this rises for 10 of the 12 countries (excepting only Laos and Cambodia) to 68 percent or more for the second generation.

---

[5]Among children age 5 years and older, those who speak only English in the home are categorized as speaking English exclusively, and those who speak a language other than English in the home are distinguished according to 4 categories, whether they speak English very well, well, not well, or not at all.

Looking to the future, it will be important to assess whether and to what extent factors that may result from the expanding Spanish-speaking immigrant population, such as growing up in homogeneously Spanish-speaking neighborhoods or watching Spanish-language TV, will affect the acquisition of fluent English among children in immigrant families from Spanish-speaking countries.

Linguistic Isolation

Lack of English fluency may not pose enormous difficulties for immigrants in communities that have a large number of people with the same national origin—but it can isolate them from mainstream society. The Census Bureau defines a linguistically isolated household as one in which no person age 14 or older speaks English either "exclusively" or "very well." In 1990, 76 to 78 percent of children in immigrant families lived with a mother or a father who did not speak English at home. In households with both mother and father at home, the proportion was 70 percent. No language information was collected in the 1960 census, but historical changes are best measured by comparing data on "mother tongue" for 1910 with data on "language spoken" in 1990. In 1910, 84 to 85 percent of children in immigrant families lived with either a father or a mother whose mother tongue was not English. For 79 percent of children in immigrant families in 1910 with two parents in the home, neither parent spoke English as a mother tongue. Although these measures of language are not identical, they are similar, and the similarity of the results for 1910 and 1990 suggests that differences in the proportion of children in immigrant families with parents speaking or not speaking English were about the same at the beginning and the end of the century.

Among children in immigrant families from each of the 12 high-poverty countries, 30 percent or more lived in linguistically isolated households. The proportion was over 40 percent for 9 of these countries, and at 60 percent for two of them (Laos and Cambodia). Four additional countries of origin had 30 percent or more children living in linguistically isolated households (China, Hong Kong, Taiwan, Colombia).

Citizenship

Of the 8.4 million children in immigrant families in 1990, 75 percent were U.S. citizens by birth, 4 percent were naturalized citizens, and 21 percent (1.7 million) were not citizens. Of the citizen children, 54 percent (3.6 million) had at least one parent in the home who was not a citizen; thus, approximately two-thirds of children in immigrant families in 1990 were either themselves not a citizen or lived with a noncitizen parent. Children who are illegal immigrants are ineligible for most public benefits and services and, under welfare reform, those who are legal immigrants but not citizens may also be ineligible for important medical and social services (see Chapter 4). Equally important, U.S.-born children in immigrant families who are eligible for such services may not receive them, because immigrant parents who are not themselves eligible may not be aware that their children are eligible, or they may fear or resist contact with government agencies administering the services. Because legal immigrants and citizens experienced essentially the same eligibility prior to welfare reform, for legal immigrants the fact of not being a U.S. citizen has only recently become a potential risk factor.

Welfare eligibility exclusions are most significant to children living in poverty. In 1990, the official poverty rate was 34 percent among children who were not citizens and 23 percent among citizen children with at least one noncitizen parent. For all children in immigrant families, the poverty rate in 1990 was 27 percent.

Children in immigrant families from 8 of the 12 high-poverty countries of origin were especially likely to be noncitizens, with rates of 30 percent or more. For children from the four remaining high-poverty countries (the Dominican Republic, Mexico, Honduras, Haiti), the proportion who were not citizens was 20 to 29 percent. For three additional countries of origin (Venezuela, Romania, Guyana) with child poverty rates at least as high as the rate for third- and later-generation white children (11 percent), the proportion of children who were not citizens was 30 percent or more (see Appendix Table B-1E).

In 1990, among children from 10 of the 12 high-poverty countries or origin, the proportion of children who were not citizens or had at least one parent who was not a citizen was 73 percent or more. Among the two remaining high-poverty countries, the former Soviet Union and Vietnam, the proportions of children who were not citizens or who had at least one parent who was not a citizen were 62 to 63 percent. The figure was 50 percent or more for 18 of the other 26 countries of origin with child poverty rates at least as high as the rate for third- and later-generation white children. Thus eligibility rules that exclude persons who are not citizens from public benefits and services may have important consequences for children from many different countries of origin.

Traumatic Circumstances

Children who have witnessed the horrors of war firsthand, including the killing of parents or siblings, may have special needs, particularly for mental health services, that are especially serious. Children with these experiences and others who enter the United States unaccompanied by an adult and without documentation face severe difficulties. However, very little information is available about them.

The Immigration and Naturalization Service (INS) arrested 2,028 minors in 1995, the last year for which data were available (McDonnell, 1997). In 1990, the INS arrested 8,500 undocumented minors (under age 18), 70 percent of whom were unaccompanied by an adult (Human Rights Watch, 1997). Most detained children are placed in foster care or a relative's care or are deported in a matter of days. At any one time, several hundred to more than 1,000 undocumented children are in longer-term detention centers. Minors are held in about 100 detention centers that range from nonsecure foster care facilities to adult correctional facilities. About one-third of children in the legal guardianship of the INS in places of detention are younger than 15 years old, and some are under age 10.

In addition to lack of legal counsel, one brief survey of undocumented children in INS detention revealed that they were exposed to physical and sexual assaults, verbal abuse, denial of medical services, and nutritional deprivation (one meal per day) in some facilities. Lack of health care, especially mental health services, is a particular concern, because these minors may have been seriously traumatized prior to entering the United States or while held in detention (Nadeau et al., 1997). The number of minors imprisoned by the INS does not appear to be large, but the lack of publicly available information about unaccompanied children in detention is an important gap in the knowledge about immigrant children at risk.

Summary

Children in immigrant families may be subject to risk factors that grow out of their immigrant circumstances. Lack of English fluency can limit effective communication and functioning in health facilities, schools, and other settings that provide resources essential to children and their families. However, although most children in immigrant families speak a language other than English at home, the vast majority of them (73 percent) speak English exclusively or very well, and language assimilation occurs rapidly across generations (National Research Council, 1997).

With the passage of welfare reform legislation, lack of U.S. citizenship became a potentially important risk factor, by limiting eligibility and access of noncitizens to public benefits and services. A large majority of children in immigrant families may be ineligible for important benefits, or have parents who are ineligible and who are therefore hesitant to secure benefits on behalf of their children. Moreover, reductions in benefits available to such families will reduce their overall resources.

One other very high risk group merits attention: children who have emigrated under traumatic circumstances, especially from Southeast Asia and Central America, including those with first-hand experience of the horrors of war.

CHAPTER 3

Health Status and Adjustment

The health of children in immigrant families and the extent to which they adapt successfully to American society are very broad topics. Because few surveys or health monitoring systems in the United States use a generational perspective to distinguish among foreign-born children, U.S.-born children with immigrant parents, and U.S.-born children with U.S.-born parents, the scientific evidence is limited. Nevertheless, on the basis of available data, it appears that, along a small number of important dimensions, children in immigrant families experience better health and adjustment than do U.S.-born children in U.S.-born families. This relative advantage tends to deteriorate with length of time in the United States and from one generation to the next. Moreover, as we discuss in this chapter, children in immigrant families may be at particular risk for certain health conditions.

Care must be taken not to overgeneralize, because children from different countries of origin differ greatly, the variation among children from the same country of origin is often substantial, and the available evidence for preliminary conclusions is quite limited. This chapter reviews what is known about the physical and mental health and adjustment of children in immigrant families. It identifies areas in which more research is needed, as well as areas in which children in immigrant families may face risks to healthy development and adjustment.

BIRTHWEIGHT AND INFANT MORTALITY

The two most commonly used indicators of infant health are the rate of infants born with low birthweight (defined as less than 2,500 grams) and infant mortality (defined as deaths before age 1 per 1,000 births) (Institute of Medicine, 1985; U.S. Department of Health and Human Services, 1986). A number of studies report significantly *lower* rates for these two indicators among the immigrant population than among U.S.-born mothers of the same ethnicity, a phenomenon that is referred to as the *epidemiological paradox*.

Initial studies of this phenomenon focused on the Mexican-origin population (Guendelman, 1995; Guendelman and English, 1995; Guendelman et al., 1995; Markides and Coreil, 1986; Scribner and Dwyer, 1989; Ventura, 1983, 1984; Williams et al., 1986).[1] Subsequent research has documented a similar pattern for other ethnic groups, although the differences in rates of low birthweight and infant mortality in these groups have often been smaller than they are for Mexican immigrants. For example, in an analysis conducted for the committee, based on single births in the 1989-1991 Linked Birth/Infant Death Data Sets (Landale et al., 1998), the percentages of foreign-born and U.S.-born mothers with low-birthweight infants are, respectively, 4.1 and 5.4 percent for Mexicans, 4.4 and 4.7 percent for Cubans, and 4.8 and 5.2 percent for Central and South Americans. The more favorable measures hold for most Asian immigrants as well (Figure 3-1).

Although it is well documented that prenatal care contributes to positive birth outcomes, the more favorable health outcomes of immigrants often occur in the context of lower utilization of pre-

---

[1]Among the hypotheses that might explain the epidemiological paradox are several that point to possible data limitations. Some have argued, for example, that the unexpectedly low rate of infant mortality among Mexican-origin women, especially immigrants, may be due to underreporting of infant deaths or ethnic misclassifications on birth and/or death certificates. These hypotheses have received little support in research on the Mexican-origin population (Guendelman, 1995; Guendelman and English, 1995; Williams et al., 1986). There is no reason to believe that birthweight would be recorded more accurately for immigrants or ethnic minorities than for others, because birthweight is recorded on the birth certificate according to information provided by medical personnel.

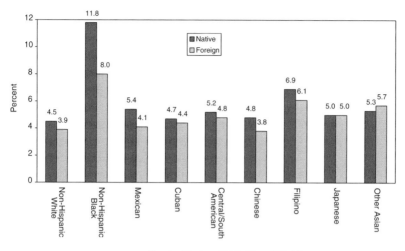

FIGURE 3-1   Percent with low birthweights among births to immigrant and native-born women by country or region of origin and race or ethnicity: 1990. Source: Landale et al. (1998).

natal care. There are indications that other factors may be of equal or greater importance. The role of lifestyle, for example, is only beginning to be documented and understood. More detailed studies of previously unmeasured lifestyle differences, such as nutrition and stress, that compare immigrants and natives, coupled with greater attention to alternative sources of information for pregnant immigrant women, could shed light on the precise role of formal medicine in protecting the health of children in immigrant families during infancy.

Consistent with the pattern for low birthweight, infant mortality rates are also lower for children of immigrants than for U.S.-born children of U.S.-born women, although sometimes the differences are slight. Among Hispanics, the infant mortality rates for single infants born to foreign-born and U.S.-born women are, respectively, 5.3 and 6.6 percent for Mexicans, 4.7 and 5.3 percent for Cubans, and for 5.0 and 5.2 percent for Central and South Americans. For Asians, infant mortality rates for infants of foreign-born and U.S.-born mothers are 4.3 and 4.6 percent for Chinese, 4.8 and 6.8 percent for Filipinos, 3.7 and 3.7 percent for Japa-

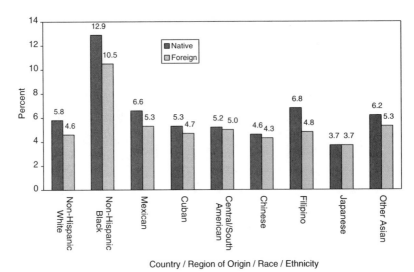

FIGURE 3-2 Infant mortality rate for children of immigrant and native-born women by country or region of origin or race or ethnicity: 1990. Source: Landale et al. (1998).

nese, and 5.3 and 6.2 percent for other Asians and Pacific Islanders. The infant mortality rates for non-Hispanic whites and blacks are also lower for foreign-born than for U.S.-born mothers (4.6 and 5.8 percent for whites, and 10.5 and 12.9 percent for blacks) (Figure 3-2) (Landale et al., 1998).

The pattern is less consistent for neonatal mortality rates (deaths at less than 28 days of age). The rate is lower for infants of foreign-born than for U.S.-born mothers for some groups (non-Hispanic whites, non-Hispanic blacks, Mexicans, Cubans, Filipinos), and higher for others (Central and South Americans, Chinese, Japanese, other Asians and Pacific Islanders). In contrast, the post-neonatal mortality rates (deaths between 28 days and 1 year of age) are lower for all immigrant groups except for Cubans, for whom the rates are somewhat higher (Landale et al., 1998).

A number of factors may contribute to these positive outcomes for infants in immigrant families. The relatively high levels of educational and occupational attainment among Asian immigrants may explain their superior infant health outcomes.

However, most immigrants from Latin America (particularly from Mexico) are neither affluent nor well educated; alternative explanations take into consideration the possible protective influence provided by their cultures of origin. For example, there is convincing evidence that cigarette smoking during pregnancy, a well-recognized cause of low birthweight, is substantially lower among immigrant women; statistically excluding the effect of that single factor substantially reduces the differential rates (Landale et al., 1998).

With regard to infant mortality, a nurturing and protective prebirth environment for the mother is most important. Along these lines, immigrant women of Mexican origin are less likely to use alcohol and drugs and may have a healthier diet than U.S.-born women (Cabral et al., 1990; Guendelman and Abrams, 1995). These healthful behaviors may be reinforced by strong family bonds among immigrant groups and communities that sustain cultural orientations that lead to healthful behavior, factors that become diluted with duration of residence in the United States. As we look to the future, however, it is possible that the increasing size and the geographic concentration of the immigrant population, especially from Mexico, will act to sustain these protective factors.

Additional study will allow researchers to identify the protective factors that contribute to the epidemiological paradox and to determine why, for some groups, acculturation leads to deteriorating health outcomes for infants. Such research should assess another possible explanation, as well: that women who are especially healthy may be more likely to immigrate to the United States than women who are less healthy; that is, that immigrant women are self-selected from among the more healthy women in their countries of origin, and they continue to have comparatively good health after they immigrate.

CHILDREN'S GENERAL HEALTH

Very little is known about the health of school-age children in immigrant families, and much of what is known derives from parental and self-reports. The 1994 National Health Interview Survey (NHIS) and the 1996 National Health and Nutrition Examination Survey (NHANES III) provide some health status parameters for children in immigrant families,[2] as reported by parents.

However, these data must be interpreted with caution for several reasons. The NHIS responses are not categorized by families' country of origin (across which there may be significant variations); the responses to both surveys reflect parental awareness of conditions rather than medically confirmed diagnoses; immigrant parents may be more hesitant than U.S.-born parents to reveal the existence of health problems to an interviewer, or they may have health expectations that differ from native-born parents, because they come from different cultures; and only the NHANES III has standardized translations of the survey instruments into Spanish and uses bilingual, bicultural interviews. For all these reasons, inconsistencies between parental reports of general health and of the prevalence of specific conditions should be treated as preliminary, and subject to additional study.

In the NHIS, first- and second-generation children and adolescents up to 17 years of age were reported by their parents to have fewer acute and chronic health problems (except for certain respiratory conditions) than third- and later-generation children in the same age range. This was reported for all age subcategories (i.e., 0 to 2, 3 to 5, 6 to 11, and 12 to 17).

Parents of first- and second-generation children surveyed by the NHIS also reported fewer health problems that limited the children's activity (4 percent for the first and second generations compared with 7 percent for the third and later generations), and they reported that children were less often placed in special classes or unable to attend school because of health problems (2 percent for the first and second generations compared with 5 percent for the third and later generations).

Paradoxically, despite reporting significantly fewer individual health problems, immigrant parents reported in the NHIS that their first- and second-generation immigrant children have somewhat less favorable health status than did parents of third- and later-generation children: 75 percent of immigrant parents com-

---

[2]NHANES III has data for children in Mexican-origin families only.

pared with 81 percent of U.S.-born parents reported their child to be in "excellent" or "very good" health. Comparable percentages (3 percent compared with 2 percent) reported their child to be in "fair" or "poor" health.

Parents were asked to rate their children's health as excellent, very good, good, fair, or poor in NHANES III. A clear difference was seen between all generations of Mexican-origin children and third- and later-generation white children in this measure of health. Mexican-origin children were more likely to be rated in fair or poor health by their parents than were third- and later-generation white children. Moreover, this difference was greatest for the first generation and declined with each generation (Mendoza and Dixon, 1998) (see Table 3-1).

Among first-generation Mexican-origin children, about 1 in 4 was rated by their parents to be in poor health. This compares to 1 in 25 for third- and later-generation white children. Third- and later-generation Mexican-origin children had similar rates as third- and later-generation black children, and both were twice as likely to be rated in fair or poor health compared with third- and later-generation white children. Mexican-origin children in all generations are therefore 2 to 9 times more likely to have parents who express concerns about their health than third- and later-generation white parents.

Data on migrant farmworker children, who are primarily second-generation children, provide more detail about parents' perceptions of their children's health and other aspects of health status. In a study of preschool children enrolled in the Migrant Head Start program, 56 percent of Hispanic parents considered their children to be in "excellent" or "very good" health, 34 percent to be in "good" health, and 9 percent in "fair" or "poor" health. The parents' impressions were consistent with a review of the children's health records, which indicated that 7 percent had "frequent" health problems, principally repeated upper respiratory infections (Aguirre International, 1997). Among the migrant population, it is likely that those children enrolled in Head Start have better health status than those not enrolled. Although this study did not collect data on health hazards posed by parental working conditions, particularly from pesticide residues on par-

TABLE 3-1   Percent with Selected Reported Health Conditions for First- and Second-Generation Children by Generation and for Third- and Later-Generation Children by Race and Ethnicity: 1996

Percent with Reported Condition[a]	First-Generation Mexican American	Second-Generation Mexican American	Third-Generation Mexican American
Perceived health to be fair or poor as assessed by parent			
< 5 yrs.	23.9 (3.33)	16.8 (1.05)	6.3 (0.83)
6-11 yrs.	27.6 (7.70)	20.0 (2.28)	6.6 (1.43)
12-16 yrs.	28.7 (4.99)	15.4 (2.52)	6.8 (1.63)
Asthma			
< 5 yrs.	2.2 (1.20)	5.2 (0.88)	8.1 (1.72)
6-11 yrs.	3.8 (2.74)	9.8 (2.71)	15.0 (4.09)
12-16 yrs.	3.1 (1.77)	6.6 (1.91)	8.5 (1.92)
Possible active infection on physical examination at time of survey[b]			
< 5 yrs.	8.3 (2.68)	9.1 (1.42)	12.3 (1.93)
6-11 yrs.	8.6 (3.66)	5.3 (1.43)	5.9 (1.57)
12-16 yrs.	4.0 (1.13)	2.1 (1.12)	4.7 (1.49)
Ever had anemia			
< 5 yrs.	9.7 (2.18)	14.5 (1.09)	11.0 (1.60)
6-11 yrs.	9.2 (3.14)	11.7 (2.08)	2.8 (0.93)
12 16 yrs.	8.7 (2.64)	7.2 (1.88)	4.3 (1.12)
Past 12 months any accidents, injury, or poisoning			
< 5 yrs.	3.7 (1.65)	5.5 (0.58)	10.0 (1.16)
6-11 yrs.	4.2 (3.26)	5.0 (1.16)	8.1 (1.95)
12-16 yrs.	3.6 (1.58)	7.5 (1.40)	10.7 (2.63)
Condition of Teeth - Fair to Poor			
< 5 yrs.	39.3 (5.10)	26.0 (2.49)	21.0 (1.80)
6-11 yrs.	60.1 (8.15)	42.6 (2.92)	23.5 (3.68)
12-16 yrs.	50.8 (4.65)	36.3 (3.24)	16.4 (1.99)
Problems seeing			
< 5 yrs.	0.2 (0.24)	1.1 (0.35)	0.7 (0.30)
6-11 yrs.	6.8 (2.42)	13.2 (2.42)	7.9 (1.19)
12-16 yrs.	18.8 (2.97)	15.2 (1.86)	13.3 (2.05)

[a]Parental reported condition from Household Youth Questionnaire NHANES III.
[b]Assessed by survey physicians by standardized physical examinations.

Non-Hispanic Black	Non-Hispanic White	Non-Hispanic Other
4.9 (0.73)	1.8 (0.35)	7.4(1.25)
6.9 (0.91)	2.0 (0.47)	3.5 (1.36)
7.4 (1.20)	3.5 (0.79)	8.4 (4.25)
9.0 (0.75)	5.1 (0.55)	6.6 (1.40)
9.4 (1.00)	10.6 (1.41)	12.4 (6.12)
12.6 (1.63)	12.8 (1.67)	12.9 (4.59)
12.1 (1.74)	7.1 (1.25)	5.1 (1.35)
5.9 (0.94)	5.0 (1.31)	16.0 (6.77)
3.0 (0.83)	4.6 (1.67)	4.4 (3.25)
11.2 (1.06)	6.4 (0.67)	10.7 (1.97)
7.4 (0.74)	7.2 (1.11)	7.4 (3.00)
6.4 (1.17)	8.4 (1.55)	3.6 (2.24)
6.3 (0.61)	12.8 (0.89)	7.4(1.69)
7.0 (0.96)	19.3 (2.31)	4.2 (1.92)
11.0 (1.15)	18.5 (2.15)	9.7 (3.33)
13.7 (1.37)	6.9 (0.89)	17.3 (2.37)
22.7 (1.52)	12.2 (1.20)	18.4 (4.36)
20.2 (2.05)	11.5 (1.64)	8.6 (3.23)
1.8 (0.35)	1.5 (0.34)	1.6 (1.06)
9.8 (1.17)	7.6 (1.07)	4.5 (2.19)
15.2 (1.63)	12.5 (1.80)	16.4 (6.77)

NOTE: Non-Hispanic Asians are not included because of small sample size.
Source: Mendoza and Dixon (1998).

ents' clothing and accidental contamination of the water supply, they are an additional health risk that warrants examination.

In a random sample of migrant farmworker women in Wisconsin with children age 16 or younger traveling with them, children ages 3 to 5 had immunization levels for DPT, polio, measles, and rubella roughly comparable to kindergarten children in the state (Slesinger et al., 1986). Children of migrant farmworkers had lower levels of immunization for mumps, and only half of the children under the age of 12 had received an annual checkup. The study also reported that children of migrant farmworkers were less likely to receive dental care than the general population of children in the United States. It should be noted that the sample size in this study was relatively small (330 children) and the children were primarily Mexican-origin.

Any overall conclusion from these studies about the general good health and well-being of children in migrant farmworker families must be tempered by the fact that the farmworker and migrant subpopulations are extremely heterogeneous. Factors such as ethnicity, recency of immigration, cultural and linguistic barriers to health care, widely varied living and working conditions, and availability and quality of health care make generalizations difficult. Moreover, inappropriate generalization could obscure significant health problems in specific subpopulations of migrant farmworkers.

CHRONIC HEALTH CONDITIONS

An accurate assessment of the prevalence of chronic health conditions and disability among children in immigrant families does not exist for the most part. But there is little reason to expect chronic conditions among them to differ from those for other children who belong to the same racial, ethnic, or income groups.

Children in the United States with chronic conditions often face significant financial and other barriers that complicate the provision of comprehensive services, and the barriers are likely to be more formidable for immigrants. Chronically ill children may require multiple diagnostic and therapeutic services from the medical, educational, and social service systems. These resources are often located in different institutions, each with specific and sometimes complex and changing eligibility criteria. As a result, providing for and coordinating the provision of care for a chronically ill child usually falls heavily to the family. That responsibility can be particularly difficult for the immigrant family, for whom differences in culture, language, access to care, and financial resources can complicate the process (Lequerica, 1993; Smith and Ryan, 1987).

Asthma is the most common severe chronic physical condition of children, and the rates of the disease have increased in the past few decades. It is a single condition influenced by several key factors, including access to care, utilization of medical and support services, housing conditions (notably cleanliness), and the influence of cultural values on the pattern of care provided. Asthma also provides measurable and meaningful outcomes for both short- and long-term morbidity and health care costs. Additional careful study of asthma in the immigrant population may serve as a valuable indicator of the health and well-being of immigrant children.

The prevalence of childhood asthma varies substantially across ethnic groups for reasons that reflect a combination of biological, cultural, and socioeconomic differences, although the mechanisms by which these factors work are not well understood. Children in immigrant families with asthma often have additional complicating factors. For some with pollen-sensitive forms of asthma, attacks may be exacerbated by the move from a tropical to a temperate climate with higher and more seasonably varying pollen rates (Echechipia et al., 1995; Sin et al., 1997). In addition, infection by viral pathogens to which children have not been exposed previously can trigger acute asthma episodes (Sokhandan et al., 1995). Cultural beliefs among immigrant families about the etiology and treatment of asthma may differ from the general U.S. population as well. For example, studies in the Puerto Rican community have demonstrated that the degree of acculturation is directly related to the likelihood of compliance with medically prescribed asthma therapy for children (Pachter and Weller, 1993).

New analyses conducted for the committee from NHANES III indicate that, among Mexican-origin children, the prevalence of asthma as reported by parents increased between the first, second, and third and later generations (Mendoza and Dixon, 1998) (see Table 3-1). By the third generation, parental reports of asthma among Mexican-origin parents exceeded those of U.S.-born white parents for children ages 0 to 12, but were lower for adolescents. Since these prevalences are based on parental reports, knowledge of the condition is essential. This knowledge, in turn, is most likely to be accurate for children who have been diagnosed by a health care professional. The possibility of generational differences in access to health care among children of Mexican origin may, as a result, be a factor in these results (with either underreporting or overreporting among the first generation). Clinical data are important to further assess the generational differences in the prevalence of asthma among immigrant Mexican-origin children.

Comprehensive and culturally sensitive care may be particularly important in the care of asthma, because access appears to be problematic for immigrant and minority populations. In one study, black and Hispanic children were less likely than white children to leave the hospital with appropriate home nebulization services, a cornerstone of chronic asthma therapy (Finkelstein et al., 1995).

INFECTIOUS DISEASES

The primary infectious diseases associated with significant morbidity and mortality among infants, children, and adolescents in the United States are perinatal infections, some of which are preventable with adequate prenatal care; human immunodeficiency virus (HIV) infection; vaccine-preventable illnesses among those inadequately immunized; tuberculosis among infants and children exposed to adults with tuberculosis; sexually transmitted diseases (other than HIV) among adolescents; and a range of respiratory and gastrointestinal infections responsible for minimal mortality but significant morbidity and expense.

These diseases occur among children of all racial and ethnic origins, but children of recently arrived immigrants are at particularly high risk of harboring or acquiring several of them. Rates of infection vary considerably by country of origin and socioeconomic status and are compounded if there is lack of access to health care in the United States. Furthermore, the infectious disease problems of children in immigrant families present a challenge to U.S. physicians, who may be inexperienced in diagnosing and treating conditions such as malaria, amebiasis, schistosomiasis and other helminthic infections, congenital syphilis, hepatitis B, and tuberculosis (American Academy of Pediatrics, 1997b). Tuberculosis, hepatitis B, and parasitic infections are of particular concern for the children in immigrant families, with implications for the health of the entire U.S. population.

In 1995, immigrants accounted for 7,930, or 35 percent, of total U.S. tuberculosis cases. Tuberculosis in the foreign-born population is concentrated geographically, both in terms of country of origin and state of residence. In 1995, two-thirds of immigrants with tuberculosis were from seven countries: Mexico (22 percent), the Philippines (13 percent), Vietnam (12 percent), China (5 percent), Haiti (5 percent), India (5 percent), and Korea (4 percent). Nearly 70 percent of those immigrants resided in four states: California, New York, Texas, and Florida (Binkin et al., 1996). Foreign-born people are at particular risk for drug-resistant tuberculosis infection, an important reason to identify these cases and ensure that they are provided appropriate care in order to minimize the risk of spread to the entire U.S. population (American Academy of Pediatrics, 1997a).

A diagnosis of tuberculosis infection in a child is a sentinel event, because it represents recent transmission in the community and therefore merits intensive investigation by public health authorities to identify the source. Control of this disease requires a combination of strategies, including a vigorous and adequately funded public health effort, improved policies and procedures for overseas screening of potential immigrants, and careful surveillance of cases once in the United States. It is of importance to the entire population as well as to immigrants with tuberculosis that immigrants are ensured access to appropriate health services.

Hepatitis B infection is highly endemic in China, Southeast Asia, Africa, the Pacific Islands, parts of the Middle East, and the Amazon Basin. In these areas, 8 to 15 percent of the population become chronically infected with the virus, which is a major cause of acute and chronic hepatitis, cirrhosis, and primary hepatocellular carcinoma. Universal hepatitis B vaccination is now recommended for all children born in the United States, and for children younger than 11 living in households of first-generation immigrants from countries with intermediate or high endemic rates of hepatitis B.

Parasitic infection rates ranging from 10 to 55 percent have been reported for immigrant pediatric populations in the United States, with *Trichuris* and *Giardia* the most frequently isolated parasites (Starke et al., 1994). Most intestinal parasites do not present a significant public health hazard in the United States, because effective sewage disposal and hygienic practices interrupt transmission. However, many immigrants live in crowded areas with poor sanitation, and transmission within households may occur. Intestinal parasites may be the cause of chronic or recurrent abdominal pain, diarrhea, anemia, and growth failure in children. Physicians should be particularly alert for their possible occurrence in children from Central and South America, Mexico, the Caribbean, Southeast Asia, and Africa.

One of the few measures of children's physical health status in the NHANES III that is determined by physician report is the assessment of a possible active infection in the child at the time of the survey. As seen in Table 3-1, comparisons between all generations of Mexican-origin children and third- and later-generation white children show no significant differences in the frequency of active infections (Mendoza and Dixon, 1998). There were also no differences in active infections between generations of Mexican origin nor between them and third- and later-generation black children. These data need to be interpreted with caution, given that they represent only one point in time and should not be generalized beyond immigrants of Mexican origin; however, they suggest that there may not be a significant difference in active infections between this group of foreign-born and U.S.-born children.

ENVIRONMENTAL TOXINS

High levels of lead in the blood pose a risk to brain development, particularly during the second and third years of life, and have been associated with hyperactivity, diminished intellectual ability, and impaired academic performance in school-age children.

National estimates of blood lead levels are not available for children from specific countries of origin, but it is evident that children in immigrant families may have a higher incidence of lead poisoning than third- and later-generation children for several reasons, including poverty, exposure to lead in their countries of origin, use of lead-containing products from their country of origin, and a higher likelihood of residing in lead-contaminated housing (Bellinger et al., 1989). One estimate from the most recent National Health and Nutrition Examination Survey (NHANES III) found elevated blood lead levels among Mexican-origin children, and a study of Mexican-born children in Santa Clara Valley, California, found lead levels above 10 µg/dL among 20 percent of the children, compared with 7 percent of third- and later-generation children (Snyder et al., 1995).

Although few countries sending large numbers of immigrants to the United States gather data from nationally representative samples, mean blood lead values from selected studies of children in those countries are considerably higher than the current U.S. mean of 3.5 µg/dL for 1- to 5-year-old children. For example, contemporaneous surveys of children in Mexico City indicate mean lead levels of 12.0 µg/dL in 2- to 4-year-olds (Salazar-Schettino et al., 1991) and 9.9 µg/dL in 1- to 5-year-olds (Romieu et al., 1995). Children residing in urban areas in China were reported to have mean lead levels of 21 µg/dL (Shen et al., 1996), and the mean cord blood lead level of Indian children born in Lucknow in 1990 was 17.0 µg/dL (Saxena et al., 1994).

An important source of lead exposure in Mexico is the leaded glaze on earthen pottery cookware (Rojas-Lopez et al., 1994), and elevated blood lead levels have been reported in Mexican-origin children from the same source (Gellert et al., 1993). In addition, in countries where gasoline still contains lead (including most developing countries), lead levels in children remain high, and most of this elevation is attributed to airborne lead from gasoline (Romieu et al., 1995; Shen et al., 1996). Elevated blood lead levels have been reported in children in immigrant families from the Middle East, India, and Pakistan from the use of eye cosmetics with high lead content (Al-Kaff, 1993; Sprinkle, 1995). Folk remedies that contain lead and are used to treat childhood illnesses have been reported for families of Mexican, Saudi Arabian, and

Hmong and other Asian origins (Baer and Ackerman, 1988; Yaish et al., 1992).

In an analysis of 136 Rhode Island census tracts, lead levels greater than 10 µg/dL were reported in 30 to 60 percent of children residing in census tracts with a high proportion (20 percent) of Hispanic immigrants, compared with elevated levels in less than 10 percent of children in census tracts with few immigrants (Sargent, 1997).

For migrant farmworkers, pesticides are an ever-present danger, with 1.2 billion pounds of pesticides used in U.S. agriculture annually. The Environmental Protection Agency estimates that as many as 300,000 farmworkers suffer from pesticide-related illnesses or injuries each year (U.S. General Accounting Office, 1992). One New York study found that one-third of the children interviewed who had worked in agriculture the previous year had been injured by pesticides during that time period (U.S. General Accounting Office, 1992). As harvesters, children encounter pesticide residues on crops. When children and adolescents eat, drink, or smoke in the fields, they ingest additional pesticides. And youngsters often are exposed to direct spray or drift while working in the fields or at home in adjacent migrant labor camps. These chemicals may cause acute ailments such as skin rashes, eye irritation, flu-like symptoms, and sometimes even death. They may also cause chronic harms such as birth defects, sterility, neurological damage, liver and kidney disease, and cancer (Wilk, 1993). Children are more likely to be harmed by pesticide exposures than are adults because they have lower body weight, higher metabolism, and immature immune and neurological systems (National Research Council, 1993).

NUTRITIONAL STATUS

Nutritional status is determined by measurements of children's height, weight, and dietary intake, as well as by biochemical parameters such as serum iron (Dwyer, 1991). Overall, the nutritional status of foreign-born children upon entering this country is directly related to their socioeconomic circumstances in the country of origin. Those who were better off in their home countries grow appropriately, and those who were living in poverty grow less well and proportionately to their degree of impoverishment. Given improved economic, nutritional, and health conditions, improved growth can be expected. Conversely, if poverty is unalleviated, it will continue to limit a child's growth.

There are currently only partial data on the nutritional status of children in immigrant families. For Hispanic and Asian immigrant groups, some information is available, but children from other countries, such as Eastern Europe, the former Soviet Union, Africa, and the Middle East, are for the most part invisible in the literature (Mendoza and Dixon, 1998).

For Mexican-origin immigrants, analyses of the Hispanic Health and Nutritional Examination Survey data for 1984 by Mendoza and Dixon (1998) found that, as a group, first-generation children tended to be shorter than their U.S.-born counterparts, an outcome that appeared to be the result of differences in poverty between the two groups. Weight was found to be less deviant than height from the U.S. median for both first- and second-generation children.

The greater deviation from the norm of height than weight resulted in obesity in a greater number of Mexican-origin children and adolescents in both the first and second generations. Although these children appear to have their stature affected by poverty, suggesting stunting due to poor nutrition and health, the increase in obesity would suggest the counterargument of adequate or overnutrition. Similar findings have been reported for some Asian children in immigrant families as well (Himes et al., 1992). The mechanism of this process, obesity in the face of poor linear growth, is not well understood, but one hypothesis proposes that hormonal changes during pregnancy as a result of a nutritional insult in utero may lead to changes in long-term linear growth (Popkin et al., 1996).

To explore further the issue of obesity and problems with linear growth, Mendoza and Dixon (1998) examined the daily intake of the four food groups by first- and second-generation Mexican-origin children. These data showed that consumption of the basic four food groups was similar or better for first-generation children than for second- and third- and later-generation children. In fact, for the age group 6 to 11 years, first-generation children appeared to have more balanced diets. However, the dietary intake data did not determine total caloric intake or serving size and therefore need to be viewed cautiously and confirmed by other studies.

Another way to confirm the adequacy of children's diets is by determining the prevalence of iron deficiency anemia. Iron deficiency anemia is the most commonly measured nutritional biochemical abnormality. There are other causes of anemia, but iron deficiency anemia is the most common among children, particularly for those under age 3 (Florentino and Guirriec, 1984; Looker et al., 1997; Lozoff et al., 1997).

Data on Mexican-origin children in general and reports of anemia by mothers of first-generation children suggest that high prevalences of anemia are not present, and for the most part are less than 3 percent (Looker et al., 1997; Mendoza and Dixon, 1998). Data from NHANES III show that parental reports of their children ever having anemia was about 9 percent for first-generation Mexican-origin children of all ages (see Table 3-1). For children less than age 5, there were no significant differences between first-generation Mexican-origin and third- and later-generation white children; there were also no significant differences between first- and either later-generation Mexican-origin children or third- and later-generation black children in this age group.

Data about the nutritional status of Asian children in immigrant families are limited and complicated by the diversity of Asian countries that send children to the United States. As a result, an understanding of the economic, nutritional, and health conditions of the countries of origin is essential to assessing the condition of these children.

In the 1980s, several studies reported on the growth parameters of children in immigrant families from Southeast Asia. Dewey reported significant stunting for age among Vietnamese, Hmong, Mien, and Laotian first-generation preschoolers (Dewey et al., 1986); 39 percent were below the fifth percentile for height, but only 7 percent were below the fifth percentile for weight, suggesting the presence of stunting but not wasting. In fact, Dewey found that children who had been in the United States longer were heavier but not taller. Other studies have similarly reported stunting among Southeast Asian children in immigrant families (Barry et al., 1983; Brown et al., 1986; Peck et al., 1981). Some evidence shows that, with improved economic, nutritional, and health conditions, these children have exhibited significant catch-up growth (Yip et al., 1992a, 1992b, 1993). But others have found persistent growth problems among them, including among second-generation children, which have been attributed to persistent health and nutritional problems related to poverty (Baldwin and Sutherland, 1988; Himes et al., 1992; Hyslop et al., 1996).

The limited data on the dietary intake of Asian children in immigrant families indicate that they initially consume traditional diets, but then make a transition to American foods (Story and Harris, 1988, 1989; Thuy et al., 1983). Southeast Asian mothers have been observed to reduce the practice of breastfeeding, apparently as a result of the need to work, the desire for convenience, and the sense that baby formula is superior (Serdula et al., 1991; Tuttle and Dewey, 1994). For Southeast Asians there are also findings of high levels of anemia—in some studies, among 18 to 36 percent of new immigrants (Goldenring et al., 1982; Peck et al., 1981). The prevalence of anemia indicates not only poor intake of iron-rich foods, but also possible loss of iron from gastrointestinal bleeding, commonly associated with active parasitic infections (Juckett, 1995; Sarfaty et al., 1983; Weissman, 1994; Wiesenthal et al., 1980). However, in addition to anemia from iron loss, Southeast Asian children in immigrant families also have a high prevalence of hemoglobinopathies (Craft et al., 1983; Hurst et al., 1983). It has been estimated that as many as 40 percent of Southeast Asian refugees (Vietnamese, 62%; Laotian, 22%; and Cambodian, 16%) have one or more congenital anemias (Glader and Look, 1996).

One of the few longitudinal studies of school-age children in immigrant families was done by Schumacher et al. (1987) in a Newcomers school in San Francisco. A group of 835 children from Mexico, El Salvador, Nicaragua, Honduras, Guatemala, Peru, China, Taiwan, Hong Kong, Philippines, Vietnam, Cambodia, and Laos were followed every 3 months for a year. All the children in immigrant families showed improved growth velocities that were either at or above the median for third- and later-generation white children. That is, they grew at a faster rate than the third- and later-generation children, implying that they were experiencing catch-up growth. By subgroup, 60 to 90 percent of the children, even those who started at two standard deviations below the median, showed significant catch-up growth (Schumacher et al., 1987).

OTHER HEALTH PROBLEMS

There are a number of other conditions for which children in immigrant families may be at increased risk, based on current prevalence rates among low-income U.S. ethnic groups. These include unintentional injury, the most important cause of mortality and serious disability for American children and adolescents; child maltreatment; and poor vision and dental health. Given higher rates of these conditions among children living in poverty, one might expect higher rates among children in immigrant families. However, parental report information from the NHANES III seen in Table 3-1 shows that the prevalence of accidents, injury, and poisoning among all ages of Mexican-origin children is significantly lower than that of third- and later-generation white children of similar ages (Mendoza and Dixon, 1998). Rates increase from the first to the third and later generations but remain lower than those reported by parents of third- and later-generation white children.

The opposite pattern is found for dental health. Parents of first-generation Mexican-origin children are significantly more likely to report that their children's teeth are in fair to poor condition than are parents of second- and third- and later-generation Mexican-origin children or parents of third- and later-generation white and black children (Mendoza and Dixon, 1998) (see Table 3-1). The third- and later-generation children of Mexican origin were more likely, however, to be reported as having fair to poor teeth than were third- and later-generation white children. For first-generation Mexican-origin youth and second-generation Mexican-origin 6- to 11-year-olds, vision problems were also reported at levels that exceed those of third- and later-generation children.

ADOLESCENT HEALTH

The 1995 National Longitudinal Study of Adolescent Health (called Add Health) provides estimates, based on new analyses conducted for the committee, of the perceived health status and health risk behavior of first- and second-generation adolescents compared with third-generation adolescents (Harris, 1998). Data are available for adolescents in families from countries of Central and South America, Mexico, Asia, Africa, and Europe.

As shown in Table 3-2 and Figure 3-3, overall and for most specific countries of origin, first-generation adolescents were less likely than second or third and later generations to consider themselves in poor health (specifically with neurological impairment, obesity, or asthma) or to have school absence due to health or emotional problems. By the third generation, reports of poor health often exceed those of third- and later-generation white adolescents. First-generation adolescents also reported less delinquent or violent behavior and less substance abuse than did later generations (see Table 3-2 and Figure 3-4). Among the first generation, those living in the United States for longer periods of time tended to be less healthy and to report increases in risk behaviors. (Figures 3-5 and 3-6 provide additional information by ethnic group and immigrant status.)

The Add Health survey also found that first-generation immigrant adolescents were older at age of first intercourse and had a lower probability of having had intercourse than later generations. However, first-generation adolescents were less likely to use birth control at first intercourse. These generational differences remained after statistically excluding the effects of family income, family composition, and neighborhood factors (Harris, 1998).

Other research addresses the influence of acculturation to American society among adolescents, particularly in regard to reproductive patterns and contraceptive use in the Hispanic population. A review by Brindis (1997) indicates that, with increased acculturation, Hispanic girls engage in sexual activity at earlier ages and are more likely to give birth outside marriage and to leave school. Moreover, Hispanic adolescents who consider themselves (or aspire to be) highly acculturated to American society report increased use of alcohol, tobacco, and illicit drugs (Brindis et al., 1995). Among the general population, relatively early childbearing is a common occurrence among young Hispanic women, with those age 18 to 24 almost twice as likely as white women (though less likely than black women) to have had

TABLE 3-2   Health Indicators for First- and Second-Generation Adolescents by Generation and for Third- and Later-Generation Adolescents by Race and Ethnicity: 1995 (means)

	First Generation	Second Generation	Non-Hispanic White, Third and Later Generations
Physical Health			
General health fair or poor	9.2	10.7	8.1
Missed school due to a			
health or emotional problem	33.5	36.5	33.6
Learning difficulties	9.3	12.5	16.9
Obesity	17.0	26.7	23.4
Asthma	4.8	8.1	12.2
Health and school problems index	0.74	0.94	0.93
Emotional Health			
Psychological distress	1.54	1.52	1.45
Positive well-being	2.85	2.87	3.06
Health Risk Behavior			
Ever had sex	31.3	33.9	36.7
Age at first intercourse[a]	15.1	14.9	14.8
Birth control/first intercourse[a]	56.2	57.3	67.1
Four or more delinquent acts	15.8	25.0	21.9
Three or more acts of violence	14.6	21.3	19.4
Use of three or more substances	8.3	17.4	25.1
Risk behavior index	0.7	0.98	1.03
N	1,651	2,526	10,248

NOTE: With the exception of age at first intercourse and emotional health, all differences are statistically significant at the .001 level. Non-Hispanic Asians are not included because of small sample size.

[a]These outcomes are based on the sample of adolescents who had ever had sex (N = 8,226).

Source: Harris (1998).

Non-Hispanic Black, Third and Later Generations	Non-Hispanic Other, Third and Later Generations	Hispanic, Third and Later Generations	Total
11.5	14.3	13.1	9.7
37.1	40.2	41.1	35.4
14.3	15.6	18.3	15.4
29.9	31.5	31.0	25.3
13.5	14.9	15.7	11.8
1.05	1.17	1.2	0.97
1.52	1.54	1.54	1.49
2.99	2.89	2.89	2.99
54.8	39.2	45.3	40.4
13.8	14.4	14.2	14.5
64.2	60.5	58.3	63.8
18.0	26.3	29.6	21.6
27.2	26.4	31.5	21.9
8.6	24.3	25.3	19.4
1.09	1.17	1.32	1.03
4,312	456	1,429	20,622

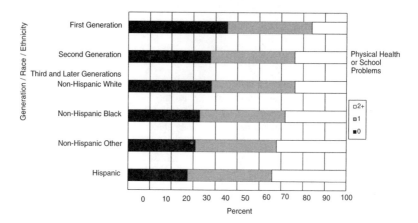

FIGURE 3-3   Percent with physical health or school problems for first- and second-generation adolescents by generation and third- and later-generation adolescents by race and ethnicity: 1995. Source: Harris (1998).

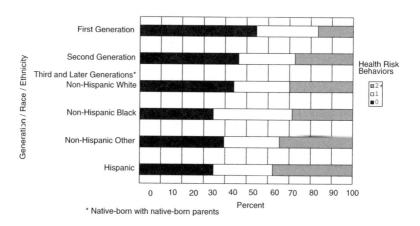

FIGURE 3-4   Percent engaging in health risk behavior for first- and second-generation adolescents by generation and third- and later-generation adolescents by race and ethnicity: 1995. Source: Harris (1998).

children. However, there are considerable differences in fertility rates among different Hispanic groups, with Mexican-origin women consistently having the highest and Cuban-origin women the lowest fertility rates.

Among adolescents in grades 7 through 12 in 1995, health risk behaviors involving early sexual activity, nonuse of birth control,

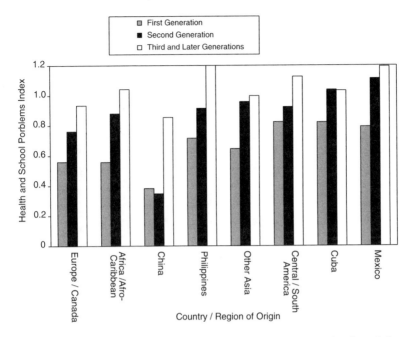

FIGURE 3-5 Mean physical health and school problems index for adolescents by generation and by country or region of origin: 1995. Source: Harris (1998).

delinquency, use of violence, and substance use tended to increase with each generation for adolescents from all countries of origin taken together (Table 3-2) (Harris, 1998). These risk behaviors also increased for each generation for children with origins in Mexico, Cuba, Central and South America, China, the Philippines, Japan, Vietnam, Africa and the Caribbean, and Europe and Canada, although the differences are not always statistically significant (Harris, 1998). For most of these behaviors, the third- and later-generation rates approach and even exceed those of third- and later-generation white children.

MENTAL HEALTH AND ADJUSTMENT

In general, the mental health and adjustment of children and youth in immigrant families appears to be similar to, if not better, than that of U.S.-born children and youth in U.S.-born families, in

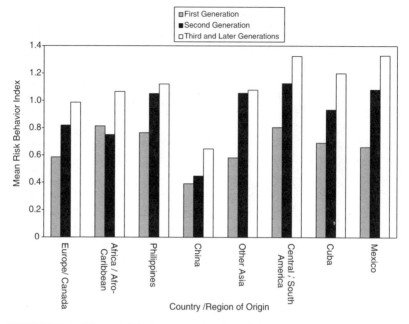

FIGURE 3-6   Mean risk behavior index for adolescents by generation and by country or region of origin: 1995. Source: Harris (1998).

most respects. There is, however, little systematic evidence available in this domain. Among the factors that have been measured with samples of children in immigrant families are acculturative stress, psychological adjustment, and academic achievement.

Acculturative Stress

A key factor in understanding psychosocial distress among children and youth in immigrant families is acculturative stress (Aronowitz, 1984; Gil et al., 1994; Gil and Vega, 1996; Zambrana and Silva-Palacios, 1989). Acculturative stress is an aspect of children's adaptation to the cultures and social structures of a new host country. The kinds of problems associated with acculturative stress include:

• Language problems as children and their families negotiate a new social system in which their native languages may not be understood and in which they may not know the language of the host country;

• Perceived discrimination from the larger society because of differences such as language, skin color, clothing, food habits, and other physical features;

• Perceived cultural incompatibilities between the home culture and the host culture resulting from different family values, interaction styles, social roles, and socialization practices; and

• Increasing gaps between the cultural affiliations of adults and children and their adherence to home country or host country cultural values and norms.

A study examining acculturative stress among Hispanic teenage boys found that second- and third- and later-generation Hispanics from low acculturation backgrounds who were primarily Spanish speaking and who experienced little family pride, high levels of language conflicts, and perceived discrimination from the larger society were at greatest risk for psychological distress. For first-generation adolescents, higher levels of acculturation corresponded with increased family conflict and decreased family pride. Bicultural individuals born in the United States experienced less acculturation stress, more family pride, and the most positive outcomes (Gil et al., 1994).

In general, mental health researchers have begun to establish that bicultural individuals are more likely to be better adjusted in a new society. This is due to the fact that they not only maintain the strengths of their home culture, but also retain supportive social links to that culture while they develop the language and social skills needed to successfully negotiate their new cultural setting (LaFromboise et al., 1993; Pawliuk et al., 1996). However, more research is needed to further validate these relationships.

Other studies have focused on the context of the receiving host communities and their impact on children's adjustment. One study differentiated the reception of Cuban and Nicaraguan immigrants in Miami (Gil and Vega, 1996). In this study, Cubans were more actively supported by the U.S. government, for example, in obtaining refugee status, work permits, and other supports; these supports were not as broadly extended to the Nicaraguans. The results of this study emphasized that supporting the family was more important than supporting an ethnic enclave. This research also established that adolescents acculturated more quickly than their parents, particularly with respect to English language acquisition, and that boys acculturated more quickly than girls. A key finding of this study was that, at equivalent stages of adjustment, the Nicaraguans experienced more acculturation conflicts and perceived more discrimination than the Cubans. Differences in the supports provided to these two Hispanic communities and differential response from the broader society in support of these groups were particularly reflected in the adolescents' adjustment.

Others have found that the degree of acceptance provided by the ethnic enclave may also affect the adjustment of children in immigrant families. McKelvey and Webb (1996) examined the expectations of Vietnamese Amerasian adolescents and young adults (born to Vietnamese mothers and American fathers) before they left Vietnam and the actual support they received from the Vietnamese community upon arrival. In general, the established Vietnamese community in the United States was not very supportive of the Amerasian Vietnamese.

The investigators found that the adolescents who had higher expectations for support from the U.S. Vietnamese community and did not receive it had the highest depressive symptoms when they were assessed several months after arrival. The investigators also discovered other factors that may have contributed to the worsening mental health of the Amerasian youth following immigration, including traveling alone or with only partial family support, close identification with other youths from whom they were separated upon arrival in this country, limited education, and little or no knowledge of English. This study underlines the importance of the local ethnic community to the mental health and adjustment of children in immigrant families. The study also provides important cautions about decisions concerning the determination of ethnicity, the appropriate ethnic community of resettlement, and the response from the local community and national government.

Although the family is the nexus of the growth and development of immigrant children, as it is for all children, differential rates of acculturation by parents and children have been associated with family problems and conflicts. Variable rates of acculturation have also been linked with psychological distress among children in immigrant families (Aronowitz, 1984; Chiu et al., 1992; Gil and Vega, 1996; Zambrana and Silva-Palacios, 1989). Common family problems include illness of a key adult, difficulties maintaining the family's financial well-being, spousal conflict, and parental drinking. Such family problems have been predictive of higher rates of adolescent distress (Zambrana and Silva-Palacios, 1989). In particular, girls seem to respond more strongly to family conflicts than boys, perhaps due to the fact that girls are thought to place more emphasis on social relations in developing their sense of self (Zambrana and Silva-Palacios, 1989). Boys may be buffered from family conflicts because they tend to spend more time outside the home. However, their tenuous family ties place them at risk for developing other kinds of problems.

In general, very little is known about the effect of the migration experience itself on children and adolescents in immigrant families. Migration from one country to another and from rural to urban areas has been found to be stressful for adults (Desjarlais et al., 1995; Hull, 1979; Kasl and Berkman, 1983; Kuo, 1976; Portes and Rumbaut, 1996; Sanua, 1970), but little is known about the sources of the stress and its manifestations at the individual level. A study by McKelvey and Webb (1996) illustrates and other research confirms that the health and well-being of children in immigrant families may be influenced by the circumstances surrounding the decision to migrate, the resources of the family, and the response of the receiving community to the immigrants (Cervantes and Castro, 1985; Portes and Rumbaut, 1996; Portes et al., 1992; Rogler, 1994; Rogler et al., 1989, 1991).

The stages of family adjustment over the course of the immigration experience also affect the psychological health of children and adolescents (Aronowitz, 1984; Gil and Vega, 1996; Pawliuk et al., 1996), although some research indicates that immigrants present fewer behavioral problems than native-born children (Gibson and Ogbu, 1991). Often, the family's first year in the United States may be characterized by feelings of euphoria over the success of their immigrating. However, the second year tends to be the most stressful, as the impact of acculturative stress is completely experienced. The third and subsequent years vary greatly psychologically, depending on the interplay of family factors and contextual variables. The response of the host community to the family may be particularly critical to the psychological well-being of children in immigrant families in the third and subsequent years.

Psychological Adjustment

Some have speculated that during adolescence the stresses of immigration are likely to be expressed as identity problems pertaining to views of the self, issues of control and efficacy, and fit into the peer group, with the school being a particularly critical context for development (Aronowitz, 1984; Gil et al., 1994; Munroe-Blum et al., 1989; Phinney, 1990; Phinney and Chavira, 1995; Rousseau et al., 1996; Rumbaut, 1998b). Aronowitz (1984) notes that children in immigrant families face a challenging double bind: if they maintain their cultural heritage over time, they risk greater discrimination and alienation from the host culture; if they abandon their cultural heritage, they risk alienation and rejection from family and friends, with no guarantees of acceptance from the wider society. Features like racial differences accentuate the differences between the immigrant child and the host society and heighten this dilemma (Phinney and Chavira, 1995).

Psychological adjustment was studied in research conducted for the committee using the National Educational Longitudinal Survey (NELS) of 1988 for 8th graders from China, the Philippines, Mexico, and other Hispanic countries (Kao, 1998) and the 1995 National Longitudinal Study of Adolescent Health (Add Health) for adolescents in grades 7 through 12 in 1995 with origins in Mexico, Cuba, Central and South America, China, the Philippines, Japan, Vietnam, Africa and the Caribbean, and Europe and Canada (Harris, 1998). The constructs assessed in Add Health were psychological distress and psychological well-being; NELS measured self-efficacy (feelings of having control over the direction of one's life), self-concept, and alienation (feelings of being unpopular among school peers).

The NELS analyses (Kao, 1998) indicated that first- and second-generation youth had significantly lower feelings of self-efficacy and higher feelings of alienation from their schoolmates than third- and later-generation white youth. In contrast, the immigrant youth and their white counterparts with U.S.-born parents did not differ in their self-concepts. The Add Health analyses (Harris, 1998) found no differences between first- and second-generation immigrant youth and third- and later-generation white youth in psychological well-being and distress (see Table 3-2). Taken together, these results may suggest that immigrant youth are able to maintain positive feelings about themselves and their general well-being, despite perceiving that they have relatively less control over their lives and are less well accepted by their school peers.

After the effects of socioeconomic status are statistically excluded, the NELS data continue to show relatively lower self-efficacy among first- and second-generation youth who are Hispanic and Asian compared with third- and later-generation white youth (see Figures 3-7 and 3-8). Black youth in immigrant families and third- and later-generation white youth, however, no longer differ significantly. With respect to alienation, after controls are added, first- and second-generation Asian youth continue to show higher feelings of alienation than third- and later-generation white youth. Among Hispanics, however, only the second generation continues to differ significantly from third- and later-generation white youth; among black youth, only the third generation shows significant differences. It is also important to note that, especially for Hispanic youth in immigrant families, low socioeconomic status is an important explanatory factor, leading to reports of lower self-efficacy and greater alienation.

When controls for socioeconomic influences such as family and neighborhood poverty are added in the Add Health data, differences in psychological well-being and distress emerge as well, but they are in the opposite direction from those found in the NELS data. When differences are found, first- and second-generation immigrant youth demonstrate better psychological well-being than third- and later-generation white youth. There is one exception, however: adolescents from the Philippines, among the most Americanized of the immigrant groups studied and a group speaking English as its native language, experienced higher psychological distress in every generation than third- and later-

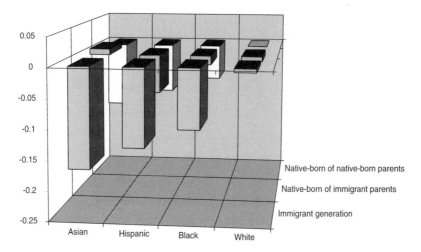

FIGURE 3-7   Estimates of adolescent self-efficacy. Note: The baseline is the score of white third-generation youths (native-born children of native-born parents). Source: Kao (1998).

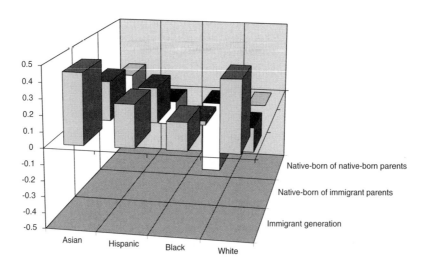

FIGURE 3-8   Estimates of adolescent alienation at school. Note: The baseline is the score of white third-generation youths (native-born children of native-born parents). Source: Kao (1998).

generation white adolescents. Family and neighborhood poverty were among the most influential predictors of psychological stress and well-being for all children. Harris (1998) interprets the data as demonstrating the protective influence of immigrant status among youth that emerges once the effects of greater exposure to poverty and inner-city neighborhoods are eliminated.

Some evidence of a protective function of immigrant status is also found in recent studies of suicide. A study of suicide trends among adolescent immigrants and ethnic groups in California found that first-generation immigrant adolescents were at a slightly lower risk of suicide, regardless of age, than third- and later-generation adolescents. The suicide rate for immigrants was the same as that of lifelong residents among third- and later-generation white and black adolescents, but the rates for Mexi-can-origin adolescents were lower than those for all third- and later-generation adolescents (Sorenson and Shen, 1996). A simi-larly low rate of suicide among Mexican-origin adolescents, com-pared with the third- and later-generation adolescent population, was found throughout the Southwest. In Miami, a longitudinal study of Cuban, Nicaraguan, other Hispanic, black, and non-His-panic white adolescent boys found the highest rate of suicide at-tempts among Nicaraguans and other Hispanics. In that study, higher levels of acculturation among minority groups were asso-ciated with an increase in suicide attempts.

The Children of Immigrants Longitudinal Study, conducted in Southern California (San Diego) and South Florida (Miami and Fort Lauderdale), is the first large-scale survey of changes in the family, community, and educational experiences of children and youth in immigrant families from nine countries of origin in the Western hemisphere and Asia (see Portes, 1996; Portes and MacLeod, 1996; Portes and Rumbaut, 1996; Rumbaut, 1994b, 1995, 1997b, 1998b). Although it does not provide nationally represen-tative estimates for children from these countries of origin and does not include comparative data from U.S.-born children and youth in U.S.-born families, the survey is a rich source of psycho-logical data and provides insights into the processes that might underlie patterns in the psychological well-being of immigrant youth. For example, Rumbaut (1998b) has recently identified the rise of a reactive ethnicity among immigrant youth. That is, some youth—notably those of Mexican and Filipino descent—increasingly identify themselves by their foreign nationality (e.g., "Filipino") or with a pan-ethnic (e.g., "Asian") label. He speculates that this pattern points to a growing identification of immigrant youth with U.S. minority groups that, if sustained, may have important implications for their later development. At the same time, the vast majority of youth in this sample agree that "there is no better country to live in than the United States."

Research was conducted for the committee based on data from this survey, focusing on children and youth in immigrant families living in San Diego who were from Mexico, the Philippines, Vietnam, Cambodia, and Laos (Rumbaut, 1998a). This study assessed possible risk and protective factors for low self-esteem and depressive symptoms, including gender, country of origin, intrafamily and extrafamily contexts and stressors, educational aspirations and achievement, language preference and skills, and physical looks and popularity with the opposite sex.

The study found lower self-esteem and higher depressive symptoms among youth in immigrant families for girls and for children experiencing high parent-child conflict, low family cohesion, recent serious illness or disability in the family, a high proportion of English-only spoken in the neighborhood, a school perceived as unsafe, dissatisfaction with physical looks, and lack of popularity with the opposite sex.[3] Also associated with low self-esteem were being of Filipino or Vietnamese origin, a recent family move to another home, low grades and educational aspirations, current limited English proficiency, and limited English proficiency in 1991 (see Table 3-3). Subsequent analyses of the Children of Immigrants Longitudinal Study (Rumbaut, 1998b) also found that self-reports of experiences of racial and ethnic discrimination were associated with a higher incidence of depressive symptoms. Self-esteem, in turn, is significantly associated

---

[3]Seven additional factors associated with higher depression were a later age at arrival in the United States, a nonintact family, a recent worsening of the family's economic situation, perceptions of poor teaching quality or unfairness, experience with stress in school, high proportion of friends not planning to attend college, and experience with racial or ethnic discrimination.

with the school performance and ambitions of these youth in immigrant families. Interestingly, the NELS data discussed above also revealed the importance of language factors and school experiences for feelings of self-efficacy among Hispanic and black youth in immigrant families, but not for Asian youth in immigrant families (see Kao, 1998).

Despite the potential importance of these factors for enhancing or reducing self-esteem and depression among children in immigrant families, national estimates of the prevalence of their experience with most of these factors are not available (exceptions are educational aspirations and achievements, as measured by NELS, and language proficiency, as measured by the decennial census).

Academic Achievement

Children from immigrant families face many potential challenges to their educational success. Many of them come from homes in which English is not the main spoken language. Parents are often unfamiliar or uncomfortable with avenues for participation in their children's schooling, and some have received little formal education. Immigrant families tend to settle in large urban areas that have troubled school systems (Fuligni, 1998). It follows that these children may experience difficulties at school— yet a handful of recent studies have begun to question this assumption.

Achievement Scores

Students in immigrant families appear to exceed prevailing assumptions about their school performance. In fact, some researchers have found that adolescents in immigrant families perform just as well if not better in school than their U.S.-born peers with U.S.-born parents (Fletcher and Steinberg, 1994; Fuligni, 1997; Kao and Tienda, 1995; Rosenthal and Feldman, 1991; Rumbaut, 1995, 1998b). Analysis commissioned by the committee from the National Educational Longitudinal Survey of 1988 corroborated this broad conclusion (Kao, 1998). Specifically, first- and second-generation children nationally have slightly higher

TABLE 3-3 Predictors of Self-Esteem and Depressive Symptoms Among Children of Immigrants: 1995-96[a]

Predictor Variables	Self-Esteem (Mean = 3.298)				CES-D Depression (Mean = 1.681)			
	Beta	T-ratio	p	ΔR^2	Beta	T-ratio	p	ΔR^2
Gender, Age at Arrival, Ethnicity:				.033 ***				.032 ***
Gender (0=male, 1=female)	-.056	(-3.12)	**		.165	(7.72)	***	
Age at arrival in the U.S.[b]			NS		.044	(1.93)	*	
Filipino	-.075	(-3.85)	***				NS	
Vietnamese	-.065	(-3.49)	***				NS	
Intra-Family Contexts and Stressors:				.147 ***				.127 ***
Intact family			NS		-.048	(-2.36)	*	
Parent-child conflict	-.180	(-9.15)	***		.200	(8.52)	***	
Family cohesion	.091	(4.85)	***		-.050	(-2.24)	*	
Family economic situation worse			NS		.055	(2.70)	**	
Family moved to another home	.068	(3.97)	***				NS	
Seriously ill or disabled since T1	-.056	(-3.34)	**		.045	(2.21)	*	
Extra-Family Contexts and Stressors:				.026 ***				.024 ***
English-only in neighborhood	-.046	(-2.57)	**		.067	(3.13)	**	
School perceived as unsafe	-.086	(-4.77)	***		.042	(1.97)	*	
Teaching quality and fairness			NS		-.042	(-1.97)	*	
School stress events experienced			NS		.050	(2.18)	*	
Friends' no-college plans			NS		.058	(2.61)	**	
Discrimination trumps education			NS		.054	(2.58)	**	

Achievement and Aspirations:	.098 ***			.001 NS		
Educational achievement (GPA)	.069	(3.49)	***			NS
Educational aspirations	.143	(7.21)	***			NS
English language proficiency	.197	(9.30)	***			NS
LEP status at T1	−.068	(−3.10)	**			NS
Looks and Opposite Sex:	.150 ***			.039 ***		
Dissatisfied with physical looks	−.343	(−19.58)	***	.185	(8.85)	***
Popular with opposite sex	.169	(9.66)	***	−.069	(−3.33)	**
R^2	.454			.223		
Adjusted R^2	.448			.215		

[a]Least-Squares Multiple Regressions for San Diego Sample, T2. Standardized regression coefficients (betas), with T-ratios in parentheses. R^2 = change in the square of the multiple correlation coefficient. Significance levels: *** p < .0001; ** p < .01; * p < .05; NS = Not Significant.

[b]A 4-point variable, where 0 = born in U.S., 1 = 0-5 years old at arrival, 2 = 6-10 years old at arrival, 3 = 11-15 years old. It is an index both of length of residence in the U.S. and, if foreign-born, age/developmental stage at arrival in U.S.

Source: Rumbaut (1998a).

grades and math test scores than third- and later-generation children, but their reading test scores are somewhat lower than those of third- and later-generation children (Kao and Tienda, 1995).

The relationship between achievement and generational status is not uniform, but varies with country of origin. As Table 3-4 shows, Mexican-origin children in every generation have similar grades and math test scores, although later generations have better reading test scores. Mexican-origin children in every generation also have substantially lower educational achievements than third- and later-generation white children; most of the difference for each generation is explained by lower parental education and family income among the Mexican-origin children (Kao, 1998).

Children in Chinese-origin immigrant families, especially the second generation, exceed third- and later-generation Chinese-origin children in grades and math test scores. However, only the second generation exceeds the third and later generations in reading test scores. First- and second-generation Chinese-origin children also exceed third- and later-generation white children in grades and math test scores; the second generation has higher reading scores as well. The superior grades and math test scores of first-generation Chinese-origin children are not explained by socioeconomic status, psychological well-being, or other school experiences. For the second generation, however, one-third to one-half of the superior performance is explained by these factors, particularly parental education and family income (Kao, 1998).

Among Filipino-origin children, the second generation also achieves better grades and math and reading test scores than the first or third and later generations (Table 3-4). Compared with third- and later-generation white children, first- and second-generation Filipino-origin children achieve higher grades. The second generation achieves higher math and reading test scores (Kao, 1998).

In the San Diego study, children in immigrant families at every grade level had higher grades than the district-wide average, and their school dropout rate was lower, even among Mexican-origin children, despite significant socioeconomic and linguistic handicaps. Factors contributing to these outcomes were these children's greater amount of time spent doing homework, lesser time spent watching television, and the higher educational aspirations of the children and parents in immigrant families (Rumbaut, 1998a).

Family and School Support for Educational Success

The National Household Education Survey was used in analyses conducted for the committee to estimate exposure to risk factors for first- and second-generation children ages 3 to 8 for Hispanics, Asians, and whites (Nord and Griffin, 1998). Estimates for specific countries of origin are not possible because of the limited sample size and lack of information on countries of origin.

Among children generally, it has been found that family members can foster school success by engaging in various activities with their young children, including teaching them letters and numbers, reading to them, and working on projects with them (Table 3-5). For seven different activities of this type in 1996, among third- and later-generation white children, the proportion of children with parents engaged in such activities during the past week ranged from 75 to 93 percent; the proportions for children in immigrant families were about the same to no more than 11 percentage points smaller. Among children in immigrant families, the proportions were usually higher for second-generation children than for the first generation, and the proportions tended to be 10 to 15 percentage points lower for Hispanic children than for Asians (Nord and Griffin, 1998).

It has also been found that, among parents generally, they can foster school achievement by taking their children on a variety of educational outings (Table 3-5). Estimates of the proportion of children whose parents took them on six different types of outings in 1996 ranged widely from 12 to 65 percent and did not vary systematically between immigrant and U.S.-born children, between first- and second-generation immigrants, or between Hispanic and Asian children in immigrant families (Nord and Griffin, 1998).

Parental involvement in their children's schools is a third set of activities that has been found for children generally to foster school achievement (Table 3-5). Among third- and later-generation children in 1996, 68 percent of whites had parents highly in-

TABLE 3-4   Descriptive Characteristics of 8th Grade Youth

	CHINESE			FILIPINOS		
	Immigrant Generation	Native-born of Foreign-born Parents	Native-born of Native-born Parents	Immigrant Generation	Native-born of Foreign-born Parents	Native-born of Native-born Parents
Self-efficacy, or locus of control	-0.241^c	0.011	0.073	-0.156	0.011	-0.006
	-0.591	-0.567	-0.757	-0.631	-0.553	-0.806
Self-concept	-0.115	-0.021	-0.058	-0.043	0.023	-0.33
	-0.644	-0.709	-0.659	-0.578	-0.641	-0.561
Alienation, or unpopularity	0.349^c	0.283^b	0.192	0.207	0.198	0.312
	-0.479	-0.453	-0.402	-0.407	-0.4	-0.479
Middle school grade point average	3.356^c	3.447^c	2.992	3.203^b	3.247^c	3.013
	-0.654	-0.568	-0.957	-0.687	-0.689	-0.74
Math test scores	56.802^c	61.363^c	53.077	50.736	56.085^c	53.651
	-9.35	-8.531	-13.564	-9.6	-9.888	-11.786
Reading test scores	49.480^b	58.204^c	49.797	49.181^b	54.587^a	55.297
	-10.166	-7.887	-10.538	-9.219	-9.239	-9.983
Parents' education	14.045^a	15.944^c	14.923	15.426^c	15.896^c	13.875
	-2.758	-3.252	-2.607	-1.973	-2.214	-1.147
Family income (in $10,000)	3.353^c	6.160^c	4.708	3.912	5.558^a	3.797
	-3.49	-4.481	-4.247	-3.044	-4.165	-1.382
Home language use Non-English language only	0.201^c	0.111^c	0.038	0.139^c	0.217^c	0
	-0.403	-0.316	-0.196	-0.347	-0.414	0

MEXICAN			OTHER HISPANICS			WHITES
Immigrant Generation	Native-born of Foreign-born Parents	Native-born of Native-born Parents	Immigrant Generation	Native-born of Foreign-born Parents	Native-born of Native-born Parents	Native-born of Native-born Parents
-0.282^c	-0.151^c	-0.113^c	-0.086^b	-0.049^a	-0.068^b	0.056
−0.619	−0.626	−0.633	−0.62	−0.684	−0.685	−0.605
-0.148^b	-0.098^b	−0.025	0.012	0.003	−0.025	−0.016
−0.62	−0.649	−0.663	−0.656	−0.642	−0.683	−0.662
0.288^c	0.263^c	0.140^a	0.219	0.166	0.206	0.17
−0.454	−0.441	−0.348	−0.416	−0.373	−0.405	−0.376
2.707^c	2.760^c	2.743^c	2.853	2.796^b	2.803^b	2.959
−0.734	−0.7	−0.743	−0.746	−0.681	−0.747	−0.751
45.393^c	45.639^c	46.383^c	46.970^c	48.547^c	46.674^c	52.547
−8.721	−7.891	−8.903	−10.121	−9.844	−9.103	−9.837
43.420^c	45.772^c	47.671^c	47.662^c	48.484^c	47.613^c	52.355
−8.59	−8.575	−9.193	−9.732	−9.591	−9.658	−9.717
11.200^c	11.887^c	13.066^c	13.512^c	14.000^b	14.033^b	14.546
−2.071	−2.165	−1.997	−2.968	−2.984	−2.4	−2.433
1.796^c	2.239^c	2.773^c	2.990^c	3.783^b	3.290^c	4.648
−1.869	−2.037	−2.103	−3.324	−4.008	−2.446	−3.9
0.251^c	0.169^c	0.112^c	0.187^c	0.218^c	0.045^c	0.007
−0.435	−0.375	−0.315	−0.391	−0.414	−0.208	−0.085

TABLE 3-4   (Continued)

	CHINESE			FILIPINOS		
	Immigrant Generation	Native-born of Foreign-born Parents	Native-born of Native-born Parents	Immigrant Generation	Native-born of Foreign-born Parents	Native-born of Native-born Parents
School experiences						
Ever repeat	0.121	0.029[b]	0.208	0.119	0.027[c]	0.2
	−0.327	−0.167	−0.415	−0.325	−0.164	−0.414
Currently enrolled in bilingual program	0.144[c]	0.037	0.043	0.091[b]	0.009	0
	−0.353	−0.191	−0.209	−0.289	−0.096	0
N	134	107	25	108	114	16

[a] $p<.05$
[b] $p<.01$
[c] $p<.001$

Source: The National Education Longitudinal Study of 1988. Kao (1998).

volved in school, somewhat more than the 59 percent for Hispanics and 56 percent for blacks. Among children in immigrant families, the proportion with parents highly involved in school was 57 percent, although most of the difference between these children and third- and later-generation white children was accounted for by the higher proportion with a moderate level of parental involvement. Parental involvement was greater for the second generation than the first (58 versus 50 percent highly involved). Among children in immigrant families, Hispanics were less likely then Asians to have highly involved parents (49 versus 57 percent) (Nord and Griffin, 1998).

Early childhood programs prior to kindergarten help children prepare for school. The proportions attending early childhood programs among third- and later-generation children were 58, 66, and 47 percent, respectively, for whites, blacks, and Hispanics, compared with 42 percent for children in immigrant families. The

MEXICAN			OTHER HISPANICS			WHITES
Immigrant Generation	Native-born of Foreign-born Parents	Native-born of Native-born Parents	Immigrant Generation	Native-born of Foreign-born Parents	Native-born of Native-born Parents	Native-born of Native-born Parents
0.273^c	0.214^c	0.214^c	0.184	0.18	0.212^b	0.148
−0.447	−0.41	−0.41	−0.39	−0.386	−0.409	−0.355
0.141^c	0.067^c	0.047	0.147^c	0.062^a	0.069^b	0.034
−0.349	−0.25	−0.212	−0.356	−0.242	−0.254	−0.182
215	578	763	121	195	242	13952

second generation was more likely than the first to attend such programs, and Hispanic children in immigrant families were slightly less likely than Asians to attend such programs (Nord and Griffin, 1998).

Children generally have been found to learn better if the schools they attend are well-disciplined and parental participation may be encouraged by a variety of school practices that foster such involvement. In parental ratings of children's schools along 10 dimensions, the proportion with favorable or very favorable parental responses was 45 to 67 percent for third- and later-generation white children. The proportions with favorable ratings were 2 to 10 percentage points lower along most dimensions for third- and later-generation blacks and Hispanics. These proportions varied between about 15 percentage points less and 15 percentage points more for third-generation children. They also varied substantially but in no specific direction for first- and

TABLE 3-5   Percent with Parents Reporting Selected Family Educational
and School Experiences for Children Ages 3 to 8 by Generation and for
Third- and Later-Generation Children by Race and Ethnicity: 1996

Characteristic	Children 3-8 Years	First and Second Generations	
		Total	First Generation
Total (thousands)	22,959	3,213	430
Family Involvement at Home			
In the past week, someone in family:			
Taught child letters, words, or numbers[a]	93%	92%	86%
Taught child songs or music[a]	76	73	68
Took child along while doing errands[a]	95	91	97
Number of times read to child:[b]			
Not at all	7	11	13
Once or twice	20	26	34
3 or more times	28	25	23
Every day	44	37	31
Told child a story	77	76	74
Worked on arts and crafts project with child	72	65	59
Played a game, sport, or exercised with child	92	86	82
Involved child in household chores	95	86	83
Worked on a project with child like building, making or fixing something[c]	67	56	51
In the past month, someone in the family:			
Visited the library with child	44	38	32
Went to a play, concert, or other live show with the child	30	26	21
Visited an art gallery, museum, or historical attraction with child	20	20	17
Visited a zoo or aquarium with child	17	23	21
Talked with child about family history or ethnic heritage	52	55	60
Attended an event with child sponsored by a community, ethnic, or religious group	50	41	39
Attended an athletic or sporting event in which child was not a player	33	22	12

				Third and Later Generations			
Second Generation	Hispanic	Asian	White	Total	White	Black	Hispanic
2,782	1,734	239	837	19,746	14,166	3,326	1,652
93%	90%	97%	94%	94%	93%	96%	91%
73	70	72	78	76	76	83	69
90	88	79	99	95	96	94	94
11	14	6	7	7	6	8	8
25	32	18	17	19	17	25	24
26	25	25	24	29	28	30	29
38	29	51	51	45	48	37	39
77	71	83	84	77	78	73	79
66	59	74	74	73	75	66	72
87	81	92	94	93	94	92	87
86	84	74	90	96	97	95	92
58	47	59	69	68	70	63	67
38	27	54	51	45	47	40	39
27	21	34	33	30	29	36	27
20	15	24	27	20	19	22	20
23	20	32	26	16	14	23	21
54	52	50	61	51	47	65	54
41	35	38	51	51	52	52	43
24	18	19	30	35	36	33	27

(Table continued on next page)

TABLE 3-5   Continued

Characteristic	Children 3-8 Years	First and Second Generations	
		Total	First Generation
Family Involvement at School			
Parents' involvement in school[d]			
Low	15	17	17
Moderate	21	26	33
High	64	57	50
Parent attended a general school meeting	83	82	78
Parent attended class or school event	67	61	60
Parent volunteered at school	51	38	24
Parent attended parent-teacher conference	79	82	84

NOTE: Hispanic children are designated as such. They are not included in any of the other racial or ethnic categories. The Total columns include all children. Because of rounding, percents may not sum to 100.

second-generation children and for Hispanic and Asian children in immigrant families (Nord and Griffin, 1998).

Educational Aspirations and School Problems

Analyses conducted for the committee based on the National Education Longitudinal Survey of 1988 (Kao, 1998) indicate that children in immigrant families, both the first and second generations, have higher educational aspirations and are more likely to aspire to graduate from college than are third- and later-generation adolescents. Among Chinese, Filipino, and Mexican children, although small sample sizes require that the findings be viewed as preliminary, educational aspirations are highest among Chinese and Filipinos in immigrant families, somewhat lower among third- and later-generation children generally, and still lower for

Second Generation	Hispanic	Asian	White	Third and Later Generations			
				Total	White	Black	Hispanic
17	21	13	10	15	13	21	17
25	30	30	20	20	19	23	24
58	49	57	70	65	68	56	59
83	79	81	87	84	84	81	82
61	54	56	73	68	71	57	64
41	29	36	54	53	56	42	46
81	83	88	86	79	79	76	78

[a]Applies only to children not yet in first grade.
[b]Applies to children age 3 years through grade 3.
[c]Applies to children in grades 1 and above.
[d]Applies to children enrolled in preschool programs or regular school.

Source: U.S. Department of Education, National Center for Education Statistics, 1996 National Household Education Survey. Nord and Griffin (1998).

third- and later-generation Chinese and Filipino children and all generations of Mexican-origin children.

Consistently, the most common school problems identified among youth in immigrant families are behavioral problems and learning difficulties (Aronowitz, 1984; Gil et al., 1994). When asked to assess children in immigrant families, teachers tend to identify more behavioral problems than do parents. It is difficult to assess from the literature whether these higher rates of behavioral problems and learning difficulties that teachers report are due to their misinterpretation of normatively different behavior or the effects of acculturative stresses, such as language difficulties and perceived discrimination at school. It is likely that both of these factors not only are present, but also interact in the school setting. In addition, the negative evaluations that teachers make may have a negative effect on the self-esteem of children in immigrant families, especially among adolescents.

Smaller-scale studies present a more complex picture of achievement motivation and school problems among different groups of youth in immigrant families. For example, Gil and colleagues (1994) found that, among second- and third-generation Hispanic adolescents, high acculturation was associated with high academic motivation. They also found that second- and third- and later-generation adolescents with low acculturation who perceived significant discrimination from the host society were most likely of all the adolescents studied to experience low self-esteem and poor school performance. Research by Rousseau and colleagues (1996) in Montreal illustrated that the school's perceptions of different immigrant groups may also interact with student motivation to produce worse outcomes for some groups of children than others. In this study, although the school performance of first-generation Southeast Asian and Central American immigrant children did not vary significantly, teachers identified more learning problems in the Central American children. They also subscribed to the stereotype of Asians as a "model minority" in their differential perceptions of these groups of students.

In another study of Canadian children, Munroe-Blum and colleagues (1989) highlighted the effect of social status on the school performance and mental health of children in immigrant families. In this large study, immigrant status was not associated with either poor school performance or more mental health problems. However, children in immigrant families were more likely to be poor, but less likely to have access to welfare and other social services. The paradoxical nature of the findings was that, given the worse social status of children in immigrant families, there were no overall statistical differences in outcomes, suggesting resilience among these children, an emerging theme in the research literature.

What cannot be ascertained from this cross-sectional study is the effect of enduring social disadvantage on children. Other studies indicate that, in the United States, the persistence of disadvantage is structured along racial lines, with black children experiencing more serious problems (Kao and Tienda, 1995;

Phinney and Chavira, 1995) and Asian children fewer problems. Better statistical analyses are needed to look more closely at different ethnic populations within these broad groupings. However, there are anecdotal indications that Hmong and other tribal people from Southeast Asia are not faring as well as other Asians; that the Cuban experience is quite different from that of Nicaraguans and Salvadorans; and that Jamaicans, Haitians, and blacks also have divergent experiences.

SUMMARY

Although we reiterate that conclusions based on the committee's analysis must be considered preliminary, many measures reported for children in immigrant families indicate that they are healthier than U.S.-born children in U.S.-born families. This relative advantage tends to decline with length of time in the United States and from one generation to the next. In addition, children in immigrant families are at particular risk for certain health problems.

Specifically, children in immigrant families experience fewer specific acute and chronic health problems than do U.S.-born children in U.S.-born families, according to parent reports, including acute infectious and parasitic diseases; acute ear infections; acute accidents; chronic respiratory conditions such as bronchitis, asthma, and hay fever; and chronic hearing, speech, and deformity impairments. For children of Mexican origin, parents in immigrant families report fewer acute injuries and poisonings and fewer limitations on major activities than U.S.-born parents in U.S.-born families. First-generation immigrant adolescents also report lower levels of neurological impairment, obesity, and asthma, and fewer health risk behaviors such as early sexual activity; use of cigarettes, alcohol, marijuana, or hard drugs; delinquency; and use of violence. Many of these health problems and risk behaviors tend, however, to increase with length of residence in the United States or from one generation to the next.

Similarly, second-generation infants are less likely to have low birthweight or to die in the first year of life than are third- and later-generation infants. Comparatively low levels of cigarette smoking and alcohol consumption during pregnancy among immigrant mothers contribute substantially to their more favorable birth outcomes; additional potentially important factors include lower levels of drug use and a healthier diet.

Perhaps as we look to the future, protective factors that lead to comparatively favorable outcomes for first- and second-generation children will be reinforced, or more easily maintained, as a result of the increasing size and the geographic concentration of the immigrant population, especially from Mexico, providing greater opportunities to retain positive cultural characteristics.

Not all indications are favorable, however. Children in immigrant families from Mexico, for example, are more likely to be reported by parents as being in fair to poor health and as having teeth in only fair to poor condition. They are also more likely to exhibit elevated blood lead levels. In addition, parents in immigrant families are, paradoxically, somewhat less likely than those in U.S.-born families to report their child's health as excellent or very good, despite the fact that they report their children to have fewer specific acute and chronic health problems. Tuberculosis, hepatitis B, parasitic infections, and elevated levels of lead in the blood are also of particular concern for children in immigrant families from certain high-risk countries of origin.

The paradoxical finding that children in immigrant families have better health than U.S.-born children in U.S.-born families on most available measures—despite their overall lower socioeconomic levels, higher poverty rates, and racial or ethnic minority status—suggests that strong family bonds among immigrants may act to sustain cultural orientations leading to healthful behavior, or that other unknown social or cultural factors may serve to protect them. Thus, children may be protected by key aspects of culture brought from their home country. It is important to also keep in mind that most of these findings (with the exception of the infant outcomes) are based on parental and self-report data, which are themselves likely to be affected by cultural factors.

The apparent deterioration of the health of children in immigrant families the longer they reside in the United States and from one generation to the next suggests that protective aspects of immigrant culture may fade as assimilation into the mainstream American culture occurs, allowing deleterious effects of low socioeconomic status, high poverty, and racial or ethnic stratification to emerge. A more complete understanding of the health situation of children in immigrant families and the reasons for change through time will depend on additional study of these children in the United States that is informed by knowledge about the health of children in countries of origin, and hence providing an explicitly cross-national comparative perspective.

Firm conclusions about similarities and differences between adolescents in immigrant and U.S.-born families regarding psychological well-being, academic success, and other measures of successful adaptation to American society are difficult to draw for reasons that include the small immigrant samples in available studies. However, adolescents in immigrant families appear to sustain positive feelings about themselves and their well-being while also perceiving that they have relatively less control over their lives and are less popular with their peers at school. They also report having higher educational aspirations, although these may deteriorate across generations.

At early ages, parents can foster school success among their young children by teaching them letters and numbers, reading to them, working on projects with them, taking them on educational outings, and getting involved in the children's school. Young children also learn better in well-disciplined schools and if parental participation is encouraged by the school. Early childhood programs prior to kindergarten help children prepare for school. Children do not differ systematically along most of these dimensions, with the exception that children in immigrant families are much less likely to be enrolled in early childhood programs or attend Head Start if they are eligible.

Children in immigrant families nationally have somewhat higher middle school grade point averages and math test scores than do U.S.-born children in U.S.-born families, although reading test scores among the first generation are lower than for later generations. Differences across children with various countries of origin appear quite large, however. For example, adolescents in Chinese-origin immigrant families have grade point averages and higher math test scores than third- and later-generation Chinese-origin or white children. In contrast, Mexican-origin children of all generations have grade point averages and math test scores that are similar to each other, but that are much lower than for third- and later-generation white children. Corresponding to the declines in educational aspirations across generations, however, there is evidence that, among Chinese-origin and Filipino-origin children, the especially strong achievement records of the second generation are not sustained.

CHAPTER 4

Public Policies

This chapter summarizes the current policy status of children in immigrant families and places this contemporary portrait in the context of previous immigration and social welfare policies that have determined their access to health and social services over time. It analyzes new data, collected for the committee, on the use of benefits by immigrant families prior to welfare reform. The chapter then provides information about health care for children in immigrant families. It examines patterns of health insurance coverage, access to and use of health services, and barriers to access.

It is beyond the scope of this report to do more than touch on the highlights of U.S. immigration history (see also Barkan, 1996; Bodnar, 1985; Daniels, 1990; Hing, 1993; Kraut, 1982; National Research Council, 1997), let alone social welfare history. Nevertheless, it is important to have some understanding of earlier practices and policies that have, by design, brought foreign-born children to the United States and provided for them once they arrived.

PROVISION OF PUBLIC BENEFITS

Current Eligibility

The most important policies affecting immigrants after arrival in the United States have been the fairly generous rules that have governed access by legal immigrants to mainstream public benefit programs, such as income support (formerly Aid to Families with Dependent Children, AFDC), health and nutrition benefits, social services, and public education. Following several years of intense national debate over the costs of immigration, particularly over the use of public benefits by immigrants, the 104th Congress enacted the Personal Responsibility and Work Opportunity Reconciliation Act of 1996 (hereafter referred to as welfare reform). This law, among other changes, fundamentally altered the legal structure for providing these public benefits to immigrants, adults and children alike.[1] The Balanced Budget Act of 1997 substantially reversed several major provisions of welfare reform, restoring roughly half of the $23 billion ($11.4 billion) in federal savings that were expected to result from the provisions targeted to immigrants (Congressional Budget Office, 1997). And, as of this writing, efforts to restore benefits to immigrants are ongoing at the federal level.

The law's impact on immigrant children derives in large part from the programmatic reach of new restrictions on immigrants' eligibility for public benefits, which encompass the benefit programs of Medicaid, Supplemental Security Income (SSI), the Food Stamp Program,[2] and noncash services (such as child care) delivered under Temporary Assistance to Needy Families (TANF, for-

---

[1]The Illegal Immigration Reform and Immigrant Responsibility Act of 1996 affected similar aspects of immigration law, but these changes were reconciled to the provisions of the welfare reform law and thus are not discussed here.

[2]On June 23, 1998, as this report was being prepared for publication, President Clinton signed the Agriculture Research, Extension, and Education Reform Act (S. 1150) which restored food stamps to 250,000 legal immigrants, including 75,000 children who lost benefits under the welfare reform bill. This figure represents about one-quarter of the approximately 935,000 legal immigrants who lost their food stamp eligibility under the welfare law.

merly Aid to Families with Dependent Children). Not only have immigrant children been direct beneficiaries of many of these programs, but also many of those who did not receive benefits themselves live in families in which a family member was eligible for and received benefits. For example, children constituted an estimated 17 percent of noncitizens losing food stamps, but almost two-thirds (64 percent) of households headed by a noncitizen that received food stamps also included children (Smolkin et al., 1996). To the extent that overall family resources for meeting basic needs are reduced, children in immigrant families will be likely to feel the impacts. These concerns about the possible negative effects of the policy changes on children in immigrant families have been met by alternative views that emphasize possible deterrent effects of the changes on future immigration and on immigrants' interest in and ability to remain in the United States.

Five shifts in public policy introduced by welfare reform are particularly significant for immigrant children. (Tables 4-1 and 4-2 summarize the major changes in eligibility for benefits that have arisen from this recent legislation.) First, the law draws a new line between legal immigrants and citizens in determining eligibility for public benefits; such a line was formerly drawn between illegal and legal immigrants. Prior to welfare reform, legal immigrants were eligible for public benefits on essentially the same terms as U.S.-born citizens (Fix and Zimmerman, 1995).[3] Currently, most immigrants (except for refugees) who are in the United States legally are barred from eligibility for food stamps,

---

[3]*Naturalized citizens* enjoyed the same entitlements as other citizens. *Refugees,* whose flight from persecution in their homeland is considered unplanned migration, were also entitled to receive full public benefits from the time of their arrival. Access of *legal permanent residents* to SSI, food stamps, and AFDC benefits was conditioned by "deeming," that is, ascribing the incomes of their sponsors to the immigrants for three to five years following entry. *Undocumented immigrants* were eligible for very few public benefits, most notably emergency medical assistance under Medicaid and the Special Supplemental Nutrition Program for Women, Infants, and Children (WIC). The Supreme Court ruled in 1982 that undocumented alien children could not be denied access to public elementary and secondary education (Plyler v. Doe, 457 U.S. 202(1982)). U.S.-born children of undocumented aliens are citizens of the United States and are eligible for public benefits on the same terms as other citizens.

TABLE 4-1 Program Eligibility Prior to Welfare Reform

	Legal Immigrants (Permanent Residents)	Refugees / Asylees	Undocumented Immigrants (Illegal Immigrants)
Food Stamps	Income of sponsor deemed for 3-5 years after entry.	Same eligibility rules as citizens.	Ineligible.
WIC	Same eligibility rules as citizens.	Same eligibility rules as citizens.	No bars to eligibility.
School Lunch	Same eligibility rules as citizens.	Same eligibility rules as citizens.	Eligible.
SSI	Income of sponsor deemed for 3-5 years after entry.	Same eligibility rules as citizens.	Ineligible.
MEDICAID	Same eligibility rules as citizens.	Same eligibility rules as citizens.	Eligible for emergency services only.
Title XX Social Services	Same eligibility rules as citizens.	Same eligibility rules as citizens.	Eligible.
AFDC	Income of sponsor deemed for 3-5 years after entry.	Same eligibility rules as citizens.	Ineligible.
State and Local Benefits	Same eligibility rules as citizens.	Same eligibility rules as citizens.	Eligibility requirements varied by state.
Head Start	Same eligibility rules as citizens.	Same eligibility rules as citizens.	No bars to eligibility.
Maternal and Child Health	Same eligibility rules as citizens.	Same eligibility rules as citizens.	No bars to eligibility.
Child Care Block Grant	Same eligibility rules as citizens.	Same eligibility rules as citizens.	No bars to eligibility.

and immigrants who arrived after August 22, 1996, are barred from a range of other federal means-tested benefits, including income assistance (TANF) and Medicaid for their first five years in the country.

Noncitizens' eligibility for SSI, which was restricted under welfare reform, was restored in the Balanced Budget Agreement of 1997. The restoration was limited, however, to elderly and disabled immigrants who were receiving SSI benefits at the time welfare reform was enacted or who were in the United States on August 22, 1996, and who later become disabled. Future immigrants will be barred—a change that will affect immigrant children largely indirectly, through a loss of benefits to adult family members who constitute the major share of immigrants receiving SSI.

In addition, many of the benefits for which undocumented children were previously eligible are likely to be withdrawn. This includes the Special Supplemental Nutrition Program for Women, Infants, and Children (WIC), most services provided under the Title XX Social Services Block Grant, and Head Start. Undocumented children retain their eligibility for emergency Medicaid, public immunization programs, and the school lunch program.

The place of the recently enacted State Children's Health Insurance Program (SCHIP) in this reformulation of eligibility remains unclear, although it appears that it will be considered a federal means-tested program and so will follow the rules that apply to Medicaid. This program, enacted as part of the Balanced Budget Act of 1997, provides funds to states to enable them to initiate and expand the provision of child health insurance to uninsured, low-income children under age 19. States may spend the new funds in one of three major ways: to extend Medicaid coverage to additional children, to support a separate state child health insurance program, or to do a combination of the two. States may also spend 10 percent of the funds for outreach activities, administrative costs, or direct purchase or provision of health services to children.

Within this overall structure, states have broad discretion in fashioning their programs with respect to specific issues such as eligibility, benefits, and cost sharing (see English, 1998; Institute of Medicine, 1998). States are still required, however, to provide

TABLE 4-2 Post-Welfare Reform Program Eligibility

	Legal Immigrants (Permanent Residents) Arriving *before* August 23, 1996	Legal Immigrants (Permanent Residents) Arriving *after* August 23, 1996	Refugees / Asylees	Undocumented Immigrants (Illegal Immigrants)
Food Stamps (Federal)	Ineligible.[a]	Ineligible.	Eligible, time limit is 5 years after admission.	Ineligible.
Food Stamps (State)	Eligibility varies by state.	Eligibility varies by state.	State option to provide benefits after refugees have been in the U.S. more than 5 years.	Ineligible.
WIC	Eligible.	Eligible.	Eligible.	Eligibility varies by state.
School Lunch	Eligible.	Eligible.	Eligible.	Eligible.
SSI	Legal aliens who were receiving SSI benefits and legal aliens in the country before August 22, 1996 who become disabled will continue to be eligible.	Ineligible with certain exceptions.	Eligible for 7 years after entry.	Ineligible.
Medicaid	State option.	Barred for first 5 years; state option afterwards.	Eligible for 7 years after entry.	Ineligible.

Emergency Medicaid	Eligible.		Eligible.	Eligible.
Title XX Social Services	Eligible.		Eligible.	Ineligible.
TANF	State option.	Barred for first 5 years; state option afterward.	Eligible for 5 years after entry.	Ineligible.
State and Local Benefits	State option.	State option.	Eligible for 5 years after entry.	Ineligible, unless state passes law explicitly authorizing.
Head Start	Same eligibility as citizens.	Same eligibility as citizens.	Same eligibility as citizens.	Not yet determined.
Maternal and Child Health	Same eligibility as citizens.	Same eligibility as citizens.	Same eligibility as citizens.	Not yet determined.
Child Care Block Grant	Same eligibility as citizens.	Same eligibility as citizens.	Same eligibility as citizens.	Not yet determined.

[a]Except lawful permanent residents who have worked 40 qualifying quarters who did not receive any means-tested federal benefits during that period, and aliens who have served in the U.S. military, who are eligible.

legal immigrants with some health and social service programs, such as those delivered under the Community Health Services Program, the Migrant Health Program, services delivered under the Public Health Services Act, and the Maternal and Child Health Block Grant, many of which are extremely important to immigrant families. Furthermore, the 10 percent funds for outreach and direct provision of health services included as part of SCHIP may presumably be used for services, such as migrant health centers, that immigrant families have traditionally used.

Second, refugees arriving after August 22, 1996, will be eligible for SSI and Medicaid for seven years and for TANF and food stamp benefits for five years following their arrival. This change represents a significant departure in refugee resettlement policy by imposing time limits on benefits, which were previously unrestricted. In addition, refugees who were here prior to welfare reform are also subject to the five-year limitation on food stamp benefits. About 10 percent of immigrants in any given year are refugees (Fix and Passel, 1994), but they comprise a substantial proportion of some immigrant groups, such as Cubans, Eastern Europeans, and Southeast Asians.

Third, the locus of many decisions affecting immigrant children's eligibility for benefits has shifted from the federal government to the states. States will be faced with an intricate array of eligibility requirements and sponsorship rules. For example, states are in the process of determining *current* immigrants' eligibility for such major benefits as income assistance and health insurance (the new federal restrictions apply largely to future immigrants). To date, none of the major immigrant-receiving states (California, Florida, Illinois, New York, and Texas) has limited current legal immigrants' access to TANF, Medicaid, or Title XX block grant programs. States are, however, showing wide variation in their decisions about whether to replace lost federal funds with state-funded programs for immigrants arriving after the enactment of welfare reform.

This devolution of responsibility for immigrant policy is likely to result in substantial state and even within-state variation in the benefits that both legal and undocumented immigrant children receive. For example, although California has decided to eliminate undocumented children from WIC, other states such as New

York have not. Furthermore, some states such as Maryland and New York have decided to use state funds to provide food assistance to immigrant children, but not to adults. In New York, these funds are provided as part of a cooperative state-county program. As a result, noncitizen children, youth, elderly, and disabled food stamp recipients in New York City have retained benefits, but their counterparts in other New York counties (e.g., Erie County) have not.

Fourth, new mandatory federal reporting requirements compel state agencies that administer federal housing, SSI, and TANF programs to furnish the U.S. Immigration and Naturalization Service (INS) four times each year with names, addresses, and other qualifying information on any immigrants known to be unlawfully in the United States. Some are concerned that enactment of this new responsibility by agencies that serve immigrant children will act as a disincentive for undocumented parents of citizen and legal, noncitizen children to seek aid for which these children are eligible and from which they could benefit. However, this remains an open question.

Fifth, the requirement for verification of immigration status has been expanded to apply to all "federal public benefits," the definition of which remains to be determined but could be quite broad. Likely to be included, for example, is Head Start, maternal and child health programs, the Child Care and Development Block Grant, and other programs that have benefited immigrant children. Children who apply to enroll in these programs will now be required to verify their immigration status, which could create a disincentive to enrollment, particularly for children whose parents are undocumented. In addition, the INS has recently promulgated long and complex new regulations that set out the new verification requirements for federal programs (*Federal Register*, November 17, 1997:61345-61416) and will be providing requirements for verification in state and local benefit programs. Complexity could give rise to confusion among implementers and, accordingly, inconsistent service delivery.

In sum, children in immigrant families, including those who have entered and are residing in the United States legally, now face major new restrictions and constraints on eligibility for benefits ranging from income supports to nutrition and health coverage. Their access to these benefits will now be conditioned by their date of arrival in the United States, entry status, state of residency, and progress through the naturalization process. This represents a marked shift in the nation's policies for immigrant children.

Access Prior to Welfare Reform

Throughout America's history, immigrants have had a profound effect on the composition of the country's population and have presented daunting social and economic challenges to successive American generations. During the last century, federal *immigration* or admissions policies have played a deliberate role in shaping the number and characteristics of foreign-born people admitted to the United States. These policies have been inclusionary by both historical and international standards (Melville, 1995), as well as comprehensive and explicit in their intent and rationale (for more information on the history of U.S. immigration, see National Research Council, 1997). More recently, they have been accompanied by policies that focus on the control of illegal immigration, including intensive border enforcement, employer sanctions, and verification and reporting requirements in the workplace and in social service agencies.

Characteristics of the current wave of immigrants have been shaped to a large extent by: (1) the 1965 amendments to the Immigration and Nationality Act, which established family reunification as a central basis for immigration[4] and removed the numerical cap on the immigration of immediate relatives of U.S. citizens (a priority that was reasserted by the 1990 Immigration Act); (2) growth in humanitarian admissions fostered by the Refugee Act of 1980, which also established a program for settling and

---

[4]It is important to note that, although public debate sharply distinguishes between family-based and employment-based admissions, this distinction is blurred in practice. Nearly half of employment-preference immigrants are the spouses and minor children of the principal beneficiary. The great majority of doctors and engineers admitted to the United States in fiscal 1995, for example, entered under family unification and other nonlabor criteria (U.S. Immigration and Naturalization Service, 1995).

assisting refugees; (3) the Immigration Reform and Control Act (IRCA) of 1986, which established inclusionary strategies, such as the legalization of 2.7 million formerly illegal immigrants, as well as exclusionary strategies to control illegal immigration; (4) the Immigration Act of 1990, with provisions for doubling the visas available for highly skilled immigrants and their families from 58,000 to 140,000 per year, authorizing the creation of a new category of "diversity immigrants" who would be admitted from countries that had sent comparatively few immigrants to the United States historically, and opening a significant new door to safe refuge in the United States by creating a temporary protected status; and (5) the Illegal Immigrant Reform and Immigrant Responsibility Act of 1996, which requires that sponsors of legal immigrants have incomes that exceed 125 percent of the poverty line, after taking into account the sponsor, his or her family, and the arriving immigrant and family members accompanying the arriving immigrant. The overall impact of these policies has been, thus far, to increase the number and share of immigrants from developing countries, notably Mexico, Southeast Asia, and Central America, many of whom have low labor market skills relative to the U.S.-born population (National Research Council, 1997).

In contrast to these relatively unrestricted, comprehensive, and explicit immigration policies, the United States has had no explicit *immigrant* policy guiding the settlement and orientation of immigrants, or determining the nature and amount of public benefits available to immigrants after arrival (Fix and Passel, 1994; Simon, 1989); the exception is resettlement policies focused on refugees. Instead, immigrants have experienced varied eligibility criteria in the context of specific legislation regarding public benefits. Different immigrant groups have had very different access to resources depending on the array of private, philanthropic, and government programs and benefits available to them at their time and place of arrival. The degree to which private agencies and federal, state, and local governments have shouldered or shared primary responsibility for providing resources needed by children in immigrant families to ensure their healthy development has also changed over time.

Private Sources of Assistance

A century ago, health care and other assistance for immigrants was provided mainly by private charities and self-help benevolent fraternal organizations. In fact, prior to the 1930s, impoverished children in need of medical services, immigrant and citizen alike, received them from health care facilities affiliated with religious institutions, such as church-affiliated hospitals, or from physicians employed by private charities or ethnic lodges and labor unions to which workers paid dues. Almshouses, supported all or in part by public funds, were available only to the destitute, including immigrants (Kraut, 1994).

Children who received medical attention upon arrival on Ellis Island or at any other immigration depot received no further attention from the federal government once they left the facility and were admitted to the United States. No federal programs existed for poor and needy children. Children's health, especially impoverished children in immigrant families, was the responsibility of state and municipal governments and private charity in the decades prior to the New Deal.

Children who attended school had the greatest access to health education and health care early in the 20th century. Initially, the public school teacher bore the main responsibility of vigilance between annual physician examinations, alerting the school doctors to suspicious signs of ill health among students. Increasingly, however, the school nurse became crucial not only in detecting disease but also in health education, including educating parents about health care for their children. School nurses treated minor ailments, thus preventing loss of instruction time, and provided health care outreach to parents.

Aside from particular ailments or disabilities, poor diet, improper personal hygiene, and insufficient health and exercise were among the most common causes of disease and disability in immigrant schoolchildren (Baker, 1939; Kraut, 1994; Riis, 1890; Spargo, 1906). In response to the problem of hunger, some reformers advocated a program of low-cost or free school lunches for poor schoolchildren. In New York, school lunches were provided in 17 schools by 1914, 11 of those in immigrant neighborhoods, with the support of philanthropists such as Andrew

Carnegie and Solomon Guggenheim. In 1919, the New York City Board of Education was funded to assume responsibility for serving school lunches—a precursor to both the federal school breakfast and lunch programs and to the federal Food Stamp Program.

Children and adolescents who were not in school presented a complex health care problem. Those working in sweatshops or doing piece work at home were not under the surveillance of teachers, school doctors, or school nurses. Yet the health of working children and youth was threatened by some of the same occupational hazards that threatened the health and shortened the lives of their elders, including such occupational diseases as lead poisoning, phosphorous necrosis, and silicosis (Gold, 1930; Kraut, 1994; Rosner and Markowitz, 1987, 1991). Children and youth living and working in congested environments were susceptible, as were their parents and older coworkers, to tuberculosis. Deprived of fresh air and healthy exercise, normal physical development was also curbed (Kraut, 1994; Stella, 1904, 1908).

In urban areas, health care for working children and adolescents was available at dispensaries or from visiting nurses financed by private charities or urban governments. However, immigrant children and youth often received care from the fraternal lodges to which they or their parents belonged. For example, Germans created and joined the *Arbeiter-Kranken-und-Starbe Kasse der Vereinigten Staaten von Amerika* (the Workingman's Sick and Death Benefit Fund of the United States), Eastern European Jews created and joined the *Landsmannschafn* (regionally based fraternal organizations), and Cuban cigar makers contributed part of their wages to the formation of *clinicas*, providing access to health insurance or services (Davis, 1921; Kalet, 1916; Kraut, 1995; Mormino and Pozzetta, 1987). In addition, visiting nurses and health educators in settlement houses, such as Lillian Wald's Henry Street Settlement and Jane Addams's Hull House, sought to bring information about health and access to basic health care to America's newest resident children and families.

Over time, however, the cooperative traditions many immigrants brought from their home countries eroded with assimilation; more recent immigrants often did not have such resources. Moreover, as the costs of health care escalated, the resources of even the most successful benevolent associations and ethnic labor unions became increasingly inadequate to the task of paying for the cost of care.

Public Assumption of Responsibility

Although the federal government assumed responsibility for inspecting the health of immigrants at the border after 1890, it was not until the 1930s that it began to provide direct financial assistance to the poor, including immigrant families. Prior to this time, however, the federal government had assumed some responsibility for gathering data on children. In 1912, the Children's Bureau was established as a fact-finding agency and was allocated $25,640 to "investigate and report upon all matters pertaining to the welfare of children and child life among all classes of our people." Staffed largely by social workers and educators of a progressive bent, the Children's Bureau through its investigators reported data on child poverty, child health, and child labor, in particular, which in time provided the justifications for federal programmatic involvement in these arenas.

The New Deal marked the first major initiative by the federal government to establish programs aimed at fostering the health of Americans, especially the poorest. Driven largely by public health concerns, funds were authorized for medical and nursing care; emergency dental work; the construction of hospitals, health clinics, and sewage plants; maternal and child care; care for physically disabled children; and the promotion of state and local public health agencies. The basic architecture of a system for distributing funds for health care, while recognizing special needs, including those of children, was well established by the late 1930s.

Since that time, punctuated by a major expansion of direct federal responsibility for the care of the country's poor in the 1960s, legal immigrant as well as U.S.-born poor children have benefited increasingly from federal assistance programs, the largest of which have been Medicaid, food stamps, SSI, and Aid to Families with Dependent Children (AFDC). Programs focused on children, such as WIC, childhood immunization programs, emergency medical services, Head Start, the school lunch and breakfast programs, and Title IV foster care and adoption assistance, have also been of great importance to immigrant children, including undocumented children who have been eligible for these programs from their inception.

As they have emerged over the past three decades, federal policies regarding immigrants' access to public benefits have incorporated three important features.

The first is the federal government's preemption of state power to determine noncitizens' eligibility for state or federally funded public benefits programs. Prior to 1972, federal statutes controlling state or local public benefit programs contained no eligibility restrictions based on immigration status; they were silent on the matter of immigrant eligibility. In the absence of federal mandates, the states established their own citizenship and alien residency requirements. In the 1970s, however, the federal government began to expressly impose restrictions on immigrant access to public benefits in response to concerns about illegal immigration, paired with concerns about major expansions in the costs of public benefits. Since then, through explicit legislative and regulatory provisions, the federal government has retained the power to establish immigrants' eligibility for federal benefits.

The second feature is the restriction of benefits for illegal and temporary immigrants—but not, for the most part, for legal permanent residents. Through the late 1970s, restrictions on immigrants' use of benefits were limited to undocumented and to temporary immigrants (students, tourists, and temporary workers, for example). Illegal immigrants were barred from AFDC, SSI, food stamps, and full Medicaid benefits, retaining their access to emergency services funded under Medicaid. In the late 1970s, concerns began to emerge that some recently arrived legal immigrants were abusing the welfare system. These concerns led to the imposition of new requirements that effectively withheld food stamp, SSI, and AFDC benefits for three years after the arrival of some immigrants who were not refugees.

This withholding of benefits was accomplished by a policy called "deeming." Under deeming the income of an immigrant's sponsor is deemed to be available to the immigrant for purposes of qualifying for means-tested benefit programs. When the incomes of sponsors and immigrants are combined, it is typically the case that they are so high that they disqualify the immigrant from receiving benefits. In addition, poor immigrants typically will not be granted a visa unless their sponsors sign an affidavit of support, which is a pledge by the sponsor to (1) support the sponsored immigrant and (2) reimburse the government for benefits provided during the period the affidavit is in effect.

Affidavits of support have not been enforced, however, because they have been determined by the courts to be a moral and not a legal obligation. In the past, the affidavit of support has been in effect during the period of deeming—typically three years. Hence, the sponsor's obligation lapsed as the government's began. The argument in favor of sponsor deeming and requiring an affidavit of support is that the government can admit immigrants who are poor at the time of entry without worrying excessively about the public fiscal burdens. The argument opposing the new laws is that they erect multiple overlapping barriers to benefit use, including affidavits of support that are in effect until the immigrant naturalizes, bars to public benefits until naturalization, and deeming in public benefit programs.

A third feature of immigrant policy in the modern era is the preferred treatment of refugees, who have experienced comparatively unrestricted access to benefits since the end of World War II. Refugees, who now represent between 10 and 15 percent of legally admitted immigrants, have been eligible for state and federal public benefit programs on the same terms as citizens from the date of their arrival. Although deeming in AFDC, SSI, and food stamps has been applied to legal permanent residents, it has not been extended to refugees (who are not sponsored).

In sum, the majority of children in immigrant families reside in the United States legally and in accord with immigration policies that have repeatedly identified family reunification as a central and explicit goal of immigration. These children now face a complex and newly redefined array of eligibility criteria for public benefits that, as of 1996, categorically exclude many of them from coverage and leave many others subject to the decisions of state governments. This new landscape of immigrant policies for children, although not unprecedented in the modern era,[5] represents a major departure from the policies of the last 25 years.

---

[5]Even prior to passage of the welfare reform legislation, public benefits for immigrants have been restricted. For example, immigrants whose status was legal-

USE OF PUBLIC BENEFITS

National attention and research have focused on the use of public benefits by immigrant adults and households (Bean et al., 1997; Blau, 1984; Borjas and Hilton, 1996; Borjas and Trejo, 1991; Fix and Passel, 1994; Jensen, 1988; Simon and Akbari, 1996; Tienda and Jensen, 1986). The literature on this issue has yielded mixed results. Studies that have focused on cash benefits (e.g., AFDC, SSI, other welfare) have generally reported that immigrants are more likely to receive various forms of public assistance than the U.S.-born, in large part because immigrants are more likely to be poor and thus eligible for benefits. Among the U.S.-born and immigrants with similar socioeconomic and demographic characteristics, immigrants are less likely to receive welfare from many specific programs. However, the proportion using at least one form of noncash benefit is higher among immigrants than comparable U.S.-born residents. It is important to determine exactly which forms of public assistance immigrants are more likely to receive, and whether this is a function of their immigrant status per se or of their disadvantaged socioeconomic and demographic circumstances independent of their immigration status.

Almost no research has examined these issues from the perspective of children (but see Currie, 1997, for an exception), even though they constitute a large share of the immigrant population and represent a sizeable fraction of the welfare caseload. To fill this gap, the committee had analyses conducted of the Survey of Income and Program Participation (SIPP) (Brandon, 1998) and the Panel Study of Income Dynamics (PSID) (Hofferth, 1998) to provide information about children in families that received public assistance.[6] The discussion in this section relies on these analy-

---

ized under the Immigration Reform and Control Act were barred from receiving public assistance for five years, and some share of legal immigrants have been barred from means-tested benefits as a result of requirements that their sponsors' income be included in determining eligibility for their first three years in the country (Fix and Passel, 1994).

[6]Analyses were conducted of the 1990-1992 waves of the Panel Study of Income Dynamics (PSID) (Hofferth, 1998) and the 1986, 1987, 1988, 1990, and 1991 panels of the Survey of Income and Program Participation (SIPP) (Brandon, 1998).

ses and is most appropriately viewed as an initial look at patterns for children in the reliance of their families on public assistance prior to welfare reform, that is, the extent to which children live in families in which at least one person in the household receives benefits from a designated public program.

The analyses conducted for the committee focused on the following public assistance programs for which children in immigrant families *or members of their families* have been eligible: AFDC, food stamps, Medicaid, SSI, heating assistance, housing assistance, school lunches, and other welfare. The indicator of cash assistance consisted of AFDC, SSI,[7] and other welfare (general assistance and miscellaneous state assistance). The indicator of noncash assistance combined Medicaid, food stamps, heating assistance, and housing assistance.

Comparisons focused on differences in receipt by immigrant generation, comparing first-generation (foreign-born) with both second-generation (U.S.-born children of immigrant parents) and third- and later-generations (U.S.-born children of U.S.-born parents), as well as by ethnicity. On one hand, first-generation children experience relatively high poverty rates and therefore might be expected to show higher rates of receipt than later-generation children. On the other hand, all persons born in the United States are eligible to apply for public benefits, and legal immigrants are eligible to apply for more benefit programs than are undocumented immigrants. This would lead us to expect U.S.-born families with U.S.-born children to have the highest likelihood of receipt, followed by U.S.-born children in immigrant families.

Patterns of Receipt by Generation and Ethnicity

Tables 4-3 and 4-4 show the incidence of public assistance participation by immigrant generation and ethnicity for the PSID and SIPP analyses, respectively. It is important to note that these analyses do not statistically exclude the effects of sociodemo-

---

[7]In most immigrant households receiving SSI benefits, the beneficiary is an adult or elderly family member, rather than the child (O'Grady, 1995).

TABLE 4-3   Percent of Children in Families Receiving Public Assistance by Race, Ethnicity, and Generation in the Panel Study of Income Dynamics: 1992

	AFDC	SSI	Other Welfare	Food Stamps	Medicaid	Housing	Heat	Cash	Non-Ncash	Total
First-generation Mexican	3	0	7	47	38	17	25	10	59	61
Second-generation Mexican	5	3	4	26	24	7	10	11	37	38
Third- and later-generation Mexican	18	5	3	30	26	11	18	23	44	45
First-generation Cuban	4	6	0	22	25	4	2	7	32	32
Second-generation Cuban	4	8	5	25	37	6	1	16	40	40
Third- and later-generation Cuban	7	20	0	10	31	5	0	27	35	35
Other Hispanic	23	3	5	24	27	11	17	23	29	29
White	4	2	1	8	8	2	5	6	14	14
Black	27	6	5	42	37	25	17	34	58	60
Other	5	3	3	14	18	7	0	11	24	27
Total	9	3	2	17	17	8	9	13	26	27

Source: Hofferth (1998).

graphic, economic, or other differences that characterize these groups.

In general, first-generation immigrant children are more likely than later-generation children to live in families receiving public assistance, and second-generation children are about as likely as third- and later-generation children to live in families receiving public assistance (see the Total rows for the generations, overall, in Tables 4-3 and 4-4). Compared with white children, higher probabilities of receipt of public assistance from specific programs were usually found for Mexican, Cuban, other Hispanic, and Asian children.

In the PSID analyses, which encompassed Mexican-origin, Cuban-origin, and other Hispanic children, the range of those living in families that received at least one form of public assistance among those listed was from 29 to 61 percent. First-generation Mexican-origin children accounted for the 61 percent figure, which dropped to 38 percent in the second generation and 45 percent in the third generation. These children lived in families that were substantally more likely to rely on noncash than on cash benefits. In the SIPP analyses, which encompassed immigrants from a wider range of regions of the world, the range was from 16 to 57 percent. The range for Mexican-origin children was from 44 to 47 percent across the generations, with greater reliance on non-cash than on cash benefits for the first and second generations. However, third- and later-generation black children have high rates of receipt as well (59 and 60 percent across all programs in the SIPP and PSID analyses, respectively). Indeed, the gap between third- and later-generation black and white children in receipt of public assistance is greater than that between each of these groups and virtually every immigrant generation group, and it is greater than the differences within the immigrant population.

In general, these analyses correspond to the previous literature on adult immigrant populations, showing higher rates of assistance among immigrants—especially first-generation immigrants—than among U.S.-born families (see Borjas and Hilton, 1996).

Determinants of Receipt of Public Assistance

Having discussed patterns of receipt of public assistance by immigrant generation and ethnicity, it is important to determine whether these patterns are explained by other characteristics of the families, particularly their demographic characteristics and poverty level. In general, the comparatively high rates of public benefit receipt among first-generation families were found to result from greater need—that is, from their disadvantaged socioeconomic and demographic circumstances, not from their immigration status per se. When controls were added for group differences along such dimensions as poverty, marital and health status of the parents, parental education, and number of children in the family, the generational differences either disappeared or were reversed (Brandon, 1998; Hofferth, 1998). In addition, the refugee status of many immigrants from certain countries, such as Cuba and Southeast Asia, is likely to account for higher levels of receipt among these groups.

Among children in families with similar socioeconomic and demographic circumstances, first- and second-generation children as a whole are less likely than third- and later-generation children to receive both cash and noncash benefits. The same is true for Mexican-origin children with similar characteristics: first- and second-generation children are less likely than the third and later generations to receive cash and noncash public assistance. For a wide range of benefits (AFDC, SSI, food stamps, Medicaid, and other welfare), first- and second-generation Mexican-origin children are either no more likely or are less likely than both third- and later-generation white and third- and later-generation Mexican-origin children with similar socioeconomic and demographic characteristics to live in families that receive benefits. Third- and later-generation Mexican children, however, are generally more likely than third-and later-generation white children with the same socioeconomic and demographic characteristics to receive benefits.

The situation is quite different for Asian children in immigrant families. At specific socioeconomic levels, first-generation Asian children are more likely than second-generation children

TABLE 4-4 Percent of Children in Families Receiving Public Assistance by Race, Ethnicity, Country of Origin, and Generation in the Survey of Income and Program Participation: 1986-1992

Generation with Ethnicity	AFDC	SSI	Other Welfare	Food Stamps	Medicaid	Housing	Heat	Cash	Non-Cash	Total
First generation	17	11	1	28	22	10	8	21	35	36
Second generation	10	6	1	22	16	7	8	13	28	29
First and second generation	12	7	1	23	17	8	8	15	29	31
Third and later generation	13	5	1	21	15	8	10	14	27	28
First-generation Mexican	17	4	2	36	24	10	9	20	45	46
Second-generation Mexican	12	8	1	36	22	10	13	15	43	44
Third- and later-generation Mexican	24	6	2	40	29	11	19	25	46	47
Cuban	3	8	0	22	13	2	4	5	32	32
First-generation Asian	27	20	0	31	31	16	7	34	36	39
Second-generation Asian	14	10	0	17	14	7	2	20	20	24
Third- and later-generation Asian	18	6	3	23	7	9	1	25	25	28

First-generation Western European	4	0	0	26	10	0	5	4	27	28
Second-generation Western European	7	4	0	13	10	3	4	8	17	18
Third- and later-generation Western European	7	3	1	13	9	6	6	8	18	19
First-generation Eastern European	4	0	0	15	5	13	9	4	27	27
Second-generation Eastern European	3	0	0	5	14	1	3	3	17	17
Third- and later-generation Eastern European	4	1	0	9	7	5	7	5	16	16
Other Hispanic	26	9	1	38	32	18	12	27	53	57
White	7	4	1	14	9	5	6	8	19	19
Black	35	14	2	51	40	23	22	37	58	59
Other	22	7	4	45	37	12	5	27	53	57
Total	13	6	1	21	15	8	8	14	27	28

Source: Brandon (1998).

to live in families receiving benefits from these programs, and second-generation children are more likely to receive benefits than third- and later-generation children only for SSI. This pattern in part reflects the refugee status of children from Vietnam, Cambodia, Laos, and Thailand, which allows them automatic and unrestricted eligibility for many public benefits. In 1990, children from these countries accounted for about 27 percent of all first-generation Asian children, but only 7 percent of all second-generation Asian children. Among those with similar socioeconomic and demographic characteristics, Asian children of all generations are more likely to live in families that receive AFDC than third- and later-generation white children.

Many Cuban-origin children in immigrant families are also entitled to refugee benefits and, not surprisingly, their patterns of reliance on public assistance are similar to those of Asian children. Among those with similar demographic and socioeconomic circumstances, first- and second-generation Cuban-origin children are more likely than either third- and later-generation Cuban children or third- and later-generation white children to live in families that receive SSI and food stamps. Comparable proportions of first- and second-generation Cuban-origin children and of third- and later-generation white children with similar demographic and socioeconomic characteristics live in families that receive AFDC, but third-generation Cuban-origin children are more likely than third- and later-generation white children to live in families that receive AFDC.

Among children from Western Europe, first-generation children are no more likely or are less likely than later-generation children in similar demographic and socioeconomic circumstances to live in families receiving public assistance. The pattern for Eastern Europeans is more similar to that of Asians. At specific socioeconomic levels, first-generation children with Eastern European origins are more likely than second-, and third-, and later-generation children with Eastern European origins to live in families receiving other welfare, Medicaid, and housing and heat assistance.

Assessment of Recent Changes

It is premature to assess the effects of the recent changes in policies affecting immigrants' access to public benefits, because many federal and state decisions have yet to be made regarding definitions, eligibility, and implementation of these policies with special relevance to immigrant children, and because the impacts of the reforms are only beginning to be felt. However, given the sizeable numbers of children in immigrant families who will be affected, a full and accurate portrait of the effects of the reforms must include specific attention to the various ways in which these children are affected.

Such an assessment will need to consider: (1) the direct effects on children of their elimination from eligibility for basic benefit programs, ranging from health care and nutrition to social services; (2) the indirect effects on noncitizen and citizen children in immigrant families that are likely to ensue from family members' loss of benefits; and (3) the indirect effects that may arise from such potentially chilling practices as new verification and reporting requirements on immigrant parents' efforts to obtain benefits for their children. It will also be important to monitor the ramifications of the nation's changing policies for local agencies and institutions—formal and informal—that have traditionally provided benefits and services to children in immigrant families. Also of interest are efforts to assess the incentives and disincentives to future immigration of families with children and to return migration on behalf of these families that arise from the reforms.

With regard to direct effects, because so many programs are affected, it will be important to assess outcomes across a wide range of developmental domains. Family- and household-level effects, such as overcrowding, that may arise from diminished resources to dependent family members also warrant attention. Consideration of synergistic effects that arise from interactions among different benefits and programs, as well as cumulative effects over time, will be critical. State variation in outcomes will be especially important to assess, given the high likelihood of growing variation in states' treatment of immigrant children and their families.

Indirect effects may be just as far-reaching as direct effects, given that, as of 1997, more than 7 million citizen children (10 percent of all children) live in families that include noncitizen parents (Fix, 1997). Children of immigrants often have a different immigration status than their parents. In general, they are more likely to be citizens and hence to be entitled to different public benefits than their parents. It is critical to understand how this situation manifests itself in a policy context in which the government is curbing benefits to noncitizens, many of whom, as parents, are responsible for accessing services on behalf of their citizen and noncitizen children.

HEALTH COVERAGE AND ACCESS

All children require access to health services to ensure that preventive services are provided as recommended, acute and chronic conditions are diagnosed and treated in a timely manner, and health and development are adequately monitored so that minor health problems do not escalate into serious and costly medical emergencies. Both health insurance coverage and having a usual source of care facilitate access to health care (Holl et al., 1995; Institute of Medicine, 1998; Lieu et al., 1993; Newacheck et al., 1996; Simpson et al., 1997; U.S. General Accounting Office, 1997).

Little systematic research has examined how immigration and citizenship status are related to health insurance coverage and access to care. This gap in the research literature has been especially acute for children. The committee had analyses conducted of existing national data sets[8] to provide descriptive data on health insurance coverage and access to health services by children in immigrant families prior to implementation of both welfare reform and the new State Children's Health Insurance Program (Brown et al., 1998). Much of the discussion in this chapter relies on these analyses and, as such, is most appropriately viewed

---

[8]Analyses of the March 1996 Current Population Survey and the 1994 National Health Interview Survey were conducted by the University of California at Los Angeles Center for Health Policy Research (Brown et al., 1998) with support from the Robert Wood Johnson Foundation.

as an initial look at an evolving system of health care financing and delivery for children in immigrant families.

Health Care Insurance

Over the past 30 years, the health care of most children in this country has been funded through one of three arrangements: employment-based insurance, public benefits, and charity arrangements. The majority of them receive health coverage through their parents' employer-sponsored health insurance (59 percent of 0- to 17-year-olds in 1995) (Institute of Medicine, 1998, citing Employee Benefit Research Institute, 1997b).[9] They receive care primarily from private physicians and private hospitals or from health maintenance organizations (HMOs). Public-sector financing for children's health care coverage comes primarily from Medicaid, a federally and state-financed program administered by states that pays for health services for children who meet low-income eligibility criteria or categorical requirements, such as being in foster care or being disabled.

In 1995, approximately 1 in 4 children was enrolled in Medicaid (Employee Benefit Research Institute, 1997a). Similarly, Medicaid provides the only source of coverage for about 1 in 4 children in immigrant families (Brown et al., 1998). Medicaid beneficiaries may receive their care from private physicians and private hospitals but, because they often have difficulty finding private providers who accept Medicaid payments, these patients obtain much of their care from public hospitals and clinics and community-based services. In general, children in immigrant families are substantially less likely to use a doctor's office or private clinic as their usual source of care than are other children. Instead, they rely more heavily on public hospitals and community and migrant health centers (Brown et al., 1998).

Since 1987, there has been a decline of 8 percent in the share of children receiving employer-based coverage and an increase of almost 8 percent in Medicaid coverage (Institute of Medicine,

---

[9]Estimates are based on data from the March 1988-1996 Current Population Survey, Bureau of the Census, U.S. Department of Commerce.

1998, citing Employee Benefit Research Institute, 1997b). This association suggests that some children may have been dropped from or lost private health insurance coverage because they became eligible for Medicaid. Most analysts suspect that some employers and employees have dropped private health insurance to take advantage of expanded eligibility for Medicaid, but the size of the effect is unknown and remains in dispute (Cutler and Gruber, 1996, 1997; Dubay and Kenney, 1997). There is, however, growing evidence that, in response to their increasing costs for health benefits, employers have raised the contributions that employees must make as their share of health insurance premiums, and that these rates have increased faster for family coverage than for individual coverage (Fronstin and Snider, 1996-1997; Kronick and Gilmer, 1997). This factor may have contributed considerably more to the decline in employment-based insurance than did expansions of Medicaid eligibility.

Approximately 14 percent of children do not have any insurance coverage. The great majority of them live in working families, but their parents either work for employers who do not offer insurance, or they perceive the health benefits offered by their employer as unaffordable. Traditionally, uninsured children have received care that is available as charity in emergency rooms, public hospitals, state and local health departments, community and migrant health centers, and other publicly funded health facilities. But many have simply gone without needed care.

Numerous studies have demonstrated that children who have neither private health insurance nor public coverage such as Medicaid have less access to both preventive and acute or chronic health care than insured children (Brown, 1989; Brown et al., 1998; Currie and Gruber, 1996; Currie and Thomas, 1995; Holl et al., 1995; Institute of Medicine, 1998; Lieu et al., 1993; Newacheck, 1992; Newacheck et al., 1996; Stoddard et al., 1994; U.S. General Accounting Office, 1997; Wood et al., 1990). Uninsured children are less likely to have seen a doctor in the past year or to receive required preventive services, such as well-child visits and immunizations, as recommended by the American Academy of Pediatrics (1995). They are also less likely to receive a doctor's care for injuries and common illnesses of childhood, such as acute earaches and asthma, that can have serious consequences if left untreated (Overpeck and Kotch, 1995; Stoddard et al., 1994). The differences between being insured and being uninsured in access and use of health care have recently been demonstrated for children in immigrant families, for whom Medicaid eligibility is associated with increases in the probability of having received at least one doctor's visit in the previous year (Currie, 1997).

Patterns of Coverage

First-generation (noncitizen) and second-generation (citizen) children are at a significantly higher risk of being uninsured than are third- and later-generation (citizen) children (see Figure 4-1).[10] With increasing time in the United States, measured by immigrant generation within ethnic groups, rates of insurance coverage increase (see also Leclere et al., 1994, comparing recent with older adult immigrants). First-generation (noncitizen) children in every ethnic group are substantially more likely to lack insurance than later-generation (citizen) children, and they are more likely to be uninsured than even third- and later-generation black children, who generally have high rates of uninsurance. Overall, first-generation children are most likely to be uninsured (36 percent), followed by second-generation children (21 percent) and third-generation children (11 percent). Even among children whose parents work full-time, year-round, children in immigrant families are more likely to be uninsured than are third- and later-generation children.

Hispanic children are the most likely to lack health insurance. They have the highest uninsured rates for each generation (rang-

---

[10]Estimates regarding health insurance coverage and access to health care in this section are based on results for first-generation children who are not citizens, first-generation children who are citizens, second-generation children who are citizens, and third- and later-generation children who are citizens. Thus, in the estimates presented here the small proportion of first-generation children who are citizens are included among the second generation. The estimates presented in this section focus on the distinction—which has become important with welfare reform—between citizen children, who are generally eligible for benefits even if they are immigrants, and noncitizen children, who are generally ineligible for benefits.

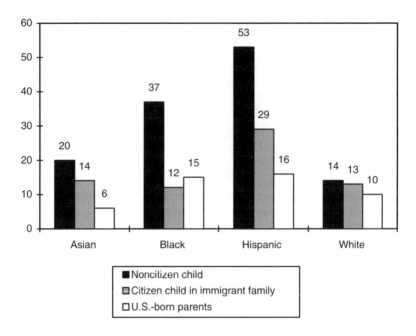

FIGURE 4-1   Percentage of children without health care insurance: 1995.
Source: March 1996 Current Population Survey. Brown et al. (1998).

ing from 53 percent for first-generation children to 16 percent for
third- and later-generation children) compared with non-Hispanic children. In contrast, by the second generation, Asian children do not differ significantly from third- and later-generation
white children in their rates of uninsurance; third- and later-generation Asian children have the lowest uninsured rate of any
group, including third- and later-generation white children.

The finding of high uninsurance rates among Hispanic immigrant children compared with immigrant children from other ethnic groups was replicated in analyses that controlled for family
structure, parents' education and employment, and family income—that is, among those with similar demographic and socioeconomic circumstances, first-generation Hispanics are more
likely to lack health insurance coverage than other first-generation children. Among second-generation children, however, Hispanics, Asians, and whites had quite comparable rates of

uninsurance when they had similar family structure and socioeconomic status. This suggests that these demographic and socioeconomic factors may play a larger role in explaining ethnic differences in insurance coverage among second-generation children than among first-generation children, for whom such factors as legal status, English proficiency, and knowledge of the U.S. health care system and benefits may play important roles as well.

As is true for all children, the cost of health insurance is the main reason for lack of coverage among children in immigrant families, regardless of ethnicity. Beliefs about coverage (e.g., that it is not needed, dissatisfaction with coverage, or lack of belief in health insurance) are not important reasons for lack of coverage for any immigrant group (Brown et al., 1998).

Sources of Coverage

Among insured children in immigrant families, the source of insurance varies by ethnic group and by immigration and citizenship status (see Table 4-5). For every ethnic group (Hispanic, Asian, black, and white), second-generation (citizen) children are more likely to have employment-based coverage than first-generation (noncitizen) children. An even larger share of third- and later-generation (citizen) children have employer-sponsored coverage.

These generational trends, however, camouflage large differences by ethnicity. Hispanic children—whether first- or second-generation—are less likely to receive employment-based coverage than corresponding generations of white, black, and Asian children. It is especially striking that, by the second generation, about two-thirds of Asian, black, and white children and adolescents have employment-based health insurance, compared with only 35 percent of second-generation Hispanic children. Among third-generation children, a substantially lower share of both black and Hispanic children have employment-based insurance than Asian and white children.

Medicaid has compensated for some of these disparities, reducing the risks of uninsurance for some children in immigrant families, despite their participation rates, which are lower than low-income third- and later-generation children. Second-genera-

TABLE 4-5   Children's Health Care Insurance Coverage: 1995

	Uninsured	Employment-based Insurance	Medicaid	Other[c]	Total
All Children[a]					
Citizen child with U.S.-born parents	11%	66%	17%	6%	100% (N=58,3000,000)
Citizen child in immigrant family	21%	52%	23%	5%	100% (N=9,621,939)
Noncitizen child	36%	35%	23%	6%	100% (N=2,340,744)
Asian[b]					
Citizen child with U.S.-born parents	6%	69%	12%	12%	100% (N=474,005)
Citizen child in immigrant family	14%	66%	13%	7%	100% (N=1,774,134)
Noncitizen child	20%	45%	26%	9%	100% (N=607,263)
Black[b]					
Citizen child with U.S.-born parents	15%	42%	40%	4%	100% (N=10,180,000)
Citizen child in immigrant family	12%	69%	17%	3%	100% (N=709,113)
Noncitizen child	37%	40%	17%	6%	100% (N=181,155)
Hispanic[b]					
Citizen child with U.S.-born parents	16%	45%	36%	3%	100% (N=3,703,829)
Citizen child in immigrant family	29%	35%	34%	2%	100% (N=4,638,045)
Noncitizen child	53%	22%	22%	3%	100% (N=1,148796)
White[b]					
Citizen child with U.S.-born parents	10%	74%	10%	7%	100% (N=43,210,000)
Citizen child in immigrant family	13%	68%	12%	7%	100% (N=2,465,344)
Noncitizen child	14%	53%	23%	10%	100% (N=400,260)

Source: March 1996 Current Population Survey. Brown et al. (1998).

[a]Includes individuals with "Other race/ethnicity"

[b]"Hispanic" includes all Hispanic persons from the Americas, "Asian," "Black," and "White" do not include any persons of Hispanic heritage.

[c]"Other" includes privately purchased health insurance, Medicare, and other public programs.

tion Hispanic children are more likely than any other second-generation group to receive Medicaid. Among first-generation children, however, Hispanic, Asian, and white children enroll in Medicaid at similar levels (ranging from 22 to 26 percent); only first-generation black children enroll at lower rates (17 percent). Among third- and later-generation children, black and Hispanic children enroll in Medicaid at similar and relatively high rates (40 percent and 36 percent, respectively), whereas a much smaller share of Asian (12 percent) and white children (10 percent) rely on Medicaid.

Looking beyond these broad ethnic categories to patterns of insurance coverage among children from specific countries of origin reveals wide variation within ethnic groups. Approximately half of first-generation children from Cuba, Mexico, and Central America are uninsured, probably reflecting the generally low educational attainment that characterizes recent immigrants from these countries, which in turn tends to limit employment to jobs that do not offer health benefits. Those from South America are more likely to have health insurance, although 39 percent are still not covered.

Children in more advantaged families from other sending countries—such as Hong Kong, Japan, Singapore, and Taiwan; Europe; China; and the Philippines, Malaysia, and Indonesia—all rank higher in their rates of insurance coverage than those from Latin American countries. These children have higher rates of employment-based health insurance, which workers with higher levels of educational attainment typically can obtain. In contrast, rates of uninsurance among Korean-origin children are very high (38 percent) and, by the second generation, exceed levels for children in immigrant families from all other sending countries, perhaps as a result of the relatively high rates of self-employment among Korean families.[11]

First-generation children from Cambodia, Laos, and Vietnam are most likely to be insured, reflecting very high levels of Medic-

---

[11]Asian children (citizen and noncitizen) in immigrant families with self-employed parents are twice as likely to lack insurance as their counterparts with parents who work part-time or part-year. They are more than three times as likely to lack insurance as those whose parents do not work (Brown et al., 1998).

aid coverage (64 percent) rather than employment-based health insurance (24 percent). This holds as well for second-generation children in families from these sending countries, despite their parents' relatively low educational levels, high poverty rates, and low participation in the labor force. These children and families from Southeast Asia have been granted refugee status since 1975, which opens the door to relatively generous Medicaid eligibility provisions.

USE OF HEALTH CARE

Given that health insurance facilitates the access of children to care, differences in coverage should be reflected in differential patterns of access to and use of health care. But access to health care services depends on more than health insurance coverage; it also requires that families develop a connection to the health care system for their children—a regular practitioner or place that can provide continuity of care over time and even across family members and serve as a guide to appropriate preventive care and needed specialized services. Having a regular source of care has been found consistently to increase the use of health care services and to enhance referrals to complex care when needed (Andersen and Davidson, 1996; Berk et al., 1995; Newacheck et al., 1996). Children who are publicly or privately insured are more likely to be connected to the health care system through a doctor (Holl et al., 1995; Kogan et al., 1995; Lieu et al., 1993; Newacheck et al., 1996).

There is virtually no research on the access of immigrant children and adolescents to health care, nor on the factors that affect access for this population. The analyses conducted for the committee (Brown et al., 1998) used the number of physician visits "during the past 12 months" as the best available measure of access. This measure combines visits for illness care together with those for preventive care. It is reasonable to assume that children who do not receive at least the minimum number of visits annually that are recommended by the American Academy of Pediatrics (AAP) will not be receiving adequate preventive care. Of course, even if they receive the minimum number of visits, the content of the care may not meet AAP recommendations.

These analyses revealed that first-generation children are less likely than either second- or third- and later-generation children to have had at least one doctor's visit during the previous 12 months (Table 4-6). One-third (32 percent) of first-generation children had not visited a doctor, compared with 18 percent of second- and third- and later-generation children.

These differences were found between first-generation and U.S.-born (second- and third-generation) Hispanic, Asian, and white, but not black, children. For all ethnic groups, first-generation children were also found to be more likely (28 percent) than second-generation children (8 percent) and third- and later-generation children (5 percent) to lack a usual provider or source of health care (Figure 4-2). However, Hispanic children in immigrant families were less likely to have a usual provider or source of care than are non-Hispanic children in immigrant families. The vast majority of second- and third- and later-generation children of all ethnicities, including Hispanics, are connected to a usual source of care. The patterns for first- and second-generation children hold regardless of their health insurance status—whether they are uninsured, have Medicaid coverage, or have private or other coverage.

However, as has been demonstrated repeatedly for children in general, without health care insurance, children in immigrant families are less likely to have a connection to the health care system (51 percent lack a usual source of care) than those having coverage. Other evidence indicates that the expansions in Medicaid eligibility that characterized the mid-1980s to early 1990s led to comparable and substantial decreases in the share of children who went without any doctor's visits in a 12-month period (Currie, 1997). This was the case for children in immigrant families (with at least one immigrant parent) and U.S.-born children in U.S.-born families, despite lower enrollment on the part of immigrant children relative to their eligibility rates (approximately 50 percent of the eligible children in immigrant families were covered, compared with 66 percent of the eligible children of the other group). For U.S.-born children with U.S.-born parents—but *not* for children in immigrant families—becoming eligible for Medicaid was also associated with increases in hospitalization rates.

Both health insurance coverage and having a usual source of

TABLE 4-6   Children Who Did Not See a Doctor in the Past Year
(Percentage), 1994

	All ages (0-17)	Ages 0 to 2 years	Ages 3 to 5 years	Ages 6 to 17 years
All Children				
Immigrant Child	32	8	16	35
	(28,36)	(0,19)	(7,24)	(31,40)
Child U.S.-Born,	18	6	10	26
Immigrant Parents	(16,19)	(4,8)	(8,13)	(23,28)
Child and Parents	18	5	10	23
U.S.-Born	(17,19)	(4,6)	(9,12)	(23,24)
Hispanic				
Immigrant Child	39	*	19	42
	(33,45)		(4,34)	(35,49)
Child U.S.-Born,	20	7	11	30
Immigrant Parents	(17,23)	(4,11)	(6,15)	(26,34)
Child and Parents	17	3	9	25
U.S.-Born	(15,20)	(1,6)	(5,13)	(22,29)
Asian				
Immigrant Child	34	*	8	39
	(26,43)		(0,43)	(30,48)
Child U.S.-Born,	20	5	13	28
Immigrant Parents	(16,24)	(0,11)	(6,21)	(22,34)
Child and Parents	17	*	*	25
U.S.-Born	(8,26)			(12,38)
Black				
Immigrant Child	19	*	*	21
	(8,30)			(9,33)
Child U.S.-Born,	14	9	10	18
Immigrant Parents	(8,19)	(0,18)	(0,20)	(10,27)
Child and Parents	23	8	12	29
U.S.-Born	(21,24)	(5,11)	(9,15)	(27,32)
White				
Immigrant Child	27	7	19	29
	(21,33)	(0,25)	(4,34)	(22,36)
Child U.S.-Born,	16	4	9	22
Immigrant Parents	(13,18)	(1,8)	(5,13)	(19, 26)
Child and Parents	17	4	10	22
U.S.-Born	(16,18)	(3,5)	(9,12)	(21,23)

Note: Numbers in parentheses are 95% confidence intervals.

Source: 1994 National Health Interview Survey. Brown et al. (1998).

*Sample size too small to make a reliable estimate.

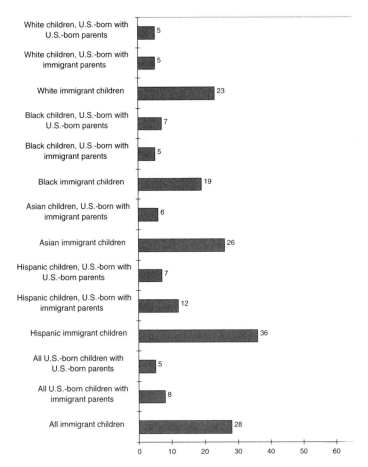

FIGURE 4-2   Children without a usual person or place for medical care: 1994. Note: Sample size of "Asian Children, U.S.-Born with U.S.-Born Parents" was too small to make a reliable estimate. Source: 1994 National Health Interview Survey. Brown et al. (1998).

care independently and strongly affected the probability that a child in an immigrant family made at least one doctor's visit during the year. Children in immigrant families who are uninsured and who have no usual source of care have the lowest probability of having seen a doctor. Those who are uninsured but have a usual source of care, as well as those who have private health insurance or Medicaid coverage but no usual source of care, both have a substantially greater probability of seeing a doctor. Finally, children who have health care coverage and a usual source of care have the greatest probability of having visited a doctor (Brown et al., 1998).

These relationships applied to children regardless of whether they were first, second, or third and later generation. They characterized Hispanic, black, Asian, and white children alike. Analyses that focused on second-generation children and controlled for family income and maternal education, however, found that some ethnic groups fared worse than others when they lacked insurance or a usual source of care. Specifically, Asian children were substantially less likely than other children to have seen a doctor in the past 12 months when they lacked both health insurance and a usual source of care.

In sum, children in immigrant families show patterns of primary health care use, as measured by having had a doctor's visit in the past year, that correspond closely to their patterns of insurance coverage and reports of having a usual source of care. These patterns and relationships, in turn, replicate those found in the pediatric health services research literature for children in general. Health care for children in immigrant families, as for all children, benefits from insurance coverage and from families' efforts to establish an ongoing connection with the health care system.

BARRIERS TO HEALTH CARE

Children do not always get appropriate health care when it is needed. They are dependent on their parents and guardians to seek care and to accept, understand, and implement the advice of health care providers. Having insurance and a regular source of health care facilitates all children's use of health services, but these factors do not guarantee entry into the health care system.

Systemic and personal factors can pose barriers that deter children from receiving the care they need (Institute of Medicine, 1994a). With the exception of isolated ethnographic studies (Baer, 1996; Baer and Bustillo, 1993; Gold et al., 1996), there is a dearth of research in this area that is specific to children in immigrant families. It is reasonable to expect, however, that some children in immigrant families may experience the kind of barriers that primarily affect children in low-income families who lack insurance or who receive Medicaid coverage, because they are similarly poor. Children in immigrant families may also experience barriers arising from their parents' lack of knowledge about the health care system in the United States, attitudes about accepting public benefits, or from language and cultural differences between parents and providers.

Medicaid and Reduced Access to Care

Limited availability of neighborhood-based primary health care facilities is frequently cited as a barrier to appropriate and timely health care by low-income families. Physicians are not required to participate in Medicaid, and 25 percent of U.S. physicians report that they do not include Medicaid patients in their practices. Approximately a third of physicians limit the number of Medicaid patients they treat (Mitchell, 1991) in part because of low fees paid by Medicaid,[12] red tape, and potential exposure to greater liability in treating poor, sick patients (Rowland and Salganicoff, 1994). Even Medicaid patients seen by physicians may be referred to public clinics for immunizations (Ruch-Ross and O'Connor, 1994).

In view of these problems, it is not surprising that many uninsured and Medicaid-covered children receive care in emergency departments and hospital clinics. Among the Medicaid population, clinics, outpatient departments, and emergency departments account for 37 percent of all visits, compared with 17 percent of visits among the privately insured (Rowland et al., 1992). Both uninsured and lower-income children are less likely to go to a physician's office for their routine care than insured and more advantaged children and youth (Holl et al., 1995; Simpson et al., 1997).

Extensive use of emergency departments and clinics undermines continuity of care and leads to lower quality of care (Erzen et al., 1997; Evans et al., 1997; Halfon et al., 1996; Holl et al., 1995; Rodewald et al., 1997), a problem for all children that is exacer-

---

[12]For pediatric and obstetric services, Medicaid reimburses providers at about half the rate of private insurers (Physician Payment Review Commission, 1991).

bated among those with chronic conditions. Moreover, it is not clear how emergency departments and clinics that low-income families rely on and that provide important sources of care for many uninsured children and youth may be affected by the recent wave of hospital closures and mergers, the takeover of not-for-profit hospitals by for-profit companies, and declining government support for public hospitals.

The Shift to Managed Care

In principle, some features of managed care, such as coordination of care by case managers and assignment of care providers to specific patients on a long-term basis, have the potential to improve access to care in the low-income eligible population. Evidence to date is mixed, however, and there are virtually no data on how immigrant children are faring in managed care settings.

A 1995 review of more than 130 studies of Medicaid managed care by the Kaiser Foundation (Rowland et al., 1995) found that managed care reduced use of emergency department and specialist care, but it did not lead to consistent changes in the overall number of doctor's visits. Access to preventive care did not consistently rise or fall, and it remained lower for the Medicaid population than for the nonpoor population. None of the studies in the Kaiser report focused specifically on immigrants. In addition, specialized services such as transportation or language translation, which are needed by many Medicaid beneficiaries and by immigrants as well, may not be offered by conventional managed care plans.

Culture and Language

For many immigrants arriving in the United States today, access to health care is likely to be complicated by cultural perceptions of health and health care that differ from Western concepts and by communication problems caused by language barriers (de Leon Siantz, in review; Munoz et al., 1986). A rich literature has characterized the ways in which culture shapes perceptions, explanations and experiences of illness, help-seeking patterns, and responses to treatment (Angel and Thoits, 1987; Harwood, 1981;

Kleinman, 1978, 1980). The fears of immigrant parents that health care providers will fail to understand or will even disparage their beliefs about their children's health and health care, whether founded or not, may discourage health care use (Institute of Medicine, 1994b; Keefe et al., 1979), although one study of Vietnamese immigrants found that differing beliefs did not act as a barrier to accessing Western medicine (Jenkins et al., 1996). Furthermore, the dearth of bilingual health care practitioners and multilingual health messages may undermine the ability of immigrant children and their families to receive health information, communicate with health providers, and identify health services in their community (Andersen et al., 1981; Giachello, 1994; Moll et al., 1976; Solis et al., 1990; Wood et al., 1995).

There is a strong consensus among health care professionals that the delivery of high-quality health care and mental health services to immigrant children and their families must be done in ways that are *culturally competent* and *culturally sensitive* and must take into account language barriers (American Academy of Pediatrics, 1997b). In a study supported by the Health Resources Services Administration, Tirado (1995) defined cultural competence as "a level of knowledge and skills to provide effective clinical care to patients from a particular ethnic or racial group," and cultural sensitivity as "a psychological propensity to adjust one's practice styles to the needs of different ethnic or racial groups." The American Medical Association (1994) defines cultural competence as "the sensitivity, cultural knowledge, skills, and actions of practitioners that meet the needs of patients from diverse backgrounds."

Several guides have been developed to help providers become more culturally competent (see, for example, American Psychiatric Association, 1994; Cross, 1992; Isaacs and Benjamin, 1991; Lynch and Hanson, 1992). They emphasize the importance of valuing cultural diversity, assessing the culture of the health care delivery system and its interface with the cultures represented by the client population, and incorporating knowledge about the culture-based beliefs and practices of the client population into health care delivery. Efforts that involve recognizing social networks and natural helpers have also been discussed in the literature (see Institute of Medicine, 1994b). Yet few applied graduate medical training programs provide courses that address these issues or offer opportunities to work with diverse populations (Allison et al., 1994).

To date, moreover, although there is an extensive literature that argues for the need to deliver culturally competent care, it relies heavily on anecdotal evidence (e.g., case studies, providers' personal experiences) and data from small nonrepresentative samples of patients. Research is clearly needed to develop a body of knowledge about how cultural differences, distinct from differences due to other factors such as social class, function to promote or deter the delivery of appropriate and effective health care to immigrant children. The perspectives of parents and children, as well as of a range of health care professionals, are needed. Important questions concern the effects of culturally competent care or its absence on parents' willingness to seek health care for their children; on the accurate communication of symptoms and diagnoses; and on parents' acceptance, understanding, and appropriate implementation of treatment recommendations.

SUMMARY

Prior to welfare reform, second-generation children, who account for three-fourths of all children in immigrant families, were nearly identical to third- and later-generation children in their likelihood of living in families receiving public assistance. First-generation children, however, were more likely than second- and third- and later-generation children to live in families with at least one person receiving public benefits. Among Mexican-origin children, who account for about one-third of all children in immigrant families, the first, second, and third and later generations are all more likely than third- and later-generation white children to live in families receiving public benefits.

It is disadvantaged socioeconomic and demographic circumstances that account for high levels of public assistance receipt among first-generation children as a whole, and among Mexican-origin children in immigrant families. Indeed, their rates of reliance on public assistance are either similar to or lower than those of third- and later-generation black children, who are also highly disadvantaged. For children with similar socioeconomic and demographic circumstances, both first- and second-generation children, generally, as well as first- and second-generation Mexican-origin children, are less likely than third- and later-generation white children to be living in families receiving welfare from most programs.

Beyond generational patterns, it is clear that, with welfare reform, the new restrictions on eligibility for many of the benefits applied to immigrant families are likely to have a disproportionate effect on children whose families are from countries that have either tended to send relatively impoverished people to the United States, such as Mexico, or have been the source of major waves of refugees, such as Southeast Asian nations, Bosnia, and the former Soviet Union.

With regard to health care coverage and access, the committee's analyses, which pertain to the situation prior to welfare reform, indicate that substantial disparities in uninsurance rates—not fully explained by family work status or income—characterize children in immigrant families. First-generation children are about three times more likely, and second-generation children are about twice as likely to lack health insurance than are third- and later-generation children. Hispanic children are particularly disadvantaged, showing both high rates of uninsurance and low rates of employer coverage relative to Asian, black, and white children of all generations.

In large part due to the automatic eligibility of refugees for Medicaid, Southeast Asian children exhibit very low rates of uninsurance despite their very low socioeconomic status. This, combined with the high rates of employment-based coverage for children from most other Asian sending countries, leaves Asian children in immigrant families overall with rates of insurance coverage that do not differ significantly from those of third- and later-generation white children. It is critical to note that the aggregating by broad ethnic groups, which is required by the small sample sizes of existing surveys, obscures the tremendous variations in patterns of insurance coverage that no doubt characterize children from different counties of origin.

When children in immigrant families are insured, they are more likely to have a usual source of care and to have seen a physician. As is true for children in general, both health insurance coverage and an ongoing connection to the health care system are independently associated with increased reliance on appropriate preventive care. It is their combined effect, however, that most strongly affects children's chances of having seen a physician in the past year. First-generation immigrant children and, to a lesser extent, second-generation children are at higher risk than third- and later-generation children of being uninsured, less likely to have a usual health care provider, and less likely to have seen a doctor in the previous year.

The evidence reviewed by the committee consistently indicates that the health behaviors of these children and their parents are not fundamentally different from those of other children and parents. Medicaid coverage, in particular, appears to increase the number of children in immigrant families who make doctor's visits during the year, without simultaneously increasing hospitalization rates or doctor's visits beyond an annual check-up. Recent reductions in health care coverage—affecting potentially 1 in 4 first-generation children if current rates of Medicaid coverage for these children hold—are likely to result in poorer access to health care, fewer usual providers or sources of care, and fewer regular doctor's visits than is already the case for this population of children, who prior to welfare reform were already disproportionately likely to lack insurance and consistent health care.

CHAPTER 5

Conclusions and Recommendations

In assessing the health, well-being, and adjustment of children in immigrant families, the committee faced from the outset a severe lack of research and data, which impaired our ability to answer many questions related to our charge. The federal government funds a rich and diverse set of data collection systems to monitor the health and well-being of the U.S. population, but few of these efforts seek information about country of birth, parents' country of birth, or citizenship—information that is needed to ascertain the circumstances of first-, second-, and third- and later- generation children. Although available data are thin, we were able to commission original research with existing data to draw preliminary conclusions on critical issues, and to provide the foundation for important recommendations for improved data collection and new research.

Recent and continuing changes in public policy posed additional constraints. First, there are no currently available data on the effects of the recent major reduction in benefits to immigrant children and families brought about by enactment of the Personal Responsibility and Work Opportunity Reconciliation Act of 1996. Second, the political environment that will influence the implementation of these new policies is in flux. Most states are still sorting through various decisions that need to be made regarding welfare reform and children's health insurance. Third, the wide discretion that states have in making decisions on the eligibility of foreign-born children and adults for benefits is likely to produce much variation in the circumstances of these children among—and even within—states.

For these reasons, we recognized that the health of children in immigrant families, their exposure to potential risk and protective factors, their access to publicly funded benefits and programs, and their use of health care services may change markedly in the years ahead. Such changes may result both from the effects of policy reforms for children in immigrant families now residing in the United States and from the effects the policies may have on future immigration. An understanding of previous practices and policies that have provided for foreign-born children and their parents therefore represents critical baseline information on which an accurate assessment of the effects of the recent policy reforms will necessarily depend. The findings and conclusions of the committee are preliminary indications of how children in immigrant families are faring and what this implies about their future prospects. The committee's recommendations focus on data needs that are essential both to a more comprehensive understanding of the health and development of children in immigrant families and to efforts to assess the effects of recent policy reforms on them.

FINDINGS AND CONCLUSIONS

Whenever possible, we compare children in immigrant families with U.S.-born children in U.S.-born families. This provides a means of deciphering generational patterns of health and adjustment and examining immigrant families in the context of the range of life chances experienced by U.S.-born children in U.S.-born families, including black children who, like immigrant children, are often considered to be at risk. The vast diversity that characterizes children in immigrant families can be considered the most salient and most important theme that surfaces from the committee's review and synthesis of this fledgling area of inquiry.

Risk and Protective Factors

Research on risk factors and, to an even greater extent, protective factors specific to children in immigrant families is extremely sparse. Little is known about the conditions or circumstances that are associated with negative outcomes for these children, and less is known about conditions that reduce the likelihood of negative outcomes, whether conceived as the absence of risk factors or the presence of influences that act in their own right to protect development. Nevertheless, a few conclusions that point to interesting questions for future research may be drawn from the existing literature.

• **In 1990, first-generation immigrant children were substantially more likely to be poor than was the case in 1960 (32.9 percent versus 22.7 percent).** In 1960, first- and second-generation children were less likely to be poor than third- and later-generation children. By 1990, first-generation children, and to a much lesser extent, second-generation children, were more likely than third- and later-generation children to live in poverty.

• **Children in immigrant families and those with U.S.-born parents are about equally likely to have fathers and mothers who are college graduates. At the other end of the spectrum, however, first- and second-generation children are more likely than third- and later-generation children to have fathers with very low educational attainment.** Between 1960 and 1990, however, the share of children living with fathers who had completed fewer than eight years of schooling declined by almost two-fifths for the second generation and by one-sixth for the first generation.

• **Throughout the century, the vast majority of children in immigrant families have had fathers in the labor force, making them comparable to U.S.-born children with U.S.-born parents. Accordingly, poverty and low parental education are not closely associated with lower rates of father's employment in immigrant families.** Children across immigrant generations have also historically not differed in their likelihood of having a mother in the labor force, although enormous increases in maternal employment have occurred for all children over the course of the century.

To the extent that differences in parental employment are found for children in immigrant families, they emerge in fathers' rates of full-time, year-round work, which are lower for the earlier generations, particularly for the first generation.

- **In 1990, children in immigrant families, especially the second generation, were more likely to live in two-parent families than were U.S.-born children with U.S.-born parents.** This was not the case at the turn of the century or in 1960, when first-, second-, and third-generation children were about equally likely to live with two parents.

- **In both 1910 and 1990, the vast majority of children in immigrant families lived in a household in which their parents did not speak English at home. The proportion of children who speak English, however, increases rapidly from the first to the second generation, such that, in 1990, 81 percent of second-generation children spoke English "exclusively or very well."** Yet linguistic isolation remains a concern. In 1990, a sizeable number of immigrant children from several of the major sending countries, including over 40 percent of children from Laos, Cambodia, Vietnam, China, and the former Soviet Union, lived in households in which no person age 14 or older spoke English either "exclusively" or "very well."

These general patterns, however, camouflage the diversity in socioeconomic circumstances that characterizes children in immigrant families from different countries of origin. Children in immigrant families from 12 countries of origin, which account for close to half of all such children, now experience poverty rates that are comparable to those experienced by Hispanic and black children who are U.S. born with U.S.-born parents. These countries include those that are the sources of many officially recognized refugees (the former Soviet Union, Cambodia, Laos, Thailand, and Vietnam) and that provide most legal and illegal unskilled migrant laborers (Mexico, Honduras, Haiti, and the Dominican Republic). Children from most of these countries had working fathers, and most lived in two-parent families. These children were also distinguished, however, by their relatively high rates of living in linguistically isolated households and of not speaking English exclusively or very well. Children with origins in most of these countries are likely to be classified as minority—Hispanic, Asian, or black—a factor with profound implications for their exposure to both risk and protective factors as they grow up.

Physical Health

Many measures of physical health and risk behaviors that have been reported for children in immigrant families indicate that they are healthier than their U.S.-born counterparts in U.S.-born families—a finding that is counterintuitive in light of the minority status, overall lower socioeconomic status, and higher poverty rates that characterize many of the immigrant children and families that have been studied. Evidence on this issue is patchy, however, focusing on some immigrant groups and some age groups and frequently relying on parental reports rather than direct medical examinations; the research that exists, however, is quite consistent. Of concern are indications that the relatively good health of children in immigrant families appears to decline with length of time in the United States and from one generation to the next. Moreover, some children in immigrant families appear to be at risk for certain health problems (e.g., drug resistant tuberculosis) that, if left untreated, could have adverse implications for the health of the entire U.S. population.

Specifically, for many of the groups of immigrant mothers that have been studied, children born in the United States to foreign-born mothers are less likely to have low birthweight or to die in the first year of life than are children born to U.S.-born mothers from the same ethnic group, despite the generally poorer socioeconomic circumstances of the immigrant mothers for many specific countries of origin. Immigrant parents report that their children experience fewer acute and chronic health problems compared with third- and later-generation families. And adolescents in immigrant families report lower levels of neurological impairment, obesity, asthma, and health risk behaviors such as early sexual activity; use of cigarettes, alcohol, marijuana, or hard drugs; delinquency; and use of violence compared with their counterparts with U.S.-born parents.

The neonatal and adolescent health advantages of immigrants

appear to deteriorate over time as environmental conditions impinge on development and as youth become increasingly removed from their immigrant origins and assimilated into the
youth culture—and often the minority youth culture—in the
United States. These data raise the intriguing possibility that children in immigrant families are somewhat protected, albeit temporarily, from many of the deleterious health consequences that
typically accompany poverty, minority status, and other indicators of disadvantage in the United States. For example, the comparatively low levels of cigarette smoking, alcohol consumption,
and drug use during pregnancy; a more healthful diet; and highly
supportive family networks may all play a role in the positive
neonatal outcomes of babies born to immigrant women in the
United States. A central challenge involves identifying the factors—genetic, familial, behavioral, environmental—tied to the
countries of origin that play into these protective functions. Although the limited available evidence suggests that protective factors specific to immigrants may diminish with increasing duration of residence in the United States and across generations,
future research should assess the possibility that the increasing
size and the geographic concentration of the immigrant population, especially from Mexico, may help to shield against the loss
of the protective factors they brought with them from their home
countries.

Despite this generally positive portrait, not all conclusions
that can be drawn about the health of immigrant children are favorable. Children in immigrant families from Mexico, for example, are more likely than third-generation white children to be
reported by parents to be in poor general health, to have teeth in
only fair to poor condition, and to exhibit elevated blood lead
levels. In addition, epidemiological evidence as well as physician
reports indicate that children of recently arrived immigrants, and
particularly those from certain high-risk countries of origin, are
at elevated risk of harboring or acquiring tuberculosis, hepatitis
B, and parasitic infections and of having unsafe levels of lead in
the blood. Exposure to pesticides is an additional health risk of
great concern for children of migrant farmworkers, in light of its
documented links to specific ailments and chronic health conditions.

Mental Health

Adolescents in immigrant families appear as likely as third- and later-generation adolescents to experience feelings of psychological well-being and positive self-concept and to avoid serious psychological distress that can, in the extreme, contribute to adolescent suicide rates. These positive signs of adjustment are maintained despite perceptions among adolescents in immigrant families—particularly those of Hispanic and Asian origin—that they have less control over their own lives and are less popular with classmates, compared with their third- and later-generation peers. Factors of particular importance to adjustment are living in a family that is mutually supportive and cohesive and in a community that is supportive of the family's resettlement, speaking English well, and being comfortable bridging one's immigrant origins and American culture.

Children in immigrant families also, on average, perform just as well if not better in school than their third- and later-generation peers. They also have somewhat higher middle school grade point averages and math test scores, although reading test scores in the first generation are lower than for later generations, probably as a result of their poorer English proficiency. Children in immigrant families from different countries of origin differ greatly in how well they perform in school, however. Children from some Asian countries, for example China and Korea, tend to outperform students from European countries, who, in turn, receive higher grades and test scores than those from Mexico. Similarly, Chinese adolescents in immigrant families have grades and math test scores that are much higher than those of third- and later-generation Chinese and white children. But Asian groups, such as the Lao and Hmong, have scores that are well below national norms.

Use of Public Benefits

First-generation immigrant children are more likely than later-generation children to live in families receiving public assistance. This is particularly the case for Mexican, Cuban, other

Hispanic, and Asian children. This pattern derives from the disadvantaged socioeconomic and demographic circumstances of their families, rather than from their immigrant status per se. At the same socioeconomic levels, both first- and second-generation children are less likely than third- and later-generation children to live in families receiving most forms of public assistance.

Second-generation children were nearly identical to third and later-generation children in their likelihood of living in families receiving benefits from major welfare programs. When generational differences in family socioeconomic levels were controlled, second-generation children were actually less likely than third- and later-generation children to live in families receiving public assistance.

Mexican-origin children were no exception to these patterns. Among those at the same socioeconomic levels, the first and second generations were usually less likely than the third and later generations to live in families that relied on public assistance. Among West European-origin children at the same socioeconomic level, the first and second generations were usually about as likely, or less likely, than the later generations to rely on public assistance. Only among Asian, Cuban, and East European children at given socioeconomic levels was the first generation generally more likely than later generations to use public assistance, probably because of the access available in the past to these populations as refugees from Southeast Asia and the former Soviet Union.

This portrait of reliance on public assistance reflects eligibility rules prior to welfare reform, when access to public benefits and programs for children in immigrant families were essentially identical for legal immigrants and citizens. Today, however, many legal immigrants are barred from a range of federal means-tested benefits, including income assistance (TANF) and Medicaid for their first five years in the country. As a result, new analyses examining immigrant families' reliance on public benefits are urgently needed.

Health Care Coverage and Access to Care

Noncitizen children in immigrant families are about three times more likely than third- and later-generation children to lack health insurance, and second-generation children with at least one immigrant parent are about two times more likely than third- and later-generation children to lack health insurance. Both noncitizen children and, to a lesser extent, citizen children with an immigrant parent are also more likely to lack a usual provider or source of health care and, accordingly, are substantially more likely to have gone without a doctor's visit in the previous year.

All children require access to preventive and acute health care for their own well-being, as well as for the protection of the nation's public health. Yet first-generation immigrant children and, to a lesser extent, second-generation children are less likely to receive this care than their counterparts who are U.S.-born children of U.S.-born parents. The measure of "care" used in this literature is modest, namely whether the child had seen a physician in the past year.

Research now indicates that access to health care is affected in identical ways for children who are immigrants or live with an immigrant parent and those who are U.S. born with U.S.-born parents. All children are more likely to receive recommended health care when they have health insurance and an ongoing connection to the health care system through a usual provider or source of care. Of particular importance is evidence linking expansions in Medicaid coverage that occurred between 1984 and 1992 to substantially reduced odds that a child went without a doctor's visit in the past year for both children who are immigrants and those who are not, but to a larger extent for immigrant children.

Medicaid, in fact, plays a vital role in health coverage for first- and second-generation children in immigrant families, as well as for third- and later-generation children. About 1 in 4 first-generation children, overall, receive coverage from Medicaid. Children in immigrant families who are Medicaid-eligible are more likely to have visited a physician in the previous year compared with uninsured children in immigrant families. And, in large part due to the automatic eligibility of refugees for Medicaid, Southeast Asian children exhibit very low rates of uninsurance despite their very low socioeconomic status.

As with public assistance in general, it is critical to assess the effects of recent reductions in insurance coverage for children in immigrant families on their receipt of basic preventive health care and care for health problems.

RESEARCH AND DATA COLLECTION

To be effective, public policies designed to foster the adjustment of children in immigrant families to American society must be founded on rigorous scientific knowledge about their needs, the processes that generate these needs, and approaches to addressing them. Nearly a dozen federal agencies conduct or fund data collection and research efforts that constitute the core of the nation's system for monitoring and understanding the physical and mental health of children, their exposure to risk and protective factors, and their access to and use of public benefits (Box 5-1). Few of these major data collection efforts provide a scientifically sound basis for monitoring or studying the health status and resources available to children in immigrant families. This enormous gap in knowledge is of great concern, given the rapid growth of this population and the pressing need to assess how they are affected by the recent policy reforms that sharply restrict their eligibility for health care and social benefit programs.

Specifically, none of the existing federal surveys and surveillance systems collects the necessary data with a sample designed to allow nationally representative estimates for first-, second-, and third- and later-generation children by detailed country of origin or by immigration status. Similarly, none of the national education data sets, including the three critical ones in listed in Box 5-1, provides the basic data needed to identify children by immigrant generation and country of origin, and only a few research efforts have begun to make use of the capacity to approximate these measures.

Knowledge about the physical and mental health, school progress, access to and use of health and social program benefits and services, and the socioeconomic risk and protective factors experienced by children in immigrant families could be expanded substantially by additional research using existing data. Small but critical improvements in data collection and in other components of major surveillance systems and surveys could enormously expand the potential for new research that would provide policy makers with information about the growing population of children in immigrant families that is now available only for U.S.-born children in U.S.-born families.

New data collection is also essential to address large gaps in knowledge that persist about the ways in which families, schools, neighborhoods, racial and ethnic stratification, and community and national policies interact with each other, and with different home country cultures and immigration experiences, to influence healthy development and successful adaptation. No single surveillance system or survey currently collects the necessary longitudinal data for children in immigrant (and other) families on physical and mental health, access to publicly funded benefits and programs, health insurance coverage and health service utilization, and exposure to potential risk and protective factors, including those factors unique to immigrants because of their culture and immigration experiences.

In light of these major limitations of existing data, the committee makes a number of recommendations for new research studies, data collection, and information dissemination. Interdisciplinary teams will be necessary to implement many aspects of these recommendations, because the required expertise spans several scientific, medical, and health disciplines.

New Research Studies

Recommendation 1. The federal government should fund a longitudinal survey of children and youth in immigrant families, measuring physical and psychosocial development and the range of contextual factors influencing their development.

Issues and questions pertaining to children in immigrant families currently in the United States, and to children born in future years to these families, will go unstudied without a new longitudinal survey. Information on country of birth for children

BOX 5-1
SELECTED DATA COLLECTION SYSTEMS AND SURVEYS

Health Status, Risk Behaviors, Insurance, and Expenditures

- **Public Health Surveillance Systems** (tuberculosis, HIV/AIDS, sexually transmitted diseases, behavioral risk factors, youth risk behavior, birth defects, and cancer registries)
    — Centers for Disease Control and Prevention

- **Birth and Death Registration Systems**
    — National Center for Health Statistics

- **National Longitudinal Adolescent Health Survey**
    — National Institute of Child Health and Human Development

- **Youth Risk Behavior National Survey**
    — Centers for Disease Control and Prevention

- **Monitoring the Future Survey**
    — National Institute on Drug Abuse
    — Survey Research Center, University of Michigan

- **National Health Interview Survey, including Child Health Supplement**
    — National Center for Health Statistics
    — National Institute of Child Health and Human Development

- **National Health and Nutrition Examination Survey**
    — National Center for Health Statistics

- **Medical Expenditure Panel Survey[1]**
    — National Center for Health Statistics

- **National Crime Victimization Survey**
    — Bureau of Justice Statistics

- **National Survey of Family Growth**
    — National Center for Health Statistics

Education

- **Early Childhood Longitudinal Survey**
    — National Center for Education Statistics

- **National Educational Longitudinal Survey**
  — National Center for Education Statistics

- **National Household Education Survey**
  — National Center for Education Statistics

Socioeconomic Risk and Participation in Public Benefit Programs

- **Decennial Census of the Population and Housing**
  — Bureau of the Census

- **Current Population Survey**
  — Bureau of the Census

- **Survey of Income and Program Participation**
  — Bureau of the Census

- **Survey of Program Dynamics**
  -- Bureau of the Census

- **Panel Study of Income Dynamics**
  — National Science Foundation
  — Survey Research Center, University of Michigan

- **National Integrated Quality Control Survey**
  — Administration for Children and Families
  — Health Care Financing Administration
  — Food and Consumer Service

---

[1]The Medical Expenditure Panel Survey (MEPS) is the third in a series of national probability surveys conducted by the Agency for Health Care Policy and Research (AHCPR) on the financing and utilization of medical care in the United States. The National Medical Care Expenditure Survey (NMCES, also known as NMES-1) was conducted in 1977, the National Medical Expenditure Survey (NMES-2) in 1987. Beginning in 1996, the MEPS continues this series with design enhancements and efficiencies that provide a more current data resource than in previous surveys.

and their parents is obtained in few ongoing national data collection efforts. Such data are essential to distinguish between foreign-born immigrant children (first-generation), U.S.-born children in immigrant families (second-generation), and U.S.-born children in U.S.-born families (third- and later-generation), and to study country-specific outcomes and causal processes. The health and developmental outcomes of children in immigrant families and the social, community, and cultural factors that may influence these outcomes are not measured in any ongoing national study. Undocumented and legal immigrant children are not distinguished in national data collection efforts.

Two central issues that emerged during the committee's review call specifically for longitudinal research. The first pertains to some evidence that suggests that children in immigrant families from at least some countries of origin may, despite negative socioeconomic risk factors, experience physical health outcomes that are superior to those for U.S.-born children in U.S.-born families. The second issue concerns evidence that this relatively good health status declines over time, and engagement in behaviors that pose risk to health increases over time, especially from one generation to the next.

The evidence supporting these broad characterizations is quite limited, however, in four respects. First, this research has focused largely on cross-sectional samples of infants and adolescents, thus limiting efforts to understand developmental patterns over time. Second, issues of selection that have hindered the literature on immigration make it very difficult to ascertain the causes of patterns that have emerged in the research on immigrant children. In particular, possibilities are very limited for considering carefully the contribution of unmeasured differences between individuals who migrate and those who do not, and of differing histories of migration across groups. Immigrants may be self-selected from among the populations in their countries of origin for better health, greater ambition, or other unmeasured factors that account for their comparatively good outcomes in the United States. Third, only a small number of circumstances and outcomes have been measured for children and adolescents in immigrant families. Fourth, little is known about possible causal or protective factors that account for either the unexpected positive or declining well-being of these children.

If first- or second-generation children experience better outcomes than would be expected from their status on risk factors known to affect the U.S. population, a diverse set of protective factors may be involved. These factors include the social capital or culturally sanctioned behaviors that immigrants bring with them, such as nuclear and intergenerational family cohesion; gender roles; norms about smoking cigarettes, drinking alcohol, sexual activity; and reciprocal responsibilities among members of the community. To the extent that more sophisticated data collection efforts replicate the intriguing patterns to date, it will also be critical to understand whether, why, and which of these protective processes decline over time and across generations and to identify other processes and practices associated with assimilation to American culture that may account for declining health among children in immigrant families.

Knowledge about these processes could, in turn, guide the development of public policies aimed at maintaining beneficial norms and behaviors among immigrant families and promoting similar practices among other U.S. families. Research to develop this knowledge would focus on understanding the dynamics of the processes by which protective factors operate, whether and why they decay or are sustained over time, and the role of the family, the community, and public policies.

This knowledge can be obtained only through new national research of the type recommended here. Essential elements of this research are listed below:

- It is longitudinal, following a sample of children over a period of years, in order to map and analyze the causes of change in their development;
- It measures a wide range of physical, psychosocial, educational, and other developmental outcomes to identify the domains in which children in immigrant families with various characteristics may be specially advantaged or experience special risks;
- It measures pertinent family, community, and policy variables and processes to provide insights into the dynamic relationships among possible causal processes; and

• It permits explicit comparisons, not only among the various immigrant groups, but also to U.S.-born black, Hispanic, Asian, and white children with U.S.-born parents with regard to policies and practices that either have worked or failed for different groups of children.

The vast majority of children in immigrant families who will require health, education, and other services during the next decade or more are the children now living in, or who will be born to, immigrant families that already reside in the United States. To ensure that scientific knowledge about these children will be available to policy makers and the American public at the earliest possible date, the new survey must include in its sample children *currently* in immigrant families when the survey is fielded, as well as children *subsequently* born into these families. Ideally, the sample would represent:

• all children in immigrant families that currently live in the United States and children who are subsequently born into these families;
• children in immigrant families in (at a minimum) the 6 states with the largest number of such children, or alternatively, those living in the 8 or 10 metropolitan areas with the largest number of children in immigrant families supplemented with a nonmetropolitan or rural sample;
• specific countries in each of the major geographic regions that send substantial numbers of immigrants, including the Caribbean; Central and South America; East, Southeast, Central, and West Asia; East and West Europe; and Africa; and
• children in populations that are difficult to enumerate, such as children of undocumented immigrants and of migrant farmworkers.

Because limited resources may preclude selection of a sample that fully meets all of these criteria, the committee urges the National Institute of Child Health and Human Development to convene an advisory group to develop design guidelines that balance these sample characteristics, especially national, state, and metropolitan sampling frames.

In this context, we reviewed the proposal for a major new survey, the New Immigrant Study (NIS), which has fielded a pilot data collection with federal support and is currently seeking funds for full implementation. The proposed study would use federal administrative records to draw a sample of foreign-born persons who were given visas in a particular year for the purpose of establishing lawful residence, either permanently (i.e., legal permanent residents, refugees) or temporarily (i.e., students, temporary workers). A second sample would be drawn of a second cohort of "new immigrants" entering three or four years after the first. Both cohorts would be resurveyed periodically.

The proposed New Immigrant Study could provide valuable information on immigration and adaptation processes among cohorts of future immigrants and their families. Our assessment of the current NIS plans, using as criteria the four essential elements and four sample characteristics described above, indicates the following.

The NIS would, or could easily, meet two of the criteria. It would be a longitudinal study that would follow first-generation children and that could follow second-generation children through time. It could, depending on sample size, represent many important countries of origin. It is uncertain, however, to what extent the NIS would meet two additional criteria, by measuring (1) a wide range of physical, psychosocial, educational, and other developmental outcomes for children, as well as (2) family, community, and policy variables and processes pertinent to child development, adaptation, and well-being.

The proposed NIS would not meet four of the eight criteria. It would not represent children in immigrant families that currently live in the United States, or in the states or metropolitan areas with the largest number of immigrants, because sample selection would include only persons who were given a visa during specified future years. It would not permit explicit comparisons between various immigrant groups and third- and later-generation white, black, Hispanic, and Asian children, because the sample would not include persons currently in the United States. Although other selected national data sources might provide a basis for simple comparisons to the NIS of child outcomes, the limits on available data would preclude explicit comparative analyses of many child outcomes for specific racial and ethnic minorities and for important aspects of the family, community, and public policy. Finally, the NIS would not include undocumented children or the children of undocumented parents, unless they were given a visa during the sample year or lived with a person who was given a visa during a sample year.

In view of these limitations, and the fact that one of every five children in the United States today is an immigrant or the child of an immigrant, we recommend a new longitudinal survey with a sample selected from the population of children who now live in the United States, as well as children subsequently born into their families. Information should be collected longitudinally on the various children and adults within specific families. Data from this study should be made publicly available at the earliest possible time to promote their widespread use and, accordingly, the rapid accumulation of new knowledge about children currently in immigrant families.

Recommendation 2. A series of ethnographic studies on the physical and mental health of children and youth in diverse immigrant families should, insofar as possible, be embedded in the proposed longitudinal survey of children in immigrant families or in other national surveys.

The proposed longitudinal survey of children in immigrant families can provide statistically reliable estimates of major outcomes and processes for this population as a whole and for important social and cultural subgroups. But survey methodology is limited in its ability to study the meaning and interpretation that individuals give their situations. Ethnographic studies have small samples that may not statistically represent the larger population, but they are well-suited to providing rich interpretations of the processes that can only be highlighted, not probed in depth, with survey methodology.

The origins and effects of health-promoting behaviors, manifestations and effects of biculturalism, and the processes associated with the migration experience itself are examples of issues that lend themselves to this methodology, as does the study of notions about health and illness that immigrants bring and that shape their help seeking and service use in the United States. Priority should also be given to ethnographic research, as well as to research that uses other methodologies, that addresses how aspects of growing up in the sending country prior to migration interact with the experiences of children after arrival in the United States.

Recent efforts to combine survey methodology with ethnographic methodology have been quite successful, by using ethnographic techniques to study a subsample of the larger survey sample. A single study combining the two approaches will yield much more information, both scientifically and for developing public policy, than would distinct studies each of which use only one approach. Because social and cultural processes may vary enormously across immigrant communities, it is critical that ethnographic studies of multiple diverse communities be conducted to fully understand and interpret results from broader surveys. Funding sources for this ethnographic research could include the federal government as well as private foundations.

Recommendation 3. Both quantitative and qualitative research should be conducted on the effects of welfare and health care reform for children and youth in immigrant families, and on how access to and effectiveness of health care and other services are affected by the provision of culturally competent care.

The welfare and health policies that constitute the major sources of public assistance for legal foreign-born (first-generation) children and citizen children with immigrant parents (second-generation) are undergoing dramatic change and reassessment. Welfare reform, in particular, represents the most significant shift in the modern era in the treatment of immigrant children and youth. Yet these policy changes have been forged without the benefit of an informed discussion of their likely effects on these children's development, adaptation, and future prospects. The combination of current policy change and the absence of a major investment in research to ascertain the effects of reforms in welfare and health care specifically on the lives and future prospects of children in immigrant families is troubling.

The consequences of recent and continuing changes in welfare and health policies may be more immediate and profound for immigrants than for others because eligibility for noncitizen immigrants has been either cut more deeply or made a state option. Yet none of the major evaluations of welfare and health reform is focused particularly on consequences for children in immigrant families, nor have they been identified as a major subgroup for study. The effects of these changes in the provision of services and benefits to children should be studied in detail, particularly to ascertain the nature and extent of any differential effects for first-, second-, and third- and later-generation children.

Important efforts already under way to study the effects of welfare reform on children and families include the Bureau of the Census's Survey of Program Dynamics, funded under the welfare reform legislation; the 12-state study sponsored by the U.S. Department of Health and Human Services; the 50-State Database Set and the National Survey of American Families of the Assessing New Federalism Project of the Urban Institute; and the study called Welfare Reform and Children: A Three-City Study. At the present time, none of these efforts includes a specific focus on children in immigrant families, although a new federally supported effort to examine the effects of welfare reform at selected sites on the economic and health status of immigrants generally is being conducted by the Urban Institute.[1]

Efforts to assess the consequences of health and welfare reforms should include substantial subsamples of children and youth in immigrant families. They should also pay attention to factors uniquely relevant to them, such as their circumstances of immigration, the duration of child and parental residence in the United States (which affects eligibility for public benefits), the immigration status of siblings and parents, the likelihood that

---

[1]The new Urban Institute project will explore the impacts of welfare reform on immigrants and the organizations that serve them, with a particular but not exclusive focus on effects associated with the loss of food stamps. This project will focus on two cities (Los Angeles and New York) and on immigrants in the United States at the time welfare reform was enacted (versus those arriving afterward). The project includes a somewhat restricted assessment of child health given its focus on a range of outcomes for the broader immigrant populations at the study sites.

parents seek citizenship, and their access to resources through other family members and sponsors. These efforts also need to measure both direct effects on immigrant children of their elimination from eligibility for basic benefit programs and indirect effects that ensue from family members' loss of benefits and from the possibility that some parents—particularly those who are undocumented—may be reluctant to sign up for benefits for which their children are eligible.

Children in immigrant families who remain eligible for welfare and health benefits may experience detrimental effects associated with their parents' and grandparents' loss of benefits. Such families may need to compensate for lost resources, and some strategies (e.g., shifts in goods purchased and trade-offs made in either the timing or intensity of services, including health services, that are sought) may have adverse consequences for children. Evidence on this issue does not exist.

Since the early 1970s, undocumented children have been ineligible for federal health and social benefits, with important exceptions that include emergency medical care, supplemental nutrition benefits (WIC), basic public health services such as immunizations, and public education. The recent welfare reform law continues these restrictions. Little is known about the medical and health needs of undocumented children or children with undocumented parents, or their use of services, compared with legal immigrant and U.S.-born citizen children. Little more is known about citizen children in families with undocumented immigrant parents. The committee's efforts to identify research on undocumented children revealed a glaring and significant gap in the scientific literature and greatly constrained our capacity to draw any conclusions regarding these children.

Despite the inherent difficulties that face efforts to obtain information on undocumented children and citizen children with undocumented parents, it is important that the continuing reexamination of public policy be informed by a dedicated effort to gather through available public records and other sources all available knowledge about their health and nutritional status, and their access to and utilization of pertinent benefits and programs, including those for which they are not legally eligible.

The need for health care to be provided in a culturally competent manner, including immigrant involvement in programs for their own care, has being widely recognized by federal and international health agencies and professional associations of physicians and social workers. Expert professional judgment and plausible examples suggest that culturally competent care by service providers may be key to achieving positive outcomes, and that the active participation of immigrants in programs for their own care may be important. Potentially important factors include what health outcomes immigrant parents and their children view as important. Little systematic research addresses these issues.

Because immigrants from various countries are quite heterogeneous socioeconomically and culturally, these studies should encompass a wide range of countries of origin, community settings in the United States, and types of service providers. Such studies might be effectively integrated with individual ethnographic studies or with ethno-surveys focused on individual, family, and community processes that influence child outcomes.

The committee urges the Health Resources and Services Administration of the U.S. Department of Health and Human Services to establish a clearinghouse to assemble and serve as a repository for knowledge about the nature and efficacy of various programs and approaches designed to foster the development of cultural competence among service providers and to directly involve immigrants in the delivery of health care and mental health services. Efforts supported by federal and state governments, professional organizations, and health care institutions should be systematically assessed to provide the basis for implementing and evaluating community intervention programs.

Data Collection and Dissemination

In addition to these recommended new research studies, the committee recommends measures to improve existing data resources and highlight immigrant children in existing data reports, each of which would substantially improve the available knowledge about these children.

Recommendation 4. The federal government should collect and code information on country of birth, citizenship status, and

parents' country of birth in key national data collection systems. This information should be made available through public use microdata samples and other vehicles for public distribution of data.

The federal government funds public health information and surveillance systems and national surveys to monitor physical and mental health, and circumstances and risk factors related to family, education, employment, income, housing, crime, and participation in public programs (see Box 5-1). It has been recognized for decades that accurate interpretation of these data requires analysis using the basic demographic measures of age, sex, race, and ethnicity. Because children in immigrant families constitute a large and increasing proportion of the population; because their healthy development is in the national interest; and because country of origin, citizenship status, and parents' country of birth may have important implications for healthy development, the committee urges that these three data elements be added to the list of basic demographic variables obtained in the data collection systems discussed below.

The Centers for Disease Control and Prevention (CDC), which has primary responsibility for health surveillance systems and public health programs, recently proposed standards for "citizenship" data to be used in health information and surveillance systems (Centers for Disease Control and Prevention, 1997). The committee commends and urges the adoption of this proposal.[2]

---

[2]Recent experience suggests that the inclusion of questions about citizenship will not produce a disincentive to participation. Specifically, the Adolescent Health Survey asked foreign-born adolescents about their citizenship status, and of the 1,900 who were asked the question, only one refused. There were no reports from the survey field staff indicating sensitivity to the question. Since 1994 in the Current Population Survey, the Bureau of the Census has asked country of birth, citizenship, year of entry, and parents' country of birth for every household member. It has encountered no negative reaction in the field to these questions, and the nonresponse rate is quite low. For example, the nonresponse rates were about 1 percent each for respondent's country of birth, mother's country of birth, and father's country of birth, and 4.6 percent among the foreign-born for the question "Are you a citizen?"

The committee also urges that the standard be expanded to include data elements on country of birth and parents' country of birth. Country of birth data and parents' country of birth data are essential to identify the origins of immigrant citizens as well as noncitizens. The CDC surveillance systems and surveys that should collect these data include those focused on behavioral risk factors, birth defects, immunizations, cancer registration, HIV/AIDS, sexually transmitted diseases, tuberculosis, youth risk behavior, and chronic diseases.

The National Center for Health Statistics within the CDC has immediate responsibility for compiling data from the birth and death registration systems, and for conducting the National Health Interview Survey, the National Health and Nutrition Examination Survey, the National Survey of Family Growth, and the Medical Expenditure Panel Survey. Taken together, these data collections constitute the core of the nation's system for periodic monitoring of health status and expenditures, fertility behavior, and mortality. Also directly relevant to health is information on the experience of adolescents as victims of crime, including exposure to violence and injury, that is collected annually in the National Victimization Survey under the auspices of the Bureau of Justice Statistics.

Two additional surveys provide critical information on adolescent risk behavior. The Monitoring the Future survey, funded by the National Institute on Drug Abuse, provides annual estimates for high school seniors on the prevalence and incidence of illicit drug use and on important values, behaviors, and lifestyle orientations. The National Longitudinal Study of Adolescent Health, funded by the National Institute of Child Health and Human Development (NICHD), provides an extremely rich source of longitudinal information for a national sample of youth who were in grades 7 through 12 in 1995 regarding physical and mental health, health risk behaviors, and the family, school, peer, and neighborhood environments.

The educational progress of children and the role of various influences are monitored by the National Center for Education Statistics with the National Educational Longitudinal Surveys, the National Household Education Survey, and the Early Childhood Longitudinal Survey.

Family and economic risk factors for children are measured with the greatest geographic specificity for the largest number of population subgroups by the Bureau of the Census in its Decennial Census of the Population and Housing. The Current Population Survey, sponsored by the Bureau of the Census and the Bureau of Labor Statistics, provides an annual update of decennial census information, with much greater detail on labor force participation, income, and school enrollment, but with less geographic specificity and for fewer subgroups.

Participation in welfare programs as related to family economic circumstances is also assessed in greatest detail by the Bureau of the Census through its Survey of Income and Program Participation and its Survey of Program Dynamics. The Bureau of Labor Statistics is the primary sponsor of the National Longitudinal Surveys of Youth, which focus on the transition from school to work and include supplements with extremely rich data on child development funded by the National Institute on Child Health and Human Development.

Among these data collection systems and surveys, only the Current Population Survey collects the full set of immigration data recommended here beginning in 1994, with funding from the Immigration and Naturalization Service and the National Institute of Child Health and Human Development. As the immigrant population grows and these data elements become essential to a proper understanding of trends in the social, economic, and health status health of the U.S. population, the cost of adding these elements to any specific survey is judged by the committee to be quite modest. But the returns on this expenditure would be quite substantial improvements in our ability to understand the health and social needs of immigrant children.

Recommendation 5. As the federal government develops new surveys or draws new samples to supplement or extend existing surveys, it should select and include subsamples that are large enough to reliably monitor the circumstances of children and youth in immigrant families as a whole and, where feasible, for specific countries of origin.

New samples are drawn periodically for continuing surveys and will be drawn for new national surveys in the future. Despite growth of the immigrant population, samples in most national surveys are too small to sustain statistically reliable estimates for the foreign-born population as a whole. This difficulty can be resolved by oversampling—drawing samples in which the foreign-born and their families represent a larger proportion than they are in the population as a whole.

Immigrants from different countries vary enormously in socioeconomic resources, language, and culture, but samples in most surveys are too small to provide estimates by specific country of origin. This problem can be mitigated in particular surveys by oversampling immigrants from a few specific countries of origin, where criteria relevant to the primary content of the survey provide the basis for selecting specific countries for study.

For any given survey, the trade-offs involved in adding a nationally representative refresher sample of immigrants or subsamples of immigrants from specific countries of origin should be explicitly debated. At the present time, it is rare for either strategy to be seriously considered. One exception is the Panel Study of Income Dynamics (PSID) conducted at the University of Michigan,[3] which recently supplemented its core sample with a representative sample of immigrants.

Recommendation 6. Key indicators of child well-being published in the annual report of the Federal Interagency Forum on Child and Family Statistics should, insofar as possible, distinguish among foreign-born immigrant children (first generation), U.S.-born children in immigrant families (second generation), and U.S.-born children in U.S.-born families (third and later generation).

A recent presidential executive order mandates the Federal Interagency Forum on Child and Family Statistics to publish an

---

[3]The PSID receives funding from the National Science Foundation, the U.S. Department of Health and Human Services, the U.S. Department of Housing and Urban Development, and the National Institute on Aging.

annual report on children (U.S. Department of Health and Human Services, 1996, 1997), but as yet there is virtually no public dissemination of information on even the most basic indicators on the lives and well-being of children in immigrant families— the fastest-growing segment of the child population. Precedents for federal publication of annual reports on important minority groups include the Current Population Reports of the Census Bureau on the black and Hispanic populations. We recommend that key indicators of child well-being published in this annual report should distinguish, insofar as possible, between foreign-born children in immigrant families (first-generation), U.S.-born children in immigrant families (second-generation), and U.S.-born children in U.S.-born families (third- and later-generation).

References

Aguirre International
    1997   *Study of the Characteristics of Families Served by Head Start Migrant Programs*. San Mateo, CA: Aguirre International.

Alba, R.
    1990   *Ethnic Identity: The Transformation of White America*. New Haven, CT: Yale University Press.

Alba, R.D., and V. Nee
    1996   The Assimilation of Immigrant Groups: Concept, Theory, and Evidence. Paper presented at the Social Science Research Council Conference on "Becoming African/America Becoming: International Migration to the United States." January 1996, Sanibel Island, FL.
    1997   Rethinking assimilation theory for a new era of immigration. *International Migration Review* 31(4):825-873.

Al-Kaff, A.
    1993   Kohl: The traditional eyeliner: Use and analysis. *Annals of Saudi Medicine* 13:26-30.

Allison, K.W., I. Crawford, R.J. Echemendia, L. Robinson, and D. Knepp
    1994   Human diversity and professional competence: Training in clinical and counseling psychology revisited. *American Psychologist* 49(9):792-796.

Alwin, D.F.
    1984   Trends in parental socialization values: Detroit, 1958-1983. *American Journal of Sociology* 90(2):359-382.

American Academy of Pediatrics
    1997a *1997 Red Book: Report of the Committee on Infectious Diseases, 24th Edition*. Chicago: American Academy of Pediatrics.
    1997b Health care for children of immigrant families. *Pediatrics* 100(1):153-156.

American Academy of Pediatrics, Committee on Practice and Ambulatory Medicine
> 1995 Recommendations for preventive pediatric health care. *Pediatrics* 96:373-374.

American Medical Association
> 1994 *AMA Guidelines for Adolescent Preventive Services (GAPS): Recommendations and Rationale*. Baltimore: Williams and Wilkins.

American Psychiatric Association
> 1994 *Diagnostic and Statistical Manual, Fourth Edition (DSM-IV)*. Washington, DC: American Psychiatric Association.

Andersen, R.M., and P.L. Davidson
> 1996 Measuring access and trends. Pp. 13-40 in *Changing the U.S. Health Care System*. R.M. Andersen, T.H. Rice, and G.F. Kominski, eds. San Francisco, CA: Jossey-Bass, Inc.

Andersen, R.M., G.V. Fleming, A.L. Giachello, P. Andrade, and B. Spencer
> 1981 *Self-Care Behavior Among the US Population: Analysis of National Data*. Washington, DC: National Center for Health Services Research.

Angel, R., and P. Thoits
> 1987 The impact of culture on the cognitive structure of illness. *Culture, Medicine, and Psychiatry* 1:465-494.

Aronowitz, M.
> 1984 The social and emotional adjustment of immigrant children: A review of the literature. *International Migration Review* 18(2):237-257.

Baer, R.D.
> 1996 Health and mental health among Mexican American migrants: Implications for survey research. *Human Organization* 55(1):58-66.

Baer, R.D., and A. Ackerman
> 1988 Toxic Mexican folk remedies for the treatment of empacho: The case of azarcon, greta, and albayalde. *Journal of Ethnopharmacology* 24:31-39.

Baer, R.D., and M. Bustillo
> 1993 Susto and mal de ojo among Florida farmworkers: Emic and etic perspectives. *Medical Anthropology Quarterly* 7(1):90-100.

Baker, S.J.
> 1939 *Fighting for Life*. New York: Macmillan.

Baldwin, L., and S. Sutherland
> 1988 Growth patterns of first generation Southeast Asian infants. *American Journal of Diseases of Children* 142(5):526-531.

Baltes, P.B., and O.G. Brim, Jr., eds.
> 1979 *Life-Span Development and Behavior*. New York: Academic Press.

Baltes, P.B., U. Lindenberger, and U.M. Staudinger
> 1997 Life-span theory in developmental psychology. Pp. 1029-1044 in *Handbook of Child Psychology, Volume 1: Theoretical Models of Human Development*. R. Lerner, ed. New York: John Wiley & Sons, Inc.

Barkan, E.R.
> 1996 *And Still They Come: Immigrants and American Society, 1920 to the 1990s*. Wheeling, IL: Harlan Davidson, Inc.

Barry, M., J. Craft, D. Coleman, H. Coulter, and R. Horwitz
  1983 Clinical findings in Southeast Asian refugees. *Journal of the American Medical Association* 249(23):3200-3203.
Bean, F.D., J. Van Hook, and J.E. Glick
  1997 Country of origin, type of public assistance, and patterns of welfare recipiency among U.S. immigrants and natives. *Social Science Quarterly* 78(2):249-268.
Bellinger, D., A. Leviton, C. Waternaux, H. Needleman, and M. Rabinowitz
  1989 Low-level lead exposure, social class, and infant development. *Neurotoxicology and Teratology* 10:497-503.
Berk, M.L., C.L. Schur, and J.C. Cantor
  1995 Ability to obtain health care: Recent estimates from the Robert Wood Johnson Foundation National Access to Care Survey. *Health Affairs* 14(3):139-146.
Binkin, N.J., P. Zuber, C.D. Wells, M.A. Tipple, and K.G. Castro
  1996 Overseas screening for tuberculosis in immigrants and refugees to the United States: Current status. *Clinical Infectious Diseases* 23(6):1226-1232.
Blake, J.
  1985 Number of siblings and educational mobility. *American Sociological Review* 50:84-94.
Blau, F.
  1984 The use of transfer payments by immigrants. *Industrial and Labor Relations Review* 37(2):222-239.
Blau, P.M., and O.D. Duncan
  1967 *The American Occupational Structure.* New York: Wiley.
Block, J.
  1971 *Lives Through Time.* Berkeley, CA: Bancroft Books.
Bodnar, J.
  1985 *The Transplanted: A History of Immigrants in Urban America.* Bloomington: Indiana University Press.
Booth, A., A.C. Crouter, and N. Landale
  1997 *Immigration and the Family: Research and Policy on U.S. Immigrants.* Mahwah, NJ: Lawrence Erlbaum Associates.
Borjas, G.J.
  1991 *Friends or Strangers: The Impact of Immigrants on the U.S. Economy.* New York: Basic Books.
  1995 Immigration and welfare, 1970-1990. *Research in Labor Economics* 14:251-280.
Borjas, G., and L. Hilton
  1996 Immigration and the welfare state: Immigrant participation in means-tested entitlement programs. *Quarterly Journal of Economics* 111(2):575-604.
Borjas, G., and S.J. Trejo
  1991 Immigrant participation in the welfare system. *Industrial and Labor Relations Review* 44(2):195-211.

Bradley, R.H., and L. Whiteside-Mansell
    1997   Children in poverty. Pp. 13-58 in *Handbook of Prevention and Treatment with Children and Adolescents*. R.T. Ammerman and M. Hersen, eds. New York: Gardner.
Bradley, R.H., L. Whiteside, D.J. Mundfrom, P.H. Casey, K.J. Kelleher, and S.K. Pope
    1994   Early indications of resilience and their relation to experiences in the home environments of low birthweight, premature children living in poverty. *Child Development* 65:346-360.
Brandon, P.
    1998   Public assistance receipt of immigrant children and their families: evidence from the Survey of Program Participation. In *Children of Immigrants: Health, Adjustment, and Public Assistance*. D.J. Hernandez, ed. Committee on the Health and Adjustment of Immigrant Children and Families, Board on Children, Youth, and Families. Washington, DC: National Academy Press.
Brindis, C.
    1997   Teen Pregnancy and Immigrant Youth. Unpublished paper prepared for the Committee on the Health and Adjustment of Immigrant Children and Families, National Research Council and Institute of Medicine.
Brindis, C., A.L. Wolfe, V. McCarter, S. Ball, and S. Starbuck-Morales
    1995   The association between immigrant status and risk-behavior patterns in Latino adolescents. *Journal of Adolescent Health* 17:99-105.
Bronfenbrenner, U.
    1979   *The Ecology of Human Development*. Cambridge, MA: Harvard University Press.
    1992   Ecological systems theory. Pp. 187-249 in *Six Theories of Child Development*. R. Vasta, ed. London: Jessica Kingsley Publishers, Ltd.
Bronfenbrenner, U., and S.J. Ceci
    1994   Nature-nurture reconceptualized in developmental perspective: A bio-ecological model. *Psychological Review* 101:568-586.
Brooks-Gunn, J., G.J. Duncan, and J.L. Aber
    1997   *Neighborhood Poverty. Volume I: Context and Consequences for Children*. New York: Russell Sage Foundation.
Brown, E.R.
    1989   Access to health insurance in the United States. *Medical Care Review* 46(4):349-385.
Brown, E.R., R. Wyn, H. Yu, A. Valenzuela, and L. Dong
    1998   Access to health insurance and health care for children in immigrant families. In *Children of Immigrants: Health, Adjustment, and Public Assistance*. D.J. Hernandez, ed. Committee on the Health and Adjustment of Immigrant Children and Families, Board on Children, Youth, and Families. Washington, DC: National Academy Press.
Brown, J., M. Serdula, K. Cairns, J. Godes, D. Jacobs, P. Elmer, and F. Trowbridge
    1986   Ethnic group differences in nutritional status of young children from

low-income areas of an urban county. *American Journal of Clinical Nutrition* 44(6):938-944.

Buriel, R.

1984 Integration with traditional Mexican American culture and sociocultural adjustment. Pp. 95-130 in *Chicano Psychology* (second edition). J.L. Martinez and R. Mendoza, eds. New York: Academic Press.

1994 Acculturation, respect for cultural differences, and biculturalism among three generations of Mexican American and Euro American school children. *The Journal of Genetic Psychology* 154:531-543.

Buriel, R., and T. De Ment

1997 Immigration and sociocultural change in Mexican, Chinese, and Vietnamese American families. Pp. 165-200 in *Immigration and the Family: Research and Policy on U.S. Immigrants*. A. Booth, A.C. Crouter, and N. Landale, eds. Mahwah, NJ: Lawrence Erlbaum Associates.

Cabral, H., L.E. Fried, S. Levenson, H. Amaro, and B. Zuckerman

1990 Foreign-born and US-born black women: Differences in health behaviors and birth outcomes. *American Journal of Public Health* 80(1):70-72.

Cervantes, R.C., and F.G. Castro

1985 Stress, coping, and Mexican American mental health: A systematic review. *Hispanic Journal of Behavioral Sciences* 7(1):1-73.

Chiswick, B.

1977 Sons of immigrants: Are they at an earnings disadvantage? *American Economic Review* 67:376-380.

1978 The effect of Americanization on the earnings of foreign-born men. *Journal of Political Economy* 86:897-921.

1986 Is the new immigration less skilled than the old? *Journal of Labor Economics* 4:168-192.

Chiswick, B.R., and T.A. Sullivan

1995 The new immigrants. Pp. 211-270 in *State of the Union: America in the 1990s, Volume 2: Social Trends*. R. Farley, ed. New York: Russell Sage Foundation.

Chiu, M.L., S. Feldman, and D.A. Rosenthal

1992 The influence of immigration on parental behavior and adolescent distress in Chinese families residing in two Western nations. *Journal of Research on Adolescence* 2(3):205-239.

Chud, B.

1982 The threshold model: A conceptual framework for understanding and assisting children of immigrants. Pp. 95-100 in *Uprooting and Surviving*. R. Nann, ed. Hingham, MA: D. Reidel Publishing Company.

Coggon, D., D.J. Barker, H. Inskip, and G. Wield

1993 Housing in early life and later mortality. *Journal of Epidemiology and Community Health* 47(5):345-348.

Conger, R.D., and G.H. Elder, Jr.

1994 *Families in Troubled Times: Adapting to Change in Rural America*. Hawthorne, NY: Aldine de Gruyter.

Congressional Budget Office
1997 *Federal Budgetary Implications of the Personal Responsibility and Work Opportunity Reconciliation Act of 1996.* Washington, DC: U.S. Government Printing Office.

Cooper, C.R., M. Azmitia, E.E. Garcia, A. Ittel, E. Lopez, L. Rivera, and R. Martinez-Chavez
1994 Aspirations of low-income Mexican American and European parents for their children and adolescents. Pp. 65-81 in *Promoting Community-based Programs for Socialization and Learning.* F.A. Villarruel and R.M. Lerner, eds. San Francisco, CA: Jossey-Bass Inc.

Craft, J., D. Coleman, H. Coulter, R. Horwitz, and M. Barry
1983 Hematologic abnormalities in Southeast Asian refugees. *Journal of the American Medical Association* 249(23):3204-3206.

Cross, T.L.
1992 *Towards a Culturally Competent System of Care.* Washington, DC: Georgetown University Child Development Center.

Currie, J.
1997 Do children of immigrants make differential use of public health insurance? *Center for American Politics and Public Policy Occasional Paper Series (95-3).* Los Angeles, CA: Center for American Politics and Public Policy, University of California at Los Angeles.

Currie, J., and J. Gruber
1996 Health insurance eligibility, utilization of medical care, and child health. *Quarterly Journal of Economics* 111(2):431-466.

Currie, J., and D. Thomas
1995 Medical care for children: Public insurance, private insurance, and racial differences in utilization. *Journal of Human Resources* 30(1):135-162.

Cutler, D.M., and J. Gruber
1996 Does public insurance crowd out private insurance? *Quarterly Journal of Economics* 111(2):391-430.
1997 Medicaid and private insurance: Evidence and implications. *Health Affairs* 16(1):194-200.

Daniels, R.
1990 *Coming to America: A History of Immigration and Ethnicity in American Life.* New York: Harper Collins.

Davis, M.
1921 *Immigrant Health and the Community.* Reissued 1971. Montclair, NJ: Patterson Smith.

Day, J.C.
1993 Population projections of the United States, by age, sex, race, and Hispanic origin: 1993-2050. *Current Population Reports, P25-1104.* U.S. Bureau of the Census. Washington, DC: U.S. Department of Commerce.

Desjarlais, R., I. Eisenberg, B. Good, and A. Kleinman
1995 *World Mental Health: Problems and Priorities in Low-Income Countries.* New York: Oxford University Press.

Dewey, K., J. Daniels, K. Teo, and E. Hassel
 1986 Height and weight of Southeast Asian preschool children in Northern California. *American Journal of Public Health* 76(7):806-808.
Dubay, L., and G. Kenney
 1997 Did Medicaid expansions for pregnant women crowd out private coverage? *Health Affairs* 16(1):185-193.
Duncan, G.J., and J. Brooks-Gunn, eds.
 1997 *Consequences of Growing Up Poor.* New York: Russell Sage Foundation.
Dwyer, J.T.
 1991 Concept of nutritional status and its measurement. Pp. 5-28 in *Anthropometric Assessment of Nutritional Status.* J.H. Hines, ed. New York: Wiley-Liss, Inc.
Echechipia, S., P. Ventas, M. Audicana, I. Urrutia, G. Gastaminza, F. Polo, and L. Fernandez de Corres
 1995 Quantitation of major allergens in dust samples from urban populations collected in different seasons in two climatic areas of the Basque region (Spain). *Allergy* 50(6):478-482.
Eichorn, D.H., J.A. Clausen, N. Haan, M. Honzik, and P.H. Mussen, eds.
 1981 *Present and Past in Middle Life.* New York: Academic Press.
Elder, G.H., Jr.
 1974 *Children of the Great Depression: Social Change in Life Experience.* Chicago: University of Chicago Press.
 1997 The life course and human development. Pp. 939-992 in *Handbook of Child Psychology, Volume 1: Theoretical Models of Human Development.* R. Lerner, ed. New York: John Wiley & Sons, Inc.
Elliott, D.E., W.J. Wilson, D. Huisinga, R.J. Sampson, A. Elliott, and B. Rankin
 1996 The effects of neighborhood disadvantage on adolescent development. *Journal of Research in Crime and Delinquency* 33:389-426.
Employee Benefit Research Institute
 1997a *Expanding Health Insurance Coverage for Children: Examining the Alternatives.* Employee Benefit Research Institute Issue Brief no. 187, July 1997.
 1997b Special tabulations from the Bureau of the Census Current Population Survey prepared for the Institute of Medicine's Committee on Children, Health Insurance, and Access to Care. Washington, DC: Employee Benefit Research Institute.
English, A.
 1998 Expanding health insurance for children and adolescents: A preliminary analysis of the Balanced Budget Act of 1997. *Youth Law News* 18(5):39-56.
Erzen, D., K.C. Carriere, N. Dik, C. Mustard, L.L. Roos, J. Manfreda, and N.R. Anthonisen
 1997 Income level and asthma prevalence and care patterns. *American Journal of Respiratory Critical Care and Medicine* 155(3):1060-1065.

Evans, D., R. Mellins, K. Lobach, C. Ramos-Bonoan, M. Pinkett-Heller, S. Wiesemann, I. Klein, C. Donahue, D. Burke, M. Levison, B. Levin, B. Zimmerman, and N. Clark
  1997 Improving care for minority children with asthma: Professional education in public health clinics. *Pediatrics* 99(2):157-164.
Fall, C.H., P.M. Goggin, P. Hawtin, D. Fine, and S. Duggleby
  1997 Growth in infancy, infant feeding, childhood living conditions, and *Helicobacter pylori* infection at age 70. *Archives of Diseases of Children* 77(4):310-314.
Featherman, D.L.
  1983 The life-span perspectives in social science research. Pp. 1-49 in *Life-Span Development and Behavior, Volume 5*. P.B. Baltes and O.G. Brim, Jr., eds. New York: Academic Press.
Featherman, D.L., and R.M. Hauser
  1978 *Opportunity and Change*. New York: Academic Press.
Featherman, D.L., and R.M. Lerner
  1985 Ontogenesis and sociogenesis: Problematics for theory and research about development and socialization across the lifespan. *American Sociological Review* 50(5):659-676.
Finkelstein, J.A., R.W. Brown, L.C. Schneider, S.T. Weiss, J.M. Quintana, D.A. Goldmann, and C.J. Homer
  1995 Quality of care for preschool children with asthma: The role of social factors and practice setting. *Pediatrics* 95:389-394.
Fix, M.
  1997 Unpublished analyses of the March, 1997 Current Population Survey prepared for the Committee on the Health and Adjustment of Immigrant Children and Families, National Research Council and Institute of Medicine.
Fix, M., and J.S. Passel
  1994 *Immigration and Immigrants: Setting the Record Straight*. Washington, DC: The Urban Institute.
Fix, M., and W. Zimmerman
  1995 When should immigrants receive public benefits? Pp. 69-72 in *Welfare Reform: An Analysis of the Issues*. I.V. Sawhill, ed. Washington, DC: The Urban Institute.
Fletcher, A., and L. Steinberg
  1994 Generational Status and Country of Origin as Influences on the Psychological Adjustment of Asian-American Adolescents. Paper presented as part of a symposium entitled "Psychological Adjustment of Asian-American Adolescents" at the meetings of the Society for Research on Adolescence, San Diego, CA, February, 1994.
Florentino, R.F., and R.M. Guirriec
  1984 Prevalence of nutritional anemia in infancy and childhood with emphasis on developing countries. Pp. 61-74 in *Iron Nutrition in Infancy and Childhood*. A. Stekel, ed. New York: Raven Press.

Fronstin, P., and S.C. Snider
    1996-   An examination of the decline in employment-based health insurance
    1997   between 1998 and 1993. *Inquiry* 33(4):317-25.
Fuligni, A.J.
    1997   The academic achievement of adolescents from immigrant families: The
            roles of family background, attitudes and behavior. *Child Development*
            68(2):351-363.
    1998 (in press)   Adolescents from immigrant families. In *Research on Minority
            Adolescents: Conceptual, Theoretical, and Methodological Issues.* V. McLoyd
            and L. Steinberg, eds. Hillsdale, NJ: Erlbaum.
Furstenberg, F.F., T.D. Cook, J. Eccles, G.H. Elder, Jr., and A. Sameroff
    1998   *Managing to Make It: Urban Families and Adolescent Success.* Chicago:
            University of Chicago Press.
Gans, H.J.
    1992   Second-generation decline: Scenarios for the economic and ethnic fu-
            ture of the post-1965 American immigrants. *Ethnic and Racial Studies*
            15:173-192.
Garcia Coll, C., G. Lamberty, and H.V. Garcia
    1996   An integrative model for the study of developmental competencies in
            minority children. *Child Development* 67(5):91-132.
Garcia Coll, C., and K. Magnuson
    1997   The psychological experience of immigration: A developmental per-
            spective. Pp. 91-132 in *Immigration and the Family: Research and Policy on
            U.S. Immigrants.* A. Booth, A.C. Crouter, and N. Landale, eds. Mahwah,
            NJ: Lawrence Erlbaum Associates.
Garmezy, N.
    1991   Resilience in children's adaptation to negative life events and stressed
            environments. *Pediatric Annals* 20:459-466.
    1993   Children in poverty: Resilience despite risk. *Psychiatry* 56:127-136.
Garmezy, N., A.S. Masten, and A. Tellegen
    1984   The study of stress and competence in children: A building block for
            developmental psychopathology. *Child Development* 55:97-111.
Gellert, G.A., G.A. Wagner, R.M. Maxwell, D. Moore, and L. Foster
    1993   Lead poisoning among low-income children in Orange County, Cali-
            fornia: A need for regionally differentiated policy. *Journal of the Ameri-
            can Medical Association* 270(1):69-71.
Giachello, A.L.
    1994   Issues of access and use. Pp. 83-114 in *Latino Health in the US: A Grow-
            ing Challenge.* W. Molina and M. Aguirre-Molina, eds. Washington,
            DC: American Public Health Association.
Gibson, M.A., and J.U. Ogbu
    1991   *Minority Status and Schooling: A Comparative Study of Immigrant and In-
            voluntary Minorities.* New York: Garland Publishing, Inc.
Gil, A.G., and W.A. Vega
    1996   Two different worlds: Acculturation stress and adaptation among Cu-

ban and Nicaraguan families. *Journal of Social and Personal Relationships* 13(3):435-456.

Gil, A.G., W.A. Vega, and J.M. Dimas
  1994 Acculturative stress and personal adjustment among Hispanic adolescent boys. *Journal of Community Psychology* 22:43-55.

Glader, B. and K. Look
  1996 Hematologic disorders in children from Southeast Asia. *Pediatric Clinics of North America* 43(3):665-681.

Gold, M.
  1930 *Jews Without Money*. Reissued 1965. New York: Avon Books.

Gold, E.B., M. Woodby, A. Buckpitt, S. Gospe, and D. Mungas
  1996 Neurobehavioral Effects of Organophosphates in Children of Farmworkers. Paper presented to the Committee on the Health and Adjustment of Immigrant Children, National Research Council and Institute of Medicine. December 2, 1996, Irvine, CA.

Goldenring, J., J. Davis, and M. McChesney
  1982 Pediatric screening of Southeast Asian immigrants. *Clinical Pediatrics* 21(10):613-616.

Gordon, M.M.
  1964 *Assimilation in American Life: The Role of Race, Religion, and National Origins*. New York: Oxford University Press.

Guberan, E.
  1980 Mortality trends in Switzerland: Infectious diseases 1876-1977. *Schweizerische Medizinische Wochenschrift* 110(15):574-583.

Guendelman, S.
  1995 Immigrants May Hold Clues to Protecting Health During Pregnancy: Exploring a Paradox. California Wellness Foundation Lecture Series, October 11, 1995.

Guendelman, S., and B. Abrams
  1995 Dietary intake among Mexican American women: Generational differences and a comparison with white non-Hispanic women. *American Journal of Public Health* 85:20-25.

Guendelman, S., and P.B. English
  1995 Effects of United States residence on birth outcomes among Mexican immigrants: An exploratory study. *American Journal of Epidemiology* 142:S30-S38.

Guendelman, S., P. English, and G. Chavez
  1995 Infants of Mexican immigrants: Health status of an emerging population. *Medical Care* 33(1):41-52.

Gutierrez, J., and A. Sameroff
  1990 Determinants of complexity in Mexican-American and Anglo-American mothers' conceptions of child development. *Child Development* 61:384-394.

Halfon, N., P.W. Newacheck, D.L. Wood, and R.F. St. Peter
  1996 Routine emergency department use for sick care by children in the United States. *Pediatrics* 98(1):28-34.

Harris, K.M.
    1998   The health status and risk behavior of adolescents in immigrant fami-
           lies. In *Children of Immigrants: Health, Adjustment, and Public Assistance.*
           D.J. Hernandez, ed. Committee on the Health and Adjustment of Im-
           migrant Children and Families, Board on Children, Youth, and Fami-
           lies. Washington, DC: National Academy Press.
Harwood, A.
    1981   *Ethnicity and Medical Care.* Cambridge, MA: Harvard University Press.
Hauser, S.T., and M.K. Bowlds
    1990   Stress, coping, and adaptation. Pp. 388-413 in *At the Threshold: The De-
           veloping Adolescent.* S.S. Feldman and G.S. Elliott, eds. Cambridge, MA:
           Harvard University Press.
Hernandez, D.J.
    1993   *America's Children: Resources from Family, Government, and the Economy.*
           New York: Russell Sage Foundation.
Hernandez, D.J., and K. Darke
    1998   Socioeconomic and demographic risk factors and resources among chil-
           dren in immigrant and native-born families: 1910, 1960, and 1990. In
           Children of Immigrants: Health, Adjustment, and Public Assistance. D.J.
           Hernandez, ed. Committee on the Health and Adjustment of Immi-
           grant Children and Families, Board on Children, Youth, and Families.
           Washington, DC: National Academy Press.
Himes, J., M. Story, K. Czaplinski, and E. Dahlbery-Luby
    1992   Indications of early obesity in low-income Hmong children. *American
           Journal of Diseases of Children* 146(1):67-69.
Hing, B.O.
    1993   *Making and Remaking Asian America Through Immigration Policy, 1850-
           1990.* Stanford, CA: Stanford University Press.
Hirschman, C.
    1994   Problems and prospects of studying immigrant adaptation from the
           1990 population census: From generational comparisons to the process
           of becoming American. *International Migration Review* 28(4):690-713.
Hofferth, S.
    1998   Public assistance receipt of Mexican- and Cuban-American children in
           native and immigrant families. In *Children of Immigrants: Health, Ad-
           justment, and Public Assistance.* D.J. Hernandez, ed. Committee on the
           Health and Adjustment of Immigrant Children and Families, Board on
           Children, Youth, and Families. Washington, DC: National Academy
           Press.
Holahan, C.K., R.R. Sears, and L.J. Cronbach
    1995   *The Gifted Group in Later Maturity.* Stanford, CA: Stanford University
           Press.
Holl, J.L., P.G. Szilagyi, L.E. Rodewald, R.S. Byrd, and M.L. Weitzman
    1995   Profile of uninsured children in the United States. *Archives of Pediatric
           and Adolescent Medicine* 149(7):398-406.

Howard, A., and R.A. Scott
   1981   The study of minority groups in complex societies. Pp. 113-154 in *Handbook of Cross-Cultural Human Development*. R.H. Munroe, R.L. Munroe, and B. Whiting, eds. New York: Garland.

Hull, J.
   1979   Psychiatric referrals in general practice. *Archives of General Psychiatry* 36(4):406-408.

Human Rights Watch Children's Rights Project
   1997   *Slipping Through the Cracks: Unaccompanied Children Detained by the U.S. Immigration and Naturalization Service*. Washington, DC: Human Rights Watch.

Hurst, D., B. Tittle, K. Kleman, S. Embury, and B. Lubin
   1983   Anemia and hemoglobinopathies in Southeast Asian refugee children. *Pediatrics* 102(5):692-697.

Huston, A.C., V.C. McLoyd, and C. Garcia Coll
   1994   Children and poverty: Issues in contemporary research. *Child Development* 65:275-282.

Hyslop, A., A. Deinard, E. Dahlberg-Luby, and J. Himes
   1996   Growth patterns of first generation Southeast Asian Americans from birth to 5 years of age. *Journal of the American Board of Family Practice* 9(5):328-335.

Institute of Medicine
   1985   *Preventing Low Birthweight: Summary*. Washington, DC: National Academy Press.
   1994a *Overcoming Barriers to Immunization: A Workshop Summary*. J.S. Durch, ed. Washington, DC: National Academy Press.
   1994b *Reducing Risks for Mental Disorders: Frontiers for Preventive Intervention Research*. P. Mrazek and R.J. Haggerty, eds. Washington, DC: National Academy Press.
   1997   *America's Vital Interest in Global Health: Protecting Our People, Enhancing Our Economy, and Advancing Our International Interests*. Washington, DC: National Academy Press.
   1998   *America's Children: Health Insurance and Access to Care*. M. Edmunds and M.J. Coye, eds. Washington, DC: National Academy Press.

Isaacs, M.R., and M.P. Benjamin
   1991   *Towards a Culturally Competent System of Care, Volume II: Programs Which Utilize Culturally Competent Principles*. Washington, DC: CASSP Technical Assistance Center, Georgetown University Child Development Center.

Jenkins, C.N., T. Le, S.J. McPhee, S. Stewart, and N.T. Halfon
   1996   Health care access and preventive care among Vietnamese immigrants: Do traditional beliefs and practices pose barriers? *Social Science and Medicine* 43(7):1049-1056.

Jensen, L.
   1988   Patterns of immigration and public assistance utilization, 1970-1980. *International Migration Review* 22(1):51-83.

Jensen, L., and Y. Chitose
    1997 Immigrant generations. Pp. 47-62 in *Immigration and the Family: Re-search and Policy on U.S. Immigrants*. A. Booth, A.C. Crouter, and N.S. Landale, eds. Mahway, NJ: Lawrence Erlbaum.
Jessor, R., J. Van Den Bos, J. Vanderryn, F.M. Costa, and M.S. Turbin
    1995 Protective factors in adolescent problem behavior: Moderator effects and developmental change. *Developmental Psychology* 31(6):923-933.
Juckett, G.
    1995 Common intestinal helminths. *American Family Physician* 52(7):2039-2048, 2051-2052.
Kagan, J., and H.A. Moss
    1962 *Birth to Maturity: A Study in Psychological Development*. New York: Wiley.
Kalet, A.
    1916 Voluntary health insurance in New York City. *American Labor Legislation Review* 6:142-154.
Kao, G.
    1998 Psychological well-being and educational achievement among immigrant youth. In *Children of Immigrants: Health, Adjustment, and Public Assistance*. D.J. Hernandez, ed. Committee on the Health and Adjustment of Immigrant Children and Families, Board on Children, Youth, and Families. Washington, DC: National Academy Press.
Kao, G., and M. Tienda
    1995 Optimism and achievement: The educational performance of immigrant youth. *Social Science Quarterly* 76(1):1-19.
Kasl, S.V., and L. Berkman
    1983 Health consequences of the experience of migration. *Annual Review of Public Health* 4:69-90.
Keefe, S., A. Padilla, and M. Carlo
    1979 The Mexican-American extended family as an emotional support system. *Human Organization* 38:144-151.
Keith, V.M., and C. Herring
    1991 Skin tone and stratification in the black community. *American Journal of Sociology* 97(3):760-768.
Kleinman, A.
    1978 Concepts and a model for the comparison of medical systems as cultural systems. *Social Science and Medicine* 12:85-93.
    1980 *Patients and Healers in the Context of Culture*. Los Angeles: University of California Press.
Kogan, M.D., G.R. Alexander, M.A. Teitelbaum, B.W. Jack, M. Kotelchuck, and G. Pappas
    1995 The effect of gaps in health insurance on continuity of regular source of care among preschool-aged children in the United States. *Journal of the American Medical Association* 274(18):1429-1435.
Kohn, M.L.
    1969 *Class and Conformity*. Homewood, IL: Dorsey.

Kohn, M.L., and C. Schooler
1983 *Work and Personality*. Norwood, NJ: Ablex.

Kominski, R.
1987 What's it worth? Educational background and economic status. *Current Population Reports, Series P-70, No. 21*. U.S. Bureau of the Census. Washington, DC: U.S. Department of Commerce.

Kraut, A.M.
1982 *The Huddled Masses: The Immigrant in American Society 1880-1921.* Wheeling, IL: Harlan Davidson, Inc.
1994 *Silent Travelers: Germs, Genes, and the "Immigrant Menace."* New York: Basic Books.
1995 Luft, gibt mir luft: The immigrant Jewish community's social construction of disease in the late nineteenth and early twentieth centuries. Pp. 171-186 and 364-367 in *An Inventory of Promises: Essays in American Jewish History in Honor of Moses Rischin*. J.S. Gurock and M.L. Raphael, eds. Brooklyn, NY: Carlson Publishing, Inc.

Kronick, R., and T. Gilmer
1997 Explaining the Decline in Health Insurance Coverage, 1979-1995. Unpublished paper, University of California, San Diego, October 1997.

Kuo, W.
1976 Theories of migration and mental health: An empirical testing on Chinese-Americans. *Social Science and Medicine* 10(6):297-306.

LaFromboise, T., H. Coleman, and J. Gerton
1993 Psychological impact of biculturalism: Evidence and theory. *Psychological Bulletin* 114(3):395-412.

Lalonde, R.J., and R.H. Topel
1991 Labor market adjustments to increased immigration. Pp. 167-199 in *Immigration, Trade, and the Labor Market*. J. Abowd and R.B. Freeman, eds. Chicago: University of Chicago Press.

Landale, N.S., R.S. Oropesa, and B. Gorman
1998 Immigration and infant health: Birth outcomes of immigrant and native women. In *Children of Immigrants: Health, Adjustment, and Public Assistance*. D.J. Hernandez, ed. Committee on the Health and Adjustment of Immigrant Children and Families, Board on Children, Youth, and Families. Washington, DC: National Academy Press.

Landale, N.S., R.S. Oropesa, and D. Llanes
1997 Schooling, Work and Idleness among Mexican and Non-Latino White Adolescents. Unpublished manuscript, Population Research Institute, Pennsylvania State University.

Laosa, L.M.
1984 Social policies toward children of diverse ethnic, racial, and language groups in the United States. Pp. 1-109 in *Child Development Research and Social Policy, Volume 1*. H.W. Stevenson and A.E. Siegel, eds. Chicago: University of Chicago Press.

1989   Social competence in childhood: Toward a developmental, socio-
        culturally relativistic paradigm. *Journal of Applied Developmental Psy-
        chology* 10:447-468.
1990   Psychosocial stress, coping, and development of Hispanic immigrant
        children. Pp. 38-65 in *Mental Health of Ethnic Minorities*. F.C. Serafica,
        A.I. Schwebel, R.K. Russell, P.D. Isaac, and L.B. Myers, eds. New York:
        Praeger Publishers.
1997   Research perspectives on constructs of change: Intercultural migration
        and developmental transitions. Pp. 133-148 in *Immigration and the Fam-
        ily: Research and Policy on U.S. Immigrants*. A. Booth, A.C. Crouter, and
        N. Landale, eds. Mahwah, NJ: Lawrence Erlbaum Associates.
Leclere, F.B., L. Jensen, and A.E. Biddlecom
1994   Health care utilization, family context, and adaptation among immi-
        grants to the United States. *Journal of Health and Social Behavior* 35:370-
        384.
Lequerica, M.
1993   Stress in immigrant families with handicapped children: A child advo-
        cacy approach. *American Journal of Orthopsychiatry* 63(4):545-552.
Lieberson, S.
1973   Generational differences among blacks in the North. *American Journal
        of Sociology* 79:550-565.
Lieberson, S., and M. Waters
1988   *From Many Strands: Ethnic and Racial Groups in Contemporary America*.
        New York: Russell Sage Foundation.
Lieu, T.A., P.W. Newacheck, and M.A. McManus
1993   Race, ethnicity, and access to ambulatory care among U.S. adolescents.
        American Journal of Public Health 83(7):960-965.
Lind, M.
1995   *The Next American Nation: The New Nationalism and the Fourth American
        Revolution*. New York: Basic Books.
Looker, A.C., P.R. Dallman, M.D. Carroll, E.W. Gunter, and C.L. Johnson
1997   Prevalence of iron deficiency in the United States. *Journal of the Ameri-
        can Medical Association* 277(12):973-976.
Lozoff, B., A. Wolf, E. Mollen, and E. Jimenez
1997   Functional significance of early iron deficiency. *Pediatric Research*
        41:15A.
Lynch, E.W., and M.J. Hanson
1992   *Developing Cross-Cultural Competence: A Guide for Working with Young
        Children and Their Families*. Baltimore: Paul H. Brookes Publishing Com-
        pany.
Maccoby, E.E.
1980   *Social Development: Psychological Growth and the Parent-Child Relation-
        ship*. New York: Harcourt Brace.
Markides, K.S., and J.T. Coreil
1986   The health of Hispanics in the southwestern United States: An epide-
        miologic paradox. *Public Health Reports* 101(3):253-265.

Marks, G., M. Garcia, and J. Solis
   1990   Health risk behaviors in Hispanics in the United States: Findings from HHANES 1982-84. *American Journal of Public Health* 80 (supplement): 20-26.
Masten, A.S., K.M. Best, and N. Garmezy
   1991   Resilience and development: Contributions from the study of children who overcame adversity. *Development and Psychopathology* 2:425-444.
McDaniel, A.
   1995   The dynamic racial composition of the United States. *Daedalus* 124(1):179-198.
McDonnell, P.J.
   1997   INS reforms on custody of minors. *Los Angeles Times*, April 30, 1997; 116:B1 column 6.
McKelvey, R.S., and J.A. Webb
   1996   Premigratory expectations and postmigratory mental health symptoms in Vietnamese Amerasians. *Journal of the American Academy of Child and Adolescent Psychiatry* 35(2):240-245.
McLanahan, S., and G. Sandefur
   1994   *Growing Up with a Single Parent: What Hurts, What Helps*. Cambridge, MA: Harvard University Press.
McLoyd, V.C.
   1990   Minority children: Introduction to the special issue. *Child Development* 61:263-266.
McLoyd, V.C., and S. Randolph
   1984   The conduct and publication of research on Afro-American children: A content analysis. *Human Development* 27:65-75.
Melville, K.
   1995   *Admission Decisions: Should Immigration Be Restricted?* New York: McGraw Hill.
Mendoza, F.S., and L.B. Dixon
   1998   The health and nutritional status of immigrant Hispanic children: Analyses of the Hispanic Health and Nutrition Examination Survey. In *Children of Immigrants: Health, Adjustment, and Public Assistance*. D.J. Hernandez, ed. Committee on the Health and Adjustment of Immigrant Children and Families, Board on Children, Youth, and Families. Washington, DC: National Academy Press.
Mines, R.
   1998   Children of immigrant farm workers. In *Children of Immigrants, Health, Adjustment, and Public Assistance*. D.J. Hernandez, ed. Committee on the Health and Adjustment of Immigrant Children and Families, Board on Children, Youth, and Families. Washington, DC: National Academy Press.
Mitchell, J.B.
   1991   Physician participation in Medicaid revisited. *Medical Care* 29(7):645-653.

Moll, L., S. Rueda, R. Reza, J. Herrera, and L. Vasquez
  1976 Mental health services in East Los Angeles: An urban case study. *Spanish Speaking Mental Health Research Center Monograph* 3:21-34.
Mormino, G.R., and G.E. Pozzetta
  1987 *The Immigrant World of Ybor City: Italians and Their Latin Neighbors in Tampa, 1885-1985.* Urbana: University of Illinois Press.
Mouw, T., and Y. Xie
  1997 Accommodation With or Without Assimilation? Bilingualism and the Academic Achievement of Asian Immigrants. Report No. 97-402, Research Reports, Population Studies Center, University of Michigan.
Munoz, R.F., F. Chan, and R. Armas
  1986 Cross-cultural perspectives on primary prevention of mental disorders. Pp. 13-54 in *Primary Prevention in Psychiatry: State of the Art.* J.T. Barter and S.W. Talbott, eds. Washington, DC: American Psychiatric Press.
Munroe-Blum, H., M.H. Boyle, D.R. Offord, and N. Kates
  1989 Immigrant children: Psychiatric disorder, school performance, and service utilization. *American Journal of Orthopsychiatry* 59(4):510-519.
Nadeau, K., K. Hannibal, S. Sirkin, and E. Nightingale
  1997 Immigrating unaccompanied minors—A neglected minority? [Letter to the Editor] *Western Journal of Medicine* 166(3):221.
National Research Council
  1993 *Pesticides in the Diets of Infants and Children.* Committee on Pesticides in the Diets of Infants and Children. Washington, DC: National Academy Press.
  1995 *Measuring Poverty: A New Approach.* C.F. Citro and R.T. Michael, eds. Panel on Poverty and Family Assistance: Concepts, Information Needs, and Measurement Methods, Committee on National Statistics. Washington, DC: National Academy Press.
  1997 *The New Americans: Economic, Demographic, and Fiscal Effects of Immigration.* J.P. Smith and B. Edmonston, eds. Panel on the Demographic and Economic Impacts of Immigration, Committee on Population and Committee on National Statistics. Washington, DC: National Academy Press.
National Research Council and Institute of Medicine
  1997 *Improving Schooling for Language-Minority Children: A Research Agenda.* K. Hakuta and D. August, eds. Committee on Developing a Research Agenda on the Education of Limited-English-Proficient and Bilingual Students, Board on Children, Youth and Families. Washington, DC: National Academy Press.
  1998 *Children of Immigrants: Health, Adjustment, and Public Assistance.* D.J. Hernandez, ed. Committee on the Health and Adjustment of Immigrant Children and Families, Board on Children, Youth, and Families. Washington, DC: National Academy Press.
Nee, V., J. Sanders, and S. Sernau
  1994 Job transitions in an immigrant metropolis: Ethnic boundaries and the mixed economy. *American Sociological Review* 59:849-872.

Neidert, L., and R. Farley
  1985   Assimilation in the United States: An analysis of ethnic and generation differences in status and achievement. *American Sociological Review* 50:840-850.
Newacheck, P.W.
  1992   Characteristics of children with high and low usage of physician services. *Medical Care* 30(1):30-42.
Newacheck, P.W., D.C. Hughes, and J.J. Stoddard
  1996   Children's access to primary care: Differences by race, income, and insurance status. *Pediatrics* 7(1):43-72.
Nord, C.W., and J.A. Griffin
  1998   Educational profile of 3 to 8 year old children of immigrants. In *Children of Immigrants: Health, Adjustment, and Public Assistance.* D.J. Hernandez, ed. Committee on the Health and Adjustment of Immigrant Children and Families, Board on Children, Youth, and Families. Washington, DC: National Academy Press.
Ogbu, J.U.
  1994   Understanding cultural diversity and learning. *Journal for the Education of the Gifted* 17(4):355-383.
O'Grady, M.J.
  1995   Native and Naturalized Citizens and Non-Citizens: An Analysis of Poverty Status, Welfare Benefits, and Other Factors. Congressional Research Service, Washington, DC.
Oropesa, R.S., and N.S. Landale
  1995   Immigrant Legacies: The Socioeconomic Circumstances of Children by Ethnicity and Generation in the United States. Working Paper 95-01R, Population Research Institute, Pennsylvania State University.
  1997a Immigrant legacies: Ethnicity, generation, and children's familial and economic lives. *Social Science Quarterly* 78(2):399-415.
  1997b In search of the new second generation: Alternative strategies for identifying second generation children and understanding their acquisition of English. *Sociological Perspectives* 49(3):429-455.
Overpeck, M.D., and J.B. Kotch
  1995   The effect of children's access to care on medical attention for injuries. *American Journal of Public Health* 85(3):402-404.
Pachter, L.M., and S.C. Weller
  1993   Acculturation and compliance with medical therapy. *Developmental and Behavioral Pediatrics* 14(3):163-168.
Park, R.E., and E.W. Burgess
  1924   *Introduction to the Science of Sociology.* Chicago: University of Chicago Press.
Paul, E.A., S.M. Lebowitz, R.E. Moore, C.W. Hoven, B.A. Bennett, and A. Chen
  1993   Nemesis revisited: Tuberculosis infection in a New York City men's shelter. *American Journal of Public Health* 83(12):1743-1745.

Pawliuk, N., N. Grizenko, A. Chan-Yip, P. Gantous, J. Mathew, and D. Nguyen
    1996   Acculturation style and psychological functioning in children of immigrants. *American Journal of Orthopsychiatry* 66(1):111-121.
Peck, R., M. Chuang, G. Robbins, and M. Nichaman
    1981   Nutritional status of Southeast Asian refugee children. *American Journal of Public Health* 71(10):1144-1148.
Phinney, J.S.
    1990   Ethnic identity in adolescents and adults: Review of research. *Psychological Bulletin* 108(3):499-514.
Phinney, J.S., and V. Chavira
    1995   Parental ethnic socialization and adolescent coping with problems related to ethnicity. *Journal of Research on Adolescence* 5(1):31-53.
Physician Payment Review Commission
    1991   *Annual Report to Congress 1991.* Washington, DC: U.S. Government Printing Office.
Popkin, B., M. Richards, and C. Montiero
    1996   Stunting is associated with overweight in children of four nations that are undergoing the nutrition transition. *Journal of Nutrition* 126:3009-3016.
Portes, A.
    1996   *The New Second Generation.* New York: Russell Sage Foundation.
Portes, A., D. Kyle, and W.W. Eaton
    1992   Mental illness and help-seeking behavior among Mariel Cuban and Haitian refugees in South Florida. *Journal of Health and Social Behavior* 33(4):283-298.
Portes, A., and D. MacLeod
    1996   Educational progress of children of immigrants: The roles of class, ethnicity, and school context. *Sociology of Education* 69(4):255-275.
Portes, A., and R.G. Rumbaut
    1996   *Immigrant America: A Portrait.* Second edition. Berkeley: University of California Press.
Portes, A., and M. Zhou
    1993   The new second generation: Segmented assimilation and its variants among post-1965 immigrant youth. *Annals of the American Academy of Political and Social Science* 530:74-98.
Riis, J.
    1890   *How the Other Half Lives: Studies Among the Tenements of New York.* New York: Hill and Wang.
Rodewald, L.E., P.G. Szilagyi, J. Holl, L.R. Shone, J. Zwanziger, and R.F. Raubertas
    1997   Health insurance for low-income working families. Effect on the provision of immunizations to preschool-age children. *Archives of Pediatric and Adolescent Medicine* 151(8):798-803.
Rogler, L.H.
    1994   International migrations: A framework for directing research. *American Psychologist* 49(8):701-708.

Rogler, L.H., D.E. Cortes, and R.G. Malgady
  1991   Acculturation and mental health status among Hispanics: Convergence and new directions for research. *American Psychologist* 46(6):585-597.
Rogler, L.H., R.G. Malgady, and O. Rodriguez
  1989   *Hispanics and Mental Health: A Framework for Research.* Malabar, FL: Robert E. Krieger Publishing Company.
Rojas-Lopez, M., C. Santos-Burgoa, C. Rios, M. Avila-Hernandez, and I. Romieu
  1994   Use of lead-glazed ceramics is the main factor association with high lead in blood levels in two Mexican rural communities. *Journal of Toxicology and Environmental Health* 42:45-52.
Romieu, I., T. Carreon, L. Lopez, E. Palazuelos, C. Rios, Y. Manuel, and M. Hernandez-Avila
  1995   Environmental urban lead exposure and blood lead levels in children of Mexico City. *Environmental Health Perspectives* 103(11):1036-1040.
Romo, H.
  1996   "The newest outsiders": Educating Mexican migrant and immigrant youth. Pp. 61-91 in *Children of La Frontera.* J. Flores, ed. Charleston, WV: ERIC Clearinghouse on Rural Education and Small Schools.
Rosenberg, T., O. Kendall, J. Blanchard, S. Martel, C. Wakelin, and M. Fast
  1997   Shigellosis on Indian reserves in Manitoba, Canada: Its relationship to crowded housing, lack of running water, and inadequate sewage disposal. *American Journal of Public Health* 87(9):1547-1551.
Rosenthal, D.A., and S.S. Feldman
  1991   The influence of perceived family and personal factors on self-reported school performance of Chinese and Western high school students. *Journal of Research on Adolescence* 1:135-154.
Rosner, D., and G. Markowitz
  1987   *Dying for Work: Workers' Safety and Health in Twentieth Century America.* Bloomington: Indiana University Press.
  1991   *Deadly Dust: Silicosis and the Politics of Occupational Disease in Twentieth Century America.* Princeton, NJ: Princeton University Press.
Rousseau, C., A. Drapeau, and E. Corin
  1996   School performance and emotional problems in refugee children. *American Journal of Orthopsychiatry* 66(2):239-251.
Rowland, D., J. Feder, B. Lyons, and A. Salganicoff
  1992   *Medicaid at the Crossroads: A Report of the Kaiser Commission on the Future of Medicaid.* Washington, DC: Henry J. Kaiser Family Foundation.
Rowland, D., S. Rosenbaum, L. Simon, and E. Chait
  1995   *Medicaid and Managed Care: Lessons From the Literature.* Kaiser Commission on the Future of Medicaid. Washington DC: Henry J. Kaiser Family Foundation.
Rowland, D., and A. Salganicoff
  1994   Commentary: Lessons from Medicaid: Improving access to office-based physician care for the low-income population. *American Journal of Public Health* 84(4):550-552.

Ruch-Ross, H.S., and K.G. O'Connor
  1994   Immunization referral practices of pediatricians in the United States. *Pediatrics* 94(4):508-513.
Rumbaut, R.G.
  1994a Origins and destinies: Immigration to the United States since World War II. *Sociological Forum* 9:583-621.
  1994b The crucible within: Ethnic identity, self-esteem, and segmented assimilation among children of immigrants. *International Migration Review* 28:748-794.
  1995   The new Californians: Comparative research findings on the educational progress of immigrant children. Pp. 17-70 in *California's Immigrant Children: Theory, Research, and Implications for Educational Policy.* R.G. Rumbaut and W.A. Cornelius, eds. San Diego, CA: Center for U.S.-Mexican Studies, University of California.
  1996   Origins and destinies: Immigration, race, and ethnicity in contemporary America. Pp. 21-42 in *Origins and Destinies: Immigration, Race, and Ethnicity in America.* S. Pedraza and R.G. Rumbaut, eds. Belmont, CA: Wadsworth Publishing Company.
  1997a Paradoxes (and orthodoxies) of assimilation. *Sociological Perspectives* 40(3):483-511.
  1997b Ties that bind: Immigration and immigrant families in the United States. Pp. 3-46 in *Immigration and the Family: Research and Policy on U.S. Immigrants.* A. Booth, A.C. Crouter, and N. Landale, eds. Mahwah, NJ: Lawrence Erlbaum Associates.
  1998a Passages to adulthood: The adaptation of children of immigrants in Southern California. In *Children of Immigrants: Health, Adjustment, and Public Assistance.* D.J. Hernandez, ed. Committee on the Health and Adjustment of Immigrant Children and Families, Board on Children, Youth, and Families. Washington, DC: National Academy Press.
  1998b Transformations: The Post-Immigrant Generation in an Age of Diversity. Paper presented at the "American Diversity: Past, Present, and Future" annual meeting of the Eastern Sociological Society, Philadelphia, March 21, 1998.
Rumbaut, R.G., and J.R. Weeks
  1996   Unraveling a public health enigma: Why do immigrants experience superior perinatal health outcomes? *Research in the Sociology of Health Care* 13B:337-391.
Rutter, M.
  1985   Resilience in the face of adversity: Protective factors and resistance to psychiatric disorder. *British Journal of Psychiatry* 147:598-611.
  1987   Psychosocial resilience and protective mechanisms. *American Journal of Orthopsychiatry* 57:316-331.
Rutter, M., L. Champion, D. Quinton, B. Maugan, and A. Pickles
  1995   Understanding individual differences in environmental-risk exposure. Pp. 61-93 in *Examining Lives in Context: Perspectives on the Ecology of Human Development.* P. Moen, G.H. Elder, Jr., and K. Lushcer, eds. Washington, DC: American Psychological Association.

Salazar-Schettino, B., M.E. Luna-Munoz, and H. Tudon-Garces
  1991 Determination of lead levels in blood in infantile population of Mexico City 1989. Preliminary study. *Archivos de Investigacion Medica* 22(3-4):245-248.

Sameroff, A.J., R. Seifer, A. Baldwin, and C. Baldwin
  1993 Stability of intelligence from preschool to adolescence: The influence of social and family risk factors. *Child Development* 64:80-97.

Sampson, R.J., S.W. Raudenbush, and F. Earls
  1997 Neighborhoods and violent crime: A multilevel study of collective efficacy. *Science* 299:918-924.

Sanua, V.
  1970 Immigration, migration and mental illness: A review of the literature with special emphasis on schizophrenia. Pp. 291-352 in *Behavior in New Environments*. E.B. Brody, ed. Beverly Hills, CA: Sage.

Sarfaty, M., Z. Rosenberg, J. Siegel, and R.M. Levin
  1983 Intestinal parasites in immigrant children from Central America. *Western Journal of Medicine* 139(3):329-331.

Sargent, J.D.
  1997 Lead Poisoning in Immigrants. Unpublished paper prepared for the Committee on the Health and Adjustment of Immigrant Children, National Research Council and Institute of Medicine.

Saxena, D.K., C. Singh, R.C. Murthy, N. Mathur, and S.V. Chandra
  1994 Blood and placental lead levels in an Indian city: A preliminary report. *Archives of Environmental Health* 49(2):106-110.

Schumacher, L., I.G. Pawson, and N. Kretchmer
  1987 Growth of immigrant children in the Newcomer schools of San Francisco. *Pediatrics* 80(6):861-868.

Scribner, R., and J.H. Dwyer
  1989 Acculturation and low birthweight among Latinos in the Hispanic HANES. *American Journal of Public Health* 79(9):1263-1267.

Seifer, R., A.J. Sameroff, C. Baldwin, and A. Baldwin
  1992 Child and family factors that ameliorate risk between 4 and 13 years of age. *Journal of American Academy of Child and Adolescent Psychiatry* 31:893-903.

Serdula, M., K. Cairns, D. Williamson, M. Fuller, and J. Brown
  1991 Correlates of breast feeding in a low income population of whites, blacks, and Southeast Asians. *Journal of the American Dietetic Association* 91(1):41-45.

Sewell, W.H., and R.M. Hauser
  1975 *Education, Occupation, and Earnings.* New York: Academic Press.

Sewell, W.H., R.M. Hauser, and W.C. Wolf
  1980 Sex, schooling, and occupational status. *American Journal of Sociology* 83(3):551-583.

Shen, X., J.F. Rosen, D. Guo, and S. Wu
  1996 Childhood lead poisoning in China. *Science of the Total Environment* 181(2):101-109.

Shibutani, T., and K. Kwan
   1965 *Ethnic Stratification*. New York: Macmillan.
de Leon Siantz, M.L.
   1997 Factors that impact developmental outcomes of immigrant children. Pp. 149-164 in *Immigration and the Family: Research and Policy on U.S. Immigrants*. A. Booth, A.C. Crouter, and N. Landale, eds. Mahwah, NJ: Lawrence Erlbaum Associates.
   in   Fair and culturally competent care: An ethical perspective for the health
   review care professionals of the 21st century. *Journal of Western Medicine*.
Simon, J.
   1989 *The Economic Consequences of Immigration*. Cambridge, MA: Basil Blackwell, Inc.
Simon, J., and A. Akbari
   1996 Determinants of welfare payment use by immigrants and natives in the United States and Canada. Pp. 79-100 in *Immigrants and Immigration Policy: Individual Skills, Family Ties, and Group Identities*. H. Wunnava, ed. Greenwich, CT: JAI Press.
Simpson, G., B. Bloom, R.A. Cohen, and P.E. Parsons
   1997 Access to health care. Part one: Children. *Vital Health Statistics* 196(10):1-46.
Sin, A., S. Kose, E. Terzioglu, A. Kokuludag, F. Sebik, and T. Kabakci
   1997 Prevalence of atopy in young healthy population, in Izmir, Turkey. *Allergologia et Immunopathologia* 25(2):80-84.
Slesinger, D.P., B.A. Christenson, and E. Cautley
   1986 Health and mortality of migrant farm children. *Social Science and Medicine* 23(1):65-74.
Smith, M.J., and A.S. Ryan
   1987 Chinese-American families of children with developmental disabilities: An exploratory study of reactions to service providers. *Mental Retardation* 25(6):345-50.
Smolkin, S., M. Stavrianos, and J. Burton
   1996 *Characteristics of Food Stamp Households: Summer 1994*. Washington, DC: Office of Analysis and Evaluation, Food and Consumer Service, U.S. Department of Agriculture.
Snyder, D.C., J.C. Mohle-Boetani, B. Palla, and M. Fenstersheib
   1995 Development of a population-specific risk assessment to predict elevated blood lead levels in Santa Clara County, California. *Pediatrics* 96(4, part 1):643-648.
Sokhandan, M., E.R. McFadden, Jr., Y.T. Huang, and M.B. Mazanec
   1995 The contribution of respiratory viruses to severe exacerbations of asthma in adults. *Chest* 107(6):1570-1574.
Solis, J.M., G. Marks, M. Garcia, and D. Shelton
   1990 Acculturation, access to care, and use of preventive services by Hispanics: Findings from HHANES 1982-84. *American Journal of Public Health* 80(Supplement):11-19.

Sorenson, S.B., and H. Shen
 1996 Youth suicide trends in California: An examination of immigrant and ethnic group risk. *Suicide and Life-Threatening Behavior* 26(2):143-154.
Spargo, J.
 1906 *The Bitter Cry of Children.* Reissued 1969. New York: Johnson Reprint Corp.
Spencer, M.B., and C. Markstrom-Adams
 1990 Identity processes among racial and ethnic minority children in America. *Child Development* 61:290-310.
Sprinkle, R.V.
 1995 Leaded eye cosmetics: A cultural cause of elevated lead levels in children. *Journal of Family Practice* 40(4):358-362.
Starke, J.R., T.Q. Tan, M.R. Chacko, T.G. Cleary, K.K. Connelly, and M.W. Kline
 1994 Infectious disease of public health significance among children and adolescents in Texas. *Texas Medicine* 90(6):35-45.
Stella, A.
 1904 Tuberculosis and the Italians in the United States. *Charities* 12:486-489.
 1908 The effect of urban congestion on Italian women and children. *Medical Record* 74:722-732.
Stoddard, J., R. St. Peter, and P.W. Newacheck
 1994 Health insurance status and ambulatory care in children. *New England Journal of Medicine* 300:1421-1425.
Story, M., and L. Harris
 1988 Food preferences, beliefs, and practices of Southeast Asia refugee adolescents. *Journal of School Health* 58(7):273-276.
 1989 Food habits and dietary changes of Southeast Asian refugee families living in the United States. *Journal of the American Dietetic Association* 89(6):800-803.
Szapocznik, J., and W. Kurtines
 1980 Acculturation, biculturalism and adjustment among Cuban Americans. Pp. 139-159 in *Acculturation: Theory, Models, and Some New Findings.* A.M. Padilla, ed. Boulder, CO: Westview.
Takanishi, R., A.M. Mortimer, and T.J. McGourthy
 1997 Positive indicators of adolescent development: Redressing the negative image of American adolescents. Pp. 428-441 in *Indicators of Children's Well-Being.* S. Hauser, B. Brown, and W. Prosser, eds. New York: Russell Sage Foundation.
Telles, E., and E. Murguia
 1990 Phenotypic discrimination and income differences among Mexican Americans. *Social Science Quarterly* 71(4):682-696.
Thuy, T., H. Tam, W. Craig, and G. Zimmerman
 1983 Food habits and preferences of Vietnamese children. *Journal of School Health* 53(2):144-147.
Tienda, M., and L. Jensen
 1986 Immigration and public assistance participation: Dispelling the myth of dependency. *Social Science Research* 15:372-400.

Tirado, M.D.
  1995   Tools for Monitoring Cultural Competence in Health Care. Final Re-
         port to the Office of Planning and Evaluation, Health Resources and
         Services Administration. San Francisco, January 31, 1995.
Tuttle, C., and K. Dewey
  1994   Determinants of infant feeding choices among Southeast Asian immi-
         grants in Northern California. *Journal of American Dietetic Association*
         94(3):282-286.
U.S. Department of Health and Human Services
  1986   *Report of the Secretary's Task Force on Black and Minority Health Volume VI,*
         "Infant Mortality and Low Birthweight." Bethesda, MD: National Insti-
         tutes of Health.
  1996   *Trends in the Well-Being of America's Children: 1996.* Office of the Assis-
         tant Secretary for Planning and Evaluation. Washington, DC: U.S. De-
         partment of Health and Human Services.
  1997   *Trends in the Well-Being of America's Children and Youth: 1997.* Office of
         the Assistant Secretary for Planning and Evaluation. Washington, DC:
         U.S. Department of Health and Human Services.
U.S. General Accounting Office
  1992   *Hired Farmworkers: Health and Well-Being at Risk.* (GAO/HRD-92-46,
         February 14, 1992) Washington, DC: U.S. Government Printing Office.
  1997   *Health Insurance: Coverage Leads to Increased Health Care Access for Chil-*
         dren. Washington, DC: U.S. Government Printing Office.
U.S. Immigration [Dillingham] Commission
  1911   *Reports of the Immigration Commission. Volume 4: Emigration Conditions*
         in Europe. Washington, DC: U.S. Government Printing Office.
U.S. Immigration and Naturalization Service
  1995   *Statistical Yearbook of the Immigration and Naturalization Service, 1995.*
         Washington, DC: U.S. Department of Justice.
Ventura, S.J.
  1983   Births of Hispanic parentage, 1980. *Monthly Vital Statistics Report*
         32(6):1-18.
  1984   Births of Hispanic parentage, 1981. *Monthly Vital Statistics Report*
         33(8):1-17.
Warner, W.L., and L. Srole
  1945   *The Social Systems of American Ethnic Groups.* New Haven, CT: Yale Uni-
         versity Press.
Waters, M.C.
  1997   Immigrant families at risk: Factors that undermine chances for success.
         Pp. 79-90 in *Immigration and the Family: Research and Policy on U.S. Immi-*
         grants. A. Booth, A.C. Crouter, and N. Landale, eds. Mahwah, NJ:
         Lawrence Erlbaum Associates.
Weissman, A.M.
  1994   Preventive health care and screening of Latin American immigrants in
         the United States. *Journal of the American Board of Family Practice*
         7(4):310-323.

Werner, E.E.
   1989   High-risk children in young adulthood: A longitudinal study from birth
          to 32 years. *American Journal of Orthopsychiatry* 59:72-81.
   1995   Resilience in development. *Current Directions in Psychological Science*
          4:81-85.
Werner, E.E., and R.S. Smith
   1992   *Overcoming the Odds: High Risk Children from Birth to Adulthood.* Ithaca,
          NY: Cornell University Press.
Wiesenthal, A.M., M.K. Nickels, K.G. Hashimoto, T. Endo, and H.B. Ehrhard
   1980   Intestinal parasites in Southeast-Asian refugees: Prevalence in a com-
          munity of Laotians. *Journal of American Medical Association* 244(22):2543-
          2544.
Wilk, V.A.
   1993   Health hazards to children in agriculture. *American Journal of Indian
          Medicine* 24(3):283-290.
Williams, R.L., N.J. Binkin, and E.J. Clingman
   1986   Pregnancy outcomes among Spanish-surname women in California.
          American Journal of Public Health 76(4):387-391.
Wilson, W.J.
   1990   *The Truly Disadvantaged: The Inner City, the Underclass, and Public Policy.*
          Chicago: University of Chicago Press.
   1997   *When Work Disappears: The World of the New Urban Poor.* New York:
          Vintage Books.
Wood, D.L., R.A. Hayward, C.R. Corey, H.E. Freeman, and M.F. Shapiro
   1990   Access to medical care for children and adolescents in the United States.
          Pediatrics 86(5):666-673.
Wood, D., C. Donald-Sherbourne, N. Halfon, M.B. Tucker, V. Ortiz, J.S. Hamlin,
          N. Duan, R.M. Mazel, M. Grabowsky, P. Brunell, and H. Freeman
   1995   Factors related to immunization status among inner-city Latino and
          African-American preschoolers. *Pediatrics* 96(2):295-301.
Yaish, H.M., G.A. Niazi, and A. al Soby
   1992   Lead encephalopathy in Saudi Arabian children. *American Journal of
          Diseases of Children* 146(11):1257-1259.
Yip, R., I. Parvanta, I., K. Scanlon, E. Borland, C. Russell, and F. Trowbridge
   1992a Pediatric nutrition surveillance system in the United States, 1980-1991.
          Morbidity and Mortality Weekly Report Surveillance Summaries 41(7):1-24.
Yip, R., K. Scanlon, and F. Trowbridge
   1992b Improving growth status of Asian refugee children in the United States.
          Journal of the American Medical Association 2267(7):937-940.
   1993   Trends and patterns in height and weight status of low income U.S.
          children. *Critical Reviews in Food Science and Nutrition* 33(4-5):409-421.
Zambrana, R.E., and V. Silva-Palacios
   1989   Gender differences in stress among Mexican immigrant adolescents in
          Los Angeles, California. *Journal of Adolescent Research* 4(4):426-442.

Participants

WORKSHOP ON THE INVISIBLE IMMIGRANT POPULATION: YOUNG CHILDREN AND THEIR FAMILIES SEPTEMBER 1994

Christine Bachrach, Demographic and Behavioral Sciences Branch, Center for Population Research, NICHD, Bethesda, MD

Frank Bean, Population Research Center, University of Texas at Austin, Austin, TX

Rodney R. Cocking, Cognition, Learning and Memory Program, Division of Basic Brain and Behavioral Sciences, Basic Behavior and Cognitive Sciences Research Branch, National Institute of Mental Health, Rockville, MD

Glen H. Elder, Jr., Carolina Population Center, University Square East, University of North Carolina, Chapel Hill, NC

David Featherman, Institute for Social Research, University of Michigan, Ann Arbor, MI

Michael Fix, The Urban Institute, Washington, DC

Linda Gordon, Statistics Division, Immigration and Naturalization Service, Washington, DC

David Howell, U.S. Commission on Immigration Reform, Washington, DC

Guillermina Jasso, Department of Sociology, New York University, New York, NY

Frank Kessel, Social Science Research Council, New York, NY

Nancy Landale, Population Research Institute, Pennsylvania State University, University Park, PA

Luis Laosa, Educational Testing Service, Research Division, Princeton, NJ

Rose Li, Demographic and Behavioral Sciences Branch, Center for Population Research, NICHD, Bethesda, MD

Lindsay Lowell, Immigration Policy and Research, U.S. Department of Labor, Washington, DC

Susan Martin, U.S. Commission on Immigration Reform, Washington, DC

John Mollenkopf, Graduate School and University Center, City University of New York, New York, NY

Jeylan Mortimer, Life Course Center, University of Minnesota, Minneapolis, MN

Katherine Newman, Department of Anthropology, Columbia University, New York, NY

Laurie Olsen, California Tomorrow, San Francisco, CA

Mark Rosenzweig, Department of Economics, University of Pennsylvania, Philadelphia, PA

Rubén G. Rumbaut, Michigan State University, East Lansing, MI

Patricia Shiono, Research and Grants, Epidemiology, Center for the Future of Children, David and Lucile Packard Foundation, Los Altos, CA

Mary Lou de Leon Siantz, University of Washington, School of Nursing, Seattle, WA

Betty Lee Sung, Consultant, New York, NY

Robert Valdez, Public Health Service and Interagency Health Policy, Health Care Financing Administration, Washington, DC

Eric Wanner, Russell Sage Foundation, New York, NY

Sheldon H.White, Department of Psychology, Harvard University, Cambridge, MA

APPENDIX B

Socioeconomic and Demographic Indicators

TABLE B-1A   Social and Economic Risk Factors for First- and Second-Generation Children by Country of Origin, for First and Second Generations Combined, and for Third- and Later-Generation Children by Race and Ethnicity: 1990

	Number of children (thousands)	Children in official poverty (percent)	Children in relative poverty (percent)	Children in middle-class comfort (percent)
All First and Second Generations	8,373	22	33	31
All Third and Later Generations	52,685	17	24	39
Third and Later Generations by Race and Ethnicity:				
White, Non-Hispanic	40,201	11	17	42
Black, Non-Hispanic	8,031	40	51	25
Asian, Non-Hispanic	329	10	14	38
American Indian	562	38	51	24
Hispanic	3,489	31	42	31
First and Second Generations by Country of Origin:				
Laos	113	51	65	16
Cambodia	64	46	62	19
Dominican Republic	179	42	55	24
USSR	62	36	42	23
Mexico	2,618	35	52	22
Thailand	69	33	42	29
Vietnam	226	31	42	29
Guatemala	101	30	46	24
Honduras	52	29	46	26
El Salvador	203	27	44	26
Nicaragua	74	27	43	28
Haiti	105	26	39	30
Jordan	19	25	35	31
Belize	16	23	31	35
Iraq	20	21	30	39
Ecuador	64	20	31	36

Children very well-off financially (percent)	Children in one-parent families (percent)	Children whose fathers have less than a high school education (percent)	Children whose mothers have less than a high school education (percent)	Children with 5 or more siblings (percent)	Children who live in linguistically isolated households (percent)
19	17	39	42	8	26
22	26	15	16	4	1
26	18	12	12	4	0
9	62	26	29	10	0
37	25	7	9	6	1
7	40	28	29	10	4
11	42	30	35	8	9
2	15	54	73	35	60
4	26	57	76	18	60
5	48	49	55	5	41
26	10	20	18	5	46
4	19	74	74	14	38
16	13	34	56	17	42
13	19	39	54	11	45
7	28	56	61	5	43
8	31	42	44	5	34
5	31	61	65	6	46
8	27	34	40	8	43
10	36	38	43	8	34
14	7	25	31	13	10
12	29	29	29	6	4
17	5	32	42	10	16
14	24	34	35	3	29

continued on next page

TABLE B-1A   (Continued)

	Number of children (thousands)	Children in official poverty (percent)	Children in relative poverty (percent)	Children in middle-class comfort (percent)
Venezuela	22	20	25	37
Israel	60	19	25	31
Trinidad and Tobago	52	18	28	37
Colombia	117	17	27	37
Pakistan	39	16	23	36
Costa Rica	23	16	26	38
Panama	40	16	25	37
Brazil	31	16	24	39
Romania	26	15	22	32
Spain	27	15	21	39
Lebanon	36	15	23	34
Jamaica	132	15	25	37
Guyana	46	15	22	41
Nigeria	34	15	27	35
China	131	14	24	30
Indonesia	17	14	19	37
Iran	76	14	19	32
Cuba	211	14	22	38
Peru	61	13	25	37
Korea	231	12	19	38
Syria	15	12	21	33
Taiwan	97	11	15	33
Argentina	35	11	19	38
Yugoslavia	44	10	16	42
Hong Kong	56	10	16	33
Chile	21	10	18	37
Australia	18	10	16	32
Austria	21	9	14	41
France	41	9	13	34
Hungary	25	9	14	35
Egypt	29	9	15	36
Germany	258	8	14	40

Children very well-off financially (percent)	Children in one-parent families (percent)	Children whose fathers have less than a high school education (percent)	Children whose mothers have less than a high school education (percent)	Children with 5 or more siblings (percent)	Children who live in linguistically isolated households (percent)
25	12	14	15	2	19
32	5	16	19	16	12
20	37	23	19	5	1
16	23	29	30	2	31
27	6	8	18	6	13
17	19	28	31	3	17
23	23	12	16	3	7
25	14	20	20	3	22
30	8	25	25	18	21
27	14	23	26	3	12
24	6	28	29	8	11
21	36	27	22	4	0
18	31	25	28	4	1
15	16	2	5	7	4
30	9	31	35	2	41
31	8	8	11	3	21
37	9	6	11	1	18
27	21	28	27	2	16
19	18	18	19	3	25
26	9	6	18	0	34
29	4	22	25	4	17
42	10	5	8	1	36
29	11	21	20	2	15
27	10	30	32	3	11
37	8	24	29	1	35
28	15	14	17	3	18
44	9	8	11	7	1
38	8	8	8	10	2
41	11	9	9	5	6
39	9	14	13	9	10
39	6	4	8	5	10
32	11	8	11	3	2

continued on next page

TABLE B-1A   (Continued)

	Number of children (thousands)	Children in official poverty (percent)	Children in relative poverty (percent)	Children in middle-class comfort (percent)
Greece	68	8	16	42
Japan	100	8	12	37
Barbados	15	8	16	47
Poland	80	7	12	45
Turkey	15	7	13	32
Italy	179	6	11	45
Portugal	77	6	11	51
United Kingdom	209	6	10	38
Canada	263	6	11	39
South Africa	15	6	10	25
Netherlands	38	5	11	39
India	175	5	9	35
Philippines	399	5	10	45
Ireland	44	4	7	41

Note: Countries are listed from highest to lowest official poverty rate for first and second generation combined.

Source: Hernandez and Darke (1998).

Children very well-off financially (percent)	Children in one-parent families (percent)	Children whose fathers have less than a high school education (percent)	Children whose mothers have less than a high school education (percent)	Children with 5 or more siblings (percent)	Children who live in linguistically isolated households (percent)
25	6	39	32	1	12
41	7	4	7	1	28
21	39	25	21	8	0
32	10	19	15	1	22
38	8	18	18	2	11
30	6	34	29	2	7
22	8	61	58	1	23
41	10	6	9	3	0
39	9	10	10	5	1
57	5	2	7	1	1
38	7	7	6	6	1
47	4	7	12	1	11
32	12	8	13	3	9
39	8	15	14	4	0

TABLE B-1B   Household and Housing Risk Factors for First- and Second-Generation Children by Country of Origin, for First and Second Generations Combined, and for Third- and Later-Generation Children by Race and Ethnicity: 1990

	Number of children (thousands)	Children in households with no car or truck (percent)
All First and Second Generations	8,373	11
All Third and Later Generations	52,685	8
Third and Later Generations by Race and Ethnicity:		
White, Non-Hispanic	40,201	3
Black, Non-Hispanic	8,031	30
Asian, Non-Hispanic	329	4
American Indian	562	14
Hispanic	3,489	17
First and Second Generations by Country of Origin:		
Laos	113	17
Cambodia	64	29
Dominican Republic	179	54
USSR	62	23
Mexico	2,618	10
Thailand	69	15
Vietnam	226	13
Guatemala	101	18
Honduras	52	22
El Salvador	203	15
Nicaragua	74	13
Haiti	105	24
Jordan	19	8
Belize	16	19
Iraq	20	4
Ecuador	64	24
Venezuela	22	6
Israel	60	13
Trinidad and Tobago	52	29
Colombia	117	13
Pakistan	39	7
Costa Rica	23	14

Children with no telephone in their homes (percent)	Children living in houses built before 1950 (percent)	Children in crowded homes (percent)
7	24	44
8	24	12
5	23	7
18	27	26
3	18	21
32	17	34
15	25	30
4	28	78
4	31	74
19	50	52
2	32	40
15	23	69
3	24	49
1	19	58
9	33	67
9	26	56
8	29	75
10	24	71
10	33	53
2	23	31
7	35	44
1	17	34
8	41	43
4	18	30
1	28	27
7	39	30
6	27	42
2	17	35
4	28	33

continued on next page

TABLE B-1B   (Continued)

	Number of children (thousands)	Children in households with no car or truck (percent)
Panama	40	16
Brazil	31	7
Romania	26	8
Spain	27	8
Lebanon	36	4
Jamaica	132	22
Guyana	46	30
Nigeria	34	10
China	131	18
Indonesia	17	4
Iran	76	4
Cuba	211	6
Peru	61	11
Korea	231	3
Syria	15	2
Taiwan	97	3
Argentina	35	6
Yugoslavia	44	6
Hong Kong	56	9
Chile	21	6
Australia	18	5
Austria	21	5
France	41	5
Hungary	25	8
Egypt	29	4
Germany	258	3
Greece	68	4
Japan	100	3
Barbados	15	29
Poland	80	5
Turkey	15	4
Italy	179	4
Portugal	77	4
United Kingdom	209	3
Canada	263	2

Children with no telephone in their homes (percent)	Children living in houses built before 1950 (percent)	Children in crowded homes (percent)
6	25	25
2	24	24
2	32	31
3	28	20
2	26	20
5	30	29
4	40	36
3	18	50
1	33	39
1	16	29
1	12	21
3	17	28
4	26	36
1	13	33
0	20	23
0	11	24
2	20	24
1	31	16
1	26	34
2	21	28
0	23	9
0	27	11
1	29	11
2	26	14
1	24	20
3	22	8
1	26	9
1	15	12
4	41	22
1	32	10
1	22	16
1	31	7
2	43	14
2	22	7
2	20	8

continued on next page

TABLE B-1B   (Continued)

	Number of children (thousands)	Children in households with no car or truck (percent)
South Africa	15	4
Netherlands	38	2
India	175	5
Philippines	399	3
Ireland	44	4

NOTE: Countries are listed from highest to lowest official poverty rate for first and second generation combined.

Source: Hernandez and Darke (1998).

Children with no telephone in their homes (percent)	Children living in houses built before 1950 (percent)	Children in crowded homes (percent)
1	20	7
1	23	8
1	13	24
1	15	38
1	38	8

TABLE B-1C   Parents' Labor Force Participation for First- and Second-Generation Children by Country of Origin, for First and Second Generations Combined, and for Third- and Later-Generation Children by Race and Ethnicity: 1990

	Number of children (thousands)	Children with fathers not in the labor force (percent)	Children with fathers not working full-time, year-round (percent)	Children with mothers not in the labor force (percent)
All First and Second Generations	8,373	7	31	42
All Third and Later Generations	52,685	5	21	34
Third and Later Generations by Race and Ethnicity:				
White, Non-Hispanic	40,201	4	19	34
Black, Non-Hispanic	8,031	11	34	33
Asian, Non-Hispanic	329	4	18	29
American Indian	562	14	46	40
Hispanic	3,489	8	30	43
First and Second Generations by Country of Origin:				
Laos	113	48	68	66
Cambodia	64	41	60	65
Dominican Republic	179	11	38	52
USSR	62	21	54	46
Mexico	2,618	7	38	50
Thailand	69	30	46	53
Vietnam	226	19	42	46
Guatemala	101	5	31	41
Honduras	52	8	37	41
El Salvador	203	5	32	34
Nicaragua	74	5	32	31
Haiti	105	8	36	22
Jordan	19	11	30	68
Belize	16	9	33	31
Iraq	20	10	30	61
Ecuador	64	4	30	39
Venezuela	22	8	28	47
Israel	60	7	26	54
Trinidad and Tobago	52	8	34	25

TABLE B-1C (continued)

	Number of children (thousands)	Children with fathers not in the labor force (percent)	Children with fathers not working full-time, year-round (percent)	Children with mothers not in the labor force (percent)
Colombia	117	4	28	38
Pakistan	39	4	26	60
Costa Rica	23	8	31	38
Panama	40	6	27	29
Brazil	31	6	28	47
Romania	26	9	26	46
Spain	27	5	26	40
Lebanon	36	9	27	61
Jamaica	132	6	29	17
Guyana	46	6	28	26
Nigeria	34	6	38	26
China	131	5	27	31
Indonesia	17	10	29	41
Iran	76	8	28	46
Cuba	211	4	22	34
Peru	61	4	27	35
Korea	231	6	26	39
Syria	15	8	32	58
Taiwan	97	6	23	40
Argentina	35	3	21	44
Yugoslavia	44	6	26	42
Hong Kong	56	6	21	31
Chile	21	3	19	38
Australia	18	4	16	49
Austria	21	4	19	35
France	41	3	20	43
Hungary	25	5	20	41
Egypt	29	4	23	42
Germany	258	3	18	37
Greece	68	6	26	46
Japan	100	4	20	58
Barbados	15	5	23	20
Poland	80	4	21	34
Turkey	15	4	20	48

continued on next page

TABLE B-1C   (Continued)

	Number of children (thousands)	Children with fathers not in the labor force (percent)	Children with fathers not working full-time, year-round (percent)	Children with mothers not in the labor force (percent)
Italy	179	5	21	47
Portugal	77	5	27	29
United Kingdom	209	3	17	38
Canada	263	3	18	38
South Africa	15	4	17	48
Netherlands	38	2	14	39
India	175	2	19	35
Philippines	399	5	22	18
Ireland	44	4	18	42

NOTE: Countries are listed from highest to lowest official poverty rate for first and second generation combined.

Source: Hernandez and Darke (1998).

TABLE B-1D   Parents' Education for First- and Second-Generation Children by Country of Origin, for First and Second Generations Combined, and for Third- and Later-Generation Children by Race and Ethnicity: 1990

	Number of children (thousands)	Children with fathers who have 8 or fewer years of education (percent)	Children with mothers who have 8 or fewer years of education percent)	Children whose fathers have four or more years of college education percent)	Children whose mothers have four or more years of college education percent)
All First and Second Generations	8,373	25	26	24	16
All Third and Later Generations	52,685	3	3	26	18
Third and Later Generations by Race and Ethnicity:					
White, Non-Hispanic	40,201	3	2	28	20
Black, Non-Hispanic	8,031	6	4	12	9
Asian, Non-Hispanic	329	1	1	40	31
American Indian	562	8	6	9	7
Hispanic	3,489	9	10	12	7
First and Second Generations by Country of Origin:					
Laos	113	41	60	7	3
Cambodia	64	42	60	6	2
Dominican Republic	179	27	30	9	5
USSR	62	8	6	41	36
Mexico	2,618	55	52	4	2
Thailand	69	25	45	24	13
Vietnam	226	21	32	18	8
Guatemala	101	35	38	9	5
Honduras	52	23	24	13	7
El Salvador	203	37	40	6	4
Nicaragua	74	17	17	21	11
Haiti	105	14	17	14	10
Jordan	19	11	12	29	11
Belize	16	10	7	14	7
Iraq	20	13	21	25	16

continued on next page

TABLE B-1D   (Continued)

	Number of children (thousands)	Children with fathers who have 8 or fewer years of education (percent)	Children with mothers who have 8 or fewer years of education percent)	Children whose fathers have four or more years of college education percent)	Children whose mothers have four or more years of college education percent)
Ecuador	64	14	13	18	9
Venezuela	22	6	5	45	28
Israel	60	5	6	41	32
Trinidad and Tobago	52	7	5	18	12
Colombia	117	11	12	22	13
Pakistan	39	3	8	65	41
Costa Rica	23	11	12	20	13
Panama	40	2	3	26	17
Brazil	31	9	10	40	29
Romania	26	9	10	38	31
Spain	27	12	12	29	19
Lebanon	36	14	12	35	21
Jamaica	132	8	5	19	15
Guyana	46	6	8	23	12
Nigeria	34	0	2	80	45
China	131	18	20	39	28
Indonesia	17	2	4	54	34
Iran	76	2	3	68	39
Cuba	211	12	9	25	16
Peru	61	5	6	29	17
Korea	231	2	7	43	28
Syria	15	10	11	41	19
Taiwan	97	3	4	73	52
Argentina	35	9	7	34	25
Yugoslavia	44	18	19	18	14
Hong Kong	56	13	14	43	30
Chile	21	5	5	33	22
Australia	18	3	1	50	33
Austria	21	2	1	45	37
France	41	4	2	49	36
Hungary	25	6	3	39	29
Egypt	29	1	2	67	44
Germany	258	2	2	35	22

TABLE B-1D   (Continued)

	Number of children (thousands)	Children with fathers who have 8 or fewer years of education (percent)	Children with mothers who have 8 or fewer years of education percent)	Children whose fathers have four or more years of college education percent)	Children whose mothers have four or more years of college education percent)
Greece	68	23	19	21	17
Japan	100	2	2	55	32
Barbados	15	8	4	18	14
Poland	80	7	5	30	23
Turkey	15	10	9	41	32
Italy	179	19	16	19	14
Portugal	//	43	39	7	5
United Kingdom	209	1	1	43	26
Canada	263	3	2	40	26
South Africa	15	0	1	68	40
Netherlands	38	2	1	41	26
India	175	2	4	76	59
Philippines	399	3	6	39	46
Ireland	44	5	3	31	19

NOTE: Countries are listed from highest to lowest official poverty rate for first and second generation combined.

Source: Hernandez and Darke (1998).

TABLE B-1E   Children's Language Use and Citizenship for First- and Second-Generation Children by Country of Origin, for First and Second Generations Combined, and for Third- and Later-Generation Children by Race and Ethnicity: 1990

	Number of children (thousands)	Children who do not speak English at home (percent)
All First and Second Generations	8,373	67
All Third and Later Generations	52,685	6
Third and Later Generations by Race and Ethnicity:		
White, Non-Hispanic	40,201	3
Black, Non-Hispanic	8,031	3
Asian, Non-Hispanic	329	8
American Indian	562	18
Hispanic	3,489	43
First and Second Generations by Country of Origin:		
Laos	113	96
Cambodia	64	93
Dominican Republic	179	93
USSR	62	84
Mexico	2,618	91
Thailand	69	66
Vietnam	226	87
Guatemala	101	90
Honduras	52	79
El Salvador	203	94
Nicaragua	74	89
Haiti	105	75
Jordan	19	62
Belize	16	18
Iraq	20	69
Ecuador	64	85
Venezuela	22	70
Israel	60	65
Trinidad and Tobago	52	6
Colombia	117	84
Pakistan	39	72

Children who do not speak English exclusively or very well (percent)	Children not U.S. citizens (percent)	Children who are not U.S. citizens, or who have at least 1 parent in the home who is not a citizen (percent)
27	21	65
2	N/A	N/A
1	N/A	N/A
1	N/A	N/A
3	N/A	N/A
7	N/A	N/A
15	N/A	N/A
61	39	89
59	42	85
39	23	73
45	51	62
40	21	78
39	48	75
44	34	63
40	31	81
31	29	73
44	34	83
46	51	83
29	22	75
11	9	38
5	16	72
11	12	44
24	17	76
23	31	76
19	18	42
1	18	71
23	21	70
19	20	55

continued on next page

TABLE B-1E   (Continued)

	Number of children (thousands)	Children who do not speak English at home (percent)
Costa Rica	23	68
Panama	40	42
Brazil	31	67
Romania	26	73
Spain	27	64
Lebanon	36	71
Jamaica	132	6
Guyana	46	7
Nigeria	34	23
China	131	81
Indonesia	17	41
Iran	76	68
Cuba	211	81
Peru	61	81
Korea	231	65
Syria	15	61
Taiwan	97	80
Argentina	35	69
Yugoslavia	44	61
Hong Kong	56	79
Chile	21	74
Australia	18	13
Austria	21	26
France	41	46
Hungary	25	43
Egypt	29	56
Germany	258	18
Greece	68	70
Japan	100	54
Barbados	15	3
Poland	80	66
Turkey	15	55
Italy	179	37
Portugal	77	75
United Kingdom	209	7

Children who do not speak English exclusively or very well (percent)	Children not U.S. citizens (percent)	Children who are not U.S. citizens, or who have at least 1 parent in the home who is not a citizen (percent)
18	16	68
13	12	48
25	28	76
23	33	47
15	17	65
16	15	40
2	24	66
2	31	62
7	12	82
36	22	46
18	23	50
20	28	67
18	11	47
26	26	67
23	23	55
15	12	43
28	27	52
17	24	60
10	9	44
35	24	39
17	19	64
3	18	76
9	4	29
10	15	56
13	9	27
13	10	34
4	5	36
11	3	36
29	31	73
1	17	58
15	18	54
8	15	51
8	3	39
16	14	63
2	13	64

continued on next page

TABLE B-1E   (Continued)

	Number of children (thousands)	Children who do not speak English at home (percent)
Canada	263	11
South Africa	15	12
Netherlands	38	13
India	175	63
Philippines	399	35
Ireland	44	5

NOTE: Countries are listed from highest to lowest official poverty rate for first and second generation combined.

Source: Hernandez and Darke (1998).

Children who do not speak English exclusively or very well (percent)	Children not U.S. citizens (percent)	Children who are not U.S. citizens, or who have at least 1 parent in the home who is not a citizen (percent)
3	11	62
3	30	58
3	5	43
14	22	68
11	15	44
1	8	48

TABLE B-2A   Social and Economic Risk Factors for First- and Second-Generation Children by Country of Origin for First and Second Generations Separately: 1990

	Number of children (thousands)	Children in official poverty (percent)	Children in relative poverty (percent)	Children in middle-class comfort (percent)
All First-Generation Children	2,084	33	47	24
All Second-Generation Children	6,288	19	29	33
Third and Later Generations by Race and Ethnicity:				
White, Non-Hispanic	40,201	11	17	42
Black, Non-Hispanic	8,031	40	51	25
Asian, Non-Hispanic	329	10	14	38
American Indian	562	38	51	24
Hispanic	3,489	31	42	31
First- and Second-Generation Children by Country of Origin:				
Laos - 1st Generation	49	51	64	16
Laos - 2nd Generation	64	50	65	15
Cambodia - 1st Generation	30	52	68	14
Cambodia - 2nd Generation	34	41	57	23
Dominican Republic - 1st Generation	48	41	57	21
Dominican Republic - 2nd Generation	131	42	54	25
USSR - 1st Generation	38	51	60	17
USSR - 2nd Generation	24	11	14	32
Mexico - 1st Generation	643	44	63	14
Mexico - 2nd Generation	1,975	32	49	24
Thailand - 1st Generation	36	59	73	12
Thailand - 2nd Generation	33	5	10	46
Vietnam - 1st Generation	99	42	54	23
Vietnam - 2nd Generation	33	23	32	35
Guatemala - 1st Generation	35	36	54	19
Guatemala - 2nd Generation	66	27	42	27

Children very well-off financially (percent)	Children in one-parent families (percent)	Children whose fathers have less than a high school education (percent)	Children whose mothers have less than a high school education (percent)	Children with 5 or more siblings (percent)	Children who live in linguistically isolated households (percent)
11	23	49	54	17	41
21	15	36	38	9	21
26	18	12	12	4	0
9	62	26	29	10	0
37	25	7	9	6	1
7	40	28	29	10	4
11	42	30	35	8	9
1	17	60	75	29	55
2	13	50	72	39	63
3	27	65	80	19	58
6	25	50	73	17	63
2	51	63	65	6	49
7	47	44	52	4	38
14	11	26	23	7	64
45	10	11	10	2	19
2	23	83	85	19	52
5	18	71	71	12	33
3	16	63	76	33	67
29	9	6	36	1	15
7	23	51	64	15	46
19	15	30	47	9	44
3	32	66	73	6	53
9	26	52	55	5	38

continued on next page

TABLE B-2A   (Continued)

	Number of children (thousands)	Children in official poverty (percent)	Children in relative poverty (percent)	Children in middle-class comfort (percent)
Honduras - 1st Generation	17	37	59	19
Honduras - 2nd Generation	35	25	40	29
El Salvador - 1st Generation	77	32	50	21
El Salvador - 2nd Generation	126	25	41	29
Nicaragua - 1st Generation	39	36	55	20
Nicaragua - 2nd Generation	35	18	29	37
Haiti - 1st Generation	28	30	49	25
Haiti - 2nd Generation	77	24	36	32
Jordan - 1st Generation	2	47	54	26
Jordan - 2nd Generation	17	22	33	31
Belize - 1st Gen.	3	23	39	30
Belize - 2nd Gen.	12	23	28	36
Iraq - 1st Generation	4	34	46	34
Iraq - 2nd Generation	17	19	27	40
Ecuador - 1st Generation	12	26	40	30
Ecuador - 2nd Generation	52	19	28	38
Venezuela - 1st Generation	8	33	39	27
Venezuela - 2nd Generation	15	13	18	41
Israel - 1st Generation	13	23	30	35
Israel - 2nd Generation	46	18	24	30
Trinidad and Tobago - 1st Generation	12	30	43	27
Trinidad and Tobago - 2nd Generation	41	14	23	39
Colombia - 1st Generation	29	19	34	33
Colombia - 2nd Generation	88	16	24	39
Pakistan - 1st Generation	11	24	34	32
Pakistan - 2nd Generation	28	13	18	38
Costa Rica - 1st Generation	4	29	40	36
Costa Rica - 2nd Generation	19	14	23	38
Panama - 1st Generation	6	27	39	39
Panama - 2nd Generation	33	15	23	36
Brazil - 1st Generation	9	21	35	33
Brazil - 2nd Generation	21	13	20	42

Children very well-off financially (percent)	Children in one-parent families (percent)	Children whose fathers have less than a high school education (percent)	Children whose mothers have less than a high school education (percent)	Children with 5 or more siblings (percent)	Children who live in linguistically isolated households (percent)
2	41	49	56	8	49
10	27	39	39	3	26
3	36	69	75	8	48
7	29	57	60	5	45
3	30	40	46	11	54
14	24	28	34	5	30
5	39	49	57	10	39
12	35	35	38	8	32
8	16	36	40	11	23
15	6	24	30	13	8
11	34	40	42	6	10
13	27	26	26	6	3
10	6	46	59	14	14
18	5	29	38	9	16
7	32	43	49	4	42
16	22	32	32	3	26
15	19	21	23	2	36
30	9	10	I2	2	10
23	7	15	17	12	22
35	5	17	20	18	9
10	46	37	33	4	2
23	35	20	16	5	0
9	32	34	42	3	44
18	21	27	27	1	27
13	10	10	20	6	21
32	4	7	17	6	10
6	26	41	36	5	34
20	17	26	30	2	14
9	34	15	22	3	19
26	21	11	14	2	5
16	19	24	23	2	45
29	12	18	19	4	11

continued on next page

TABLE B-2A　(Continued)

	Number of children (thousands)	Children in official poverty (percent)	Children in relative poverty (percent)	Children in middle-class comfort (percent)
Romania - 1st Generation	11	18	27	33
Romania - 2nd Generation	15	13	18	31
Spain -1st Generation	6	37	47	28
Spain - 2nd Generation	22	9	15	42
Lebanon - 1st Generation	8	25	39	22
Lebanon - 2nd Generation	28	12	18	37
Jamaica - 1st Generation	40	18	30	36
Jamaica - 2nd Generation	92	14	23	37
Guyana - 1st Generation	18	18	28	38
Guyana - 2nd Generation	28	13	19	43
Nigeria - 1st Generation	5	28	37	29
Nigeria - 2nd Generation	29	13	25	36
China - 1st Generation	34	25	42	28
China - 2nd Generation	97	10	18	30
Indonesia - 1st Generation	4	45	50	22
Indonesia - 2nd Generation	13	4	9	43
Iran - 1st Generation	24	27	34	29
Iran - 2nd Generation	52	8	12	33
Cuba - 1st Generation	27	27	40	30
Cuba - 2nd Generation	184	13	19	39
Peru - 1st Generation	18	22	39	27
Peru - 2nd Generation	43	10	19	41
Korea - 1st Generation	67	20	29	33
Korea - 2nd Generation	163	9	15	40
Syria - 1st Generation	2	28	41	41
Syria - 2nd Generation	13	9	18	31
Taiwan - 1st Generation	32	19	26	35
Taiwan - 2nd Generation	65	7	10	31
Argentina - 1st Generation	10	18	32	30
Argentina - 2nd Generation	26	9	14	41
Yugoslavia - 1st Generation	5	12	19	44
Yugoslavia - 2nd Generation	39	10	15	42

Children very well-off financially (percent)	Children in one-parent families (percent)	Children whose fathers have less than a high school education (percent)	Children whose mothers have less than a high school education (percent)	Children with 5 or more siblings (percent)	Children who live in linguistically isolated households (percent)
21	9	32	32	19	34
36	7	21	21	17	13
12	19	43	43	3	29
31	12	20	23	3	8
18	11	47	47	8	21
26	5	23	24	8	9
13	44	37	31	5	0
25	33	24	18	4	0
10	36	38	40	5	2
23	28	17	21	4	1
7	22	4	8	16	7
16	15	2	5	6	4
9	10	45	53	3	59
37	9	26	28	1	35
12	15	20	29	3	48
38	6	5	6	3	11
24	14	13	19	1	34
43	6	3	7	1	10
9	25	60	60	2	39
29	21	24	22	2	13
12	21	19	23	3	42
22	16	18	18	2	19
19	11	12	18	0	48
29	9	4	18	0	28
4	5	32	39	4	40
34	4	20	22	4	12
24	17	9	13	1	47
51	6	3	6	1	31
18	13	32	32	1	32
33	10	17	15	3	9
19	11	31	35	3	27
28	10	30	31	3	9

continued on next page

TABLE B-2A   (Continued)

	Number of children (thousands)	Children in official poverty (percent)	Children in relative poverty (percent)	Children in middle-class comfort (percent)
Hong Kong - 1st Generation	17	26	35	31
Hong Kong - 2nd Generation	39	3	8	35
Chile - 1st Generation	5	19	28	33
Chile - 2nd Generation	17	8	15	38
Australia - 1st Generation	3	13	17	27
Australia - 2nd Generation	14	10	16	33
Austria - 1st Generation	1	33	42	30
Austria - 2nd Generation	20	7	12	42
France - 1st Generation	7	11	14	30
France - 2nd Generation	34	8	13	35
Hungary - 1st Generation	3	17	20	33
Hungary - 2nd Generation	22	8	13	35
Egypt - 1st Generation	5	20	29	42
Egypt - 2nd Generation	25	7	12	35
Germany - 1st Generation	16	25	32	31
Germany - 2nd Generation	243	7	12	41
Greece - 1st Generation	3	16	24	44
Greece - 2nd Generation	65	8	15	42
Japan - 1st Generation	32	11	13	26
Japan - 2nd Generation	68	6	11	41
Barbados - 1st Generation	3	6	25	36
Barbados - 2nd Generation	11	8	14	51
Poland - 1st Generation	18	14	22	42
Poland - 2nd Generation	62	5	9	45
Turkey - 1st Generation	3	11	23	20
Turkey - 2nd Generation	12	6	11	35
Italy - 1st Generation	8	14	20	36
Italy - 2nd Generation	171	6	11	45
Portugal - 1st Generation	14	11	17	50
Portugal - 2nd Generation	64	5	10	51
United Kingdom - 1st Generation	31	10	13	31
United Kingdom - 2nd Generation	178	5	9	39

Children very well-off financially (percent)	Children in one-parent families (percent)	Children whose fathers have less than a high school education (percent)	Children whose mothers have less than a high school education (percent)	Children with 5 or more siblings (percent)	Children who live in linguistically isolated households (percent)
14	15	49	57	3	54
47	5	14	17	1	26
17	18	21	28	0	37
31	14	13	14	4	12
45	11	9	14	2	3
43	9	8	10	9	1
13	18	23	26	16	24
40	7	7	7	10	0
48	11	10	14	1	24
39	11	9	9	5	3
26	8	18	21	13	37
41	9	14	12	8	6
19	12	5	10	4	27
43	5	4	8	5	7
25	22	10	18	4	11
33	11	8	10	3	1
17	10	45	51	0	33
26	6	39	31	1	11
52	3	3	4	1	63
36	9	5	8	1	12
13	54	33	35	7	0
24	35	24	17	8	0
23	15	18	15	1	44
35	8	19	15	1	16
36	4	18	23	0	16
38	9	18	17	2	9
25	10	45	48	4	23
30	6	34	28	2	6
14	12	82	83	2	37
24	7	56	53	1	20
45	16	8	15	1	2
41	9	6	8	3	0

continued on next page

TABLE B-2A   (Continued)

	Number of children (thousands)	Children in official poverty (percent)	Children in relative poverty (percent)	Children in middle-class comfort (percent)
Canada - 1st Generation	33	9	14	31
Canada - 2nd Generation	230	6	11	40
South Africa - 1st Generation	5	7	11	23
South Africa - 2nd Generation	10	6	9	27
Netherlands - 1st Generation	2	14	19	24
Netherlands - 2nd Generation	36	5	11	40
India - 1st Generation	45	10	17	39
India - 2nd Generation	130	3	6	33
Philippines - 1st Generation	83	9	15	48
Philippines - 2nd Generation	316	4	8	44
Ireland - 1st Generation	4	12	14	38
Ireland - 2nd Generation	40	4	7	42

NOTE: Countries are listed from highest to lowest official poverty rate for first and second generations combined.

Source: Hernandez and Darke (1998).

Children very well-off financially (percent)	Children in one-parent families (percent)	Children whose fathers have less than a high school education (percent)	Children whose mothers have less than a high school education (percent)	Children with 5 or more siblings (percent)	Children who live in linguistically isolated households (percent)
47	12	11	13	2	5
38	8	11	10	5	1
58	7	1	6	1	2
56	5	2	8	1	0
42	18	5	7	3	3
38	7	7	6	6	1
27	13	5	23	1	18
53	5	95	8	1	9
20	12	88	15	6	16
35	7	93	13	2	7
26	24	76	23	7	3
41	14	86	13	4	0

TABLE B-2B   Household and Housing Risk Factors for First- and Second-
Generation Children by Country of Origin for First and Second Generations
Separately: 1990

	Number of children (thousands)	Children in households with no car or truck (percent)
All First-Generation Children	2,084	17
All Second-Generation Children	6,288	9
Third and Later Generations by Race and Ethnicity:		
White, Non-Hispanic	40,201	3
Black, Non-Hispanic	8,031	30
Asian, Non-Hispanic	329	4
American Indian	562	14
Hispanic	3,489	17
First- and Second-Generation Children by Country of Origin:		
Laos - 1st Generation	49	18
Laos - 2nd Generation	64	17
Cambodia - 1st Generation	30	32
Cambodia - 2nd Generation	34	27
Dominican Republic - 1st Generation	48	60
Dominican Republic - 2nd Generation	131	51
USSR - 1st Generation	38	32
USSR - 2nd Generation	24	8
Mexico - 1st Generation	643	15
Mexico - 2nd Generation	1,975	8
Thailand - 1st Generation	36	27
Thailand - 2nd Generation	33	2
Vietnam - 1st Generation	99	18
Vietnam - 2nd Generation	33	10
Guatemala - 1st Generation	35	20
Guatemala - 2nd Generation	66	17
Honduras - 1st Generation	17	26
Honduras - 2nd Generation	35	21
El Salvador - 1st Generation	77	16
El Salvador - 2nd Generation	126	15
Nicaragua - 1st Generation	39	17
Nicaragua - 2nd Generation	35	8

Children with no telephone in their homes (percent)	Children living in houses built before 1950 (percent)	Children in crowded homes (percent)
10	26	62
6	24	38
5	23	7
18	27	26
3	18	21
32	17	34
15	25	30
4	29	78
4	27	79
5	31	76
4	30	73
22	49	63
18	51	48
3	35	54
0	28	17
21	24	83
13	23	64
4	34	79
1	14	16
2	21	67
1	17	50
10	32	79
8	34	61
12	27	71
8	25	49
8	28	82
7	30	71
13	25	84
6	22	57

continued on next page

TABLE B-2B   (Continued)

	Number of children (thousands)	Children in households with no car or truck (percent)
Haiti - 1st Generation	28	30
Haiti - 2nd Generation	77	21
Jordan - 1st Generation	2	15
Jordan - 2nd Generation	17	7
Belize - 1st Gen.	3	33
Belize - 2nd Gen.	12	16
Iraq - 1st Generation	4	10
Iraq - 2nd Generation	17	3
Ecuador - 1st Generation	12	34
Ecuador - 2nd Generation	52	22
Venezuela - 1st Generation	8	11
Venezuela - 2nd Generation	15	4
Israel - 1st Generation	13	11
Israel - 2nd Generation	46	13
Trinidad and Tobago - 1st Generation	12	40
Trinidad and Tobago - 2nd Generation	41	25
Colombia - 1st Generation	29	17
Colombia - 2nd Generation	88	11
Pakistan - 1st Generation	11	10
Pakistan - 2nd Generation	28	6
Costa Rica - 1st Generation	4	18
Costa Rica - 2nd Generation	19	13
Panama - 1st Generation	6	25
Panama - 2nd Generation	33	15
Brazil - 1st Generation	9	10
Brazil - 2nd Generation	21	6
Romania - 1st Generation	11	10
Romania - 2nd Generation	15	7
Spain -1st Generation	6	10
Spain - 2nd Generation	22	7
Lebanon - 1st Generation	8	9
Lebanon - 2nd Generation	28	3
Jamaica - 1st Generation	40	29
Jamaica - 2nd Generation	92	19
Guyana - 1st Generation	18	42
Guyana - 2nd Generation	28	23
Nigeria - 1st Generation	5	19
Nigeria - 2nd Generation	29	9

Children with no telephone in their homes (percent)	Children living in houses built before 1950 (percent)	Children in crowded homes (percent)
13	34	68
9	33	47
9	15	46
1	24	29
7	35	59
6	35	40
3	31	47
1	14	31
11	46	60
7	40	39
4	21	50
5	16	20
2	25	32
1	29	26
9	45	43
6	37	26
9	29	59
5	26	36
2	20	49
2	16	29
11	22	52
3	30	28
3	28	46
7	25	22
2	24	38
3	25	18
5	37	41
0	29	23
4	31	31
3	27	17
1	32	34
2	24	16
5	33	39
5	28	25
3	46	49
5	36	28
4	18	62
3	18	48

continued on next page

TABLE B-2B   (Continued)

	Number of children (thousands)	Children in households with no car or truck (percent)
China - 1st Generation	34	36
China - 2nd Generation	97	12
Indonesia - 1st Generation	4	11
Indonesia - 2nd Generation	13	2
Iran - 1st Generation	24	8
Iran - 2nd Generation	52	3
Cuba - 1st Generation	27	12
Cuba - 2nd Generation	184	6
Peru - 1st Generation	18	13
Peru - 2nd Generation	43	10
Korea - 1st Generation	67	5
Korea - 2nd Generation	163	2
Syria - 1st Generation	2	6
Syria - 2nd Generation	13	2
Taiwan - 1st Generation	32	4
Taiwan - 2nd Generation	65	2
Argentina - 1st Generation	10	6
Argentina - 2nd Generation	26	6
Yugoslavia - 1st Generation	5	13
Yugoslavia - 2nd Generation	39	5
Hong Kong - 1st Generation	17	19
Hong Kong - 2nd Generation	39	5
Chile - 1st Generation	5	8
Chile - 2nd Generation	17	5
Australia - 1st Generation	3	6
Australia - 2nd Generation	14	5
Austria - 1st Generation	1	20
Austria - 2nd Generation	20	4
France - 1st Generation	7	5
France - 2nd Generation	34	5
Hungary - 1st Generation	3	16
Hungary - 2nd Generation	22	7
Egypt - 1st Generation	5	7
Egypt - 2nd Generation	25	3
Germany - 1st Generation	16	5
Germany - 2nd Generation	243	3

Children with no telephone in their homes (percent)	Children living in houses built before 1950 (percent)	Children in crowded homes (percent)
2	41	59
1	30	32
2	11	53
1	17	21
1	13	38
1	12	14
4	18	48
3	17	25
4	26	53
4	27	29
1	15	49
1	12	27
0	25	42
0	19	19
0	13	34
0	10	19
3	15	35
2	22	20
4	39	38
1	30	14
1	33	57
0	23	24
3	27	37
1	19	26
1	17	9
0	24	9
0	29	35
0	27	10
2	21	11
1	30	11
2	27	33
2	25	12
2	24	35
1	24	17
3	19	17
3	22	7

continued on next page

TABLE B-2B   (Continued)

	Number of children (thousands)	Children in households with no car or truck (percent)
Greece - 1st Generation	3	7
Greece - 2nd Generation	65	3
Japan - 1st Generation	32	2
Japan - 2nd Generation	68	3
Barbados - 1st Generation	3	38
Barbados - 2nd Generation	11	26
Poland - 1st Generation	18	9
Poland - 2nd Generation	62	4
Turkey - 1st Generation	3	6
Turkey - 2nd Generation	12	4
Italy - 1st Generation	8	13
Italy - 2nd Generation	171	3
Portugal - 1st Generation	14	9
Portugal - 2nd Generation	64	3
United Kingdom - 1st Generation	31	5
United Kingdom - 2nd Generation	178	3
Canada - 1st Generation	33	3
Canada - 2nd Generation	230	2
South Africa - 1st Generation	5	2
South Africa - 2nd Generation	10	5
Netherlands - 1st Generation	2	7
Netherlands - 2nd Generation	36	1
India - 1st Generation	45	11
India - 2nd Generation	130	3
Philippines - 1st Generation	83	5
Philippines - 2nd Generation	316	2
Ireland - 1st Generation	4	7
Ireland - 2nd Generation	40	4

NOTE: Countries are listed from highest to lowest official poverty rate for first and second generations combined.

Source: Hernandez and Darke (1998).

Children with no telephone in their homes (percent)	Children living in houses built before 1950 (percent)	Children in crowded homes (percent)
2	36	15
1	26	9
0	13	14
2	16	12
3	65	39
4	34	16
1	38	19
1	30	8
1	25	20
2	22	16
3	35	18
1	31	6
2	53	23
1	41	12
1	17	11
2	23	7
1	13	12
2	21	7
0	14	10
1	23	6
1	11	9
1	23	8
1	20	42
0	11	18
1	20	58
1	14	33
3	29	15
1	39	7

TABLE B-2C   Parents' Labor Force Participation for First- and Second-
Generation Children by Country of Origin for First and Second Generations
Separately: 1990

	Number of children (thousands)	Children with fathers not in the labor force (percent)	Children with fathers not working full-time, year-round (percent)	Children with mothers not in the labor force (percent)
All First-Generation Children	2,084	12	41	45
All Second-Generation Children	6,288	6	28	41
Third and Later Generations by Race and Ethnicity:				
White, Non-Hispanic	40,201	4	19	34
Black, Non-Hispanic	8,031	11	34	33
Asian, Non-Hispanic	329	4	18	29
American Indian	562	14	46	40
Hispanic	3,489	8	30	43
First- and Second-Generation Children by Country of Origin:				
Laos - 1st Generation	49	51	68	64
Laos - 2nd Generation	64	46	68	67
Cambodia - 1st Generation	30	51	69	70
Cambodia - 2nd Generation	34	34	53	62
Dominican Republic - 1st Generation	48	12	40	45
Dominican Republic - 2nd Generation	131	10	38	54
USSR - 1st Generation	38	31	75	53
USSR - 2nd Generation	24	5	21	34
Mexico - 1st Generation	643	7	43	50
Mexico - 2nd Generation	1,975	7	37	50
Thailand - 1st Generation	36	58	73	74
Thailand - 2nd Generation	33	4	21	32
Vietnam - 1st Generation	99	30	57	52
Vietnam - 2nd Generation	33	11	33	42
Guatemala - 1st Generation	35	6	32	36
Guatemala - 2nd Generation	66	5	31	44
Honduras - 1st Generation	17	10	42	38
Honduras - 2nd Generation	35	8	35	43

TABLE B-2C   (Continued)

	Number of children (thousands)	Children with fathers not in the labor force (percent)	Children with fathers not working full-time, year-round (percent)	Children with mothers not in the labor force (percent)
El Salvador - 1st Generation	77	3	35	30
El Salvador - 2nd Generation	126	5	31	36
Nicaragua - 1st Generation	39	6	38	25
Nicaragua - 2nd Generation	35	4	26	37
Haiti - 1st Generation	28	10	43	21
Haiti - 2nd Generation	77	7	33	22
Jordan - 1st Generation	2	26	60	65
Jordan - 2nd Generation	17	9	27	68
Belize - 1st Gen.	3	11	44	29
Belize - 2nd Gen.	12	8	30	32
Iraq - 1st Generation	4	21	43	59
Iraq - 2nd Generation	17	8	28	61
Ecuador - 1st Generation	12	6	40	31
Ecuador - 2nd Generation	52	4	28	41
Venezuela - 1st Generation	8	14	38	54
Venezuela - 2nd Generation	15	5	24	44
Israel - 1st Generation	13	13	34	55
Israel - 2nd Generation	46	5	24	54
Trinidad and Tobago - 1st Generation	12	13	49	24
Trinidad and Tobago - 2nd Generation	41	6	30	25
Colombia - 1st Generation	29	5	35	34
Colombia - 2nd Generation	88	4	26	40
Pakistan - 1st Generation	11	9	35	63
Pakistan - 2nd Generation	28	3	23	59
Costa Rica - 1st Generation	4	15	43	47
Costa Rica - 2nd Generation	19	7	29	36
Panama - 1st Generation	6	8	32	34
Panama - 2nd Generation	33	6	26	28
Brazil - 1st Generation	9	8	36	46
Brazil - 2nd Generation	21	5	25	48
Romania - 1st Generation	11	12	33	45
Romania - 2nd Generation	15	6	22	47
Spain -1st Generation	6	7	48	42
Spain - 2nd Generation	22	4	21	40

continued on next page

TABLE B-2C   (Continued)

	Number of children (thousands)	Children with fathers not in the labor force (percent)	Children with fathers not working full-time, year-round (percent)	Children with mothers not in the labor force (percent)
Lebanon - 1st Generation	8	12	40	63
Lebanon - 2nd Generation	28	8	24	60
Jamaica - 1st Generation	40	5	32	12
Jamaica - 2nd Generation	92	6	28	19
Guyana - 1st Generation	18	4	30	24
Guyana - 2nd Generation	28	6	27	27
Nigeria - 1st Generation	5	7	51	30
Nigeria - 2nd Generation	29	6	36	25
China - 1st Generation	34	9	41	27
China - 2nd Generation	97	4	22	32
Indonesia - 1st Generation	4	34	63	59
Indonesia - 2nd Generation	13	4	20	35
Iran - 1st Generation	24	17	45	50
Iran - 2nd Generation	52	5	21	44
Cuba - 1st Generation	27	7	37	37
Cuba - 2nd Generation	184	4	20	34
Peru - 1st Generation	18	4	34	31
Peru - 2nd Generation	43	4	25	36
Korea - 1st Generation	67	9	38	37
Korea - 2nd Generation	163	5	22	39
Syria - 1st Generation	2	13	51	62
Syria - 2nd Generation	13	7	29	57
Taiwan - 1st Generation	32	13	36	43
Taiwan - 2nd Generation	65	4	18	39
Argentina - 1st Generation	10	6	28	41
Argentina - 2nd Generation	26	2	19	45
Yugoslavia - 1st Generation	5	4	32	42
Yugoslavia - 2nd Generation	39	6	26	42
Hong Kong - 1st Generation	17	13	41	33
Hong Kong - 2nd Generation	39	3	13	30
Chile - 1st Generation	5	4	28	42
Chile - 2nd Generation	17	3	16	36
Australia - 1st Generation	3	7	17	74
Australia - 2nd Generation	14	3	16	43
Austria - 1st Generation	1	11	32	64
Austria - 2nd Generation	20	4	18	33

TABLE B-2C   (Continued)

	Number of children (thousands)	Children with fathers not in the labor force (percent)	Children with fathers not working full-time, year-round (percent)	Children with mothers not in the labor force (percent)
France - 1st Generation	7	4	18	57
France - 2nd Generation	34	3	20	40
Hungary - 1st Generation	3	5	26	46
Hungary - 2nd Generation	22	5	19	40
Egypt - 1st Generation	5	7	32	42
Egypt - 2nd Generation	25	3	22	43
Germany - 1st Generation	16	6	22	52
Germany - 2nd Generation	243	3	18	36
Greece - 1st Generation	3	7	35	51
Greece - 2nd Generation	65	6	26	46
Japan - 1st Generation	32	5	22	90
Japan - 2nd Generation	68	3	19	43
Barbados - 1st Generation	3	1	28	14
Barbados - 2nd Generation	11	6	22	22
Poland - 1st Generation	18	4	26	31
Poland - 2nd Generation	62	4	19	35
Turkey - 1st Generation	3	11	23	52
Turkey - 2nd Generation	12	2	20	47
Italy - 1st Generation	8	6	30	55
Italy - 2nd Generation	171	5	21	47
Portugal - 1st Generation	14	5	37	31
Portugal - 2nd Generation	64	6	25	28
United Kingdom - 1st Generation	31	3	15	51
United Kingdom - 2nd Generation	178	3	17	36
Canada - 1st Generation	33	4	19	46
Canada - 2nd Generation	230	3	18	37
South Africa - 1st Generation	5	6	19	50
South Africa - 2nd Generation	10	2	15	46
Netherlands - 1st Generation	2	3	16	48
Netherlands - 2nd Generation	36	2	14	39
India - 1st Generation	45	4	27	31
India - 2nd Generation	130	2	16	37

continued on next page

TABLE B-2C   (Continued)

	Number of children (thousands)	Children with fathers not in the labor force (percent)	Children with fathers not working full-time, year-round (percent)	Children with mothers not in the labor force (percent)
Philippines - 1st Generation	83	7	29	18
Philippines - 2nd Generation	316	5	20	18
Ireland - 1st Generation	4	5	29	56
Ireland - 2nd Generation	40	4	17	41

NOTE: Countries are listed from highest to lowest official poverty rate for first and second generations combined.

Source: Hernandez and Darke (1998).

TABLE B-2D   Parents' Education for First- and Second-Generation Children by Country of Origin for First and Second Generations Separately: 1990

	Number of children (thousands)	Children with fathers who have 8 or fewer years of education (percent)	Children with mothers who have 8 or fewer years of education (percent)	Children whose fathers have four or more years of college education (percent)	Children whose mothers have four or more years of college education (percent)
All First-Generation Children	2,084	34	38	23	14
All Second-Generation Children	6,288	23	22	25	17
Third and Later Generations by Race and Ethnicity:					
White, Non-Hispanic	40,201	3	2	28	20
Black, Non-Hispanic	8,031	6	4	12	9
Asian, Non-Hispanic	329	1	1	40	31
American Indian	562	8	6	9	7
Hispanic	3,489	9	10	12	7
First- and Second-Generation Children by Country of Origin:					
Laos - 1st Generation	49	48	66	8	6
Laos - 2nd Generation	64	36	56	7	2
Cambodia - 1st Generation	30	51	68	3	2
Cambodia - 2nd Generation	34	35	53	9	2
Dominican Republic - 1st Generation	48	42	43	8	4
Dominican Republic - 2nd Generation	131	22	25	10	6
USSR - 1st Generation	38	11	8	36	32
USSR - 2nd Generation	24	4	3	49	41
Mexico - 1st Generation	643	67	69	3	2
Mexico - 2nd Generation	1,975	51	48	4	3
Thailand - 1st Generation	36	50	68	8	4
Thailand - 2nd Generation	33	2	21	39	21

continued on next page

TABLE B-2D   (Continued

	Number of children (thousands)	Children with fathers who have 8 or fewer years of education (percent)	Children with mothers who have 8 or fewer years of education (percent)	Children whose fathers have four or more years of college education (percent)	Children whose mothers have four or more years of college education (percent)
Vietnam - 1st Generation	99	32	44	11	5
Vietnam - 2nd Generation	33	14	23	22	9
Guatemala - 1st Generation	35	45	52	7	3
Guatemala - 2nd Generation	66	30	32	10	6
Honduras - 1st Generation	17	33	36	13	6
Honduras - 2nd Generation	35	19	19	13	8
El Salvador - 1st Generation	77	47	51	5	3
El Salvador - 2nd Generation	126	33	35	7	4
Nicaragua - 1st Generation	39	22	23	23	11
Nicaragua - 2nd Generation	35	11	12	19	11
Haiti - 1st Generation	28	19	23	7	4
Haiti - 2nd Generation	77	13	15	17	12
Jordan - 1st Generation	2	14	17	31	11
Jordan - 2nd Generation	17	11	11	29	11
Belize - 1st Gen.	3	20	14	7	7
Belize - 2nd Gen.	12	8	5	16	7
Iraq - 1st Generation	4	21	41	23	9
Iraq - 2nd Generation	17	12	17	25	17
Ecuador - 1st Generation	12	22	20	16	9
Ecuador - 2nd Generation	52	12	12	18	9
Venezuela - 1st Generation	8	11	11	45	25
Venezuela - 2nd Generation	15	4	3	45	30
Israel - 1st Generation	13	5	6	50	34
Israel - 2nd Generation	46	5	6	38	32
Trinidad and Tobago - 1st Generation	12	15	12	13	6
Trinidad and Tobago - 2nd Generation	41	5	4	19	13
Colombia - 1st Generation	29	15	19	20	12
Colombia - 2nd Generation	88	10	9	22	13
Pakistan - 1st Generation	11	2	12	57	38
Pakistan - 2nd Generation	28	3	7	68	41

TABLE B-2D   (Continued)

	Number of children (thousands)	Children with fathers who have 8 or fewer years of education (percent)	Children with mothers who have 8 or fewer years of education (percent)	Children whose fathers have four or more years of college education (percent)	Children whose mothers have four or more years of college education (percent)
Costa Rica - 1st Generation	4	16	21	18	10
Costa Rica - 2nd Generation	19	10	10	20	13
Panama - 1st Generation	6	2	8	24	10
Panama - 2nd Generation	33	2	3	26	18
Brazil - 1st Generation	9	11	13	44	31
Brazil - 2nd Generation	21	9	9	38	28
Romania - 1st Generation	11	13	18	34	28
Romania - 2nd Generation	15	7	5	42	34
Spain -1st Generation	6	30	28	28	15
Spain - 2nd Generation	22	8	8	30	19
Lebanon - 1st Generation	8	28	23	18	11
Lebanon - 2nd Generation	28	10	9	40	24
Jamaica - 1st Generation	40	12	8	14	9
Jamaica - 2nd Generation	92	7	4	21	18
Guyana - 1st Generation	18	12	13	14	4
Guyana - 2nd Generation	28	3	5	27	16
Nigeria - 1st Generation	5	0	4	77	41
Nigeria - 2nd Generation	29	0	1	80	46
China - 1st Generation	34	30	35	28	17
China - 2nd Generation	97	13	15	43	32
Indonesia - 1st Generation	4	9	16	56	27
Indonesia - 2nd Generation	13	1	1	53	36
Iran - 1st Generation	24	4	7	60	29
Iran - 2nd Generation	52	1	1	71	43
Cuba - 1st Generation	27	30	29	11	9
Cuba - 2nd Generation	184	10	7	26	17
Peru - 1st Generation	18	6	8	26	14
Peru - 2nd Generation	43	5	5	30	19
Korea - 1st Generation	67	5	8	46	31
Korea - 2nd Generation	163	1	7	42	27
Syria - 1st Generation	2	16	21	27	14
Syria - 2nd Generation	13	9	9	44	20

continued on next page

TABLE B-2D   (Continued)

	Number of children (thousands)	Children with fathers who have 8 or fewer years of education (percent)	Children with mothers who have 8 or fewer years of education (percent)	Children whose fathers have four or more years of college education (percent)	Children whose mothers have four or more years of college education (percent)
Taiwan - 1st Generation	32	7	7	62	35
Taiwan - 2nd Generation	65	1	3	77	60
Argentina - 1st Generation	10	14	15	31	26
Argentina - 2nd Generation	26	7	4	35	24
Yugoslavia - 1st Generation	5	14	20	28	17
Yugoslavia - 2nd Generation	39	19	19	17	14
Hong Kong - 1st Generation	17	28	31	15	7
Hong Kong - 2nd Generation	39	7	8	53	39
Chile - 1st Generation	5	9	10	28	17
Chile - 2nd Generation	17	4	4	35	23
Australia - 1st Generation	3	1	2	63	32
Australia - 2nd Generation	14	3	0	48	33
Austria - 1st Generation	1	12	3	47	38
Austria - 2nd Generation	20	1	1	45	37
France - 1st Generation	7	7	8	65	45
France - 2nd Generation	34	3	1	45	34
Hungary - 1st Generation	3	5	6	51	32
Hungary - 2nd Generation	22	6	2	38	29
Egypt - 1st Generation	5	2	5	75	59
Egypt - 2nd Generation	25	1	2	66	41
Germany - 1st Generation	16	2	5	47	27
Germany - 2nd Generation	243	2	1	34	22
Greece - 1st Generation	3	24	26	24	12
Greece - 2nd Generation	65	23	18	21	17
Japan - 1st Generation	32	2	2	78	45
Japan - 2nd Generation	68	2	2	44	26
Barbados - 1st Generation	3	10	13	19	12
Barbados - 2nd Generation	11	8	2	18	14
Poland - 1st Generation	18	7	6	32	27
Poland - 2nd Generation	62	6	5	30	22
Turkey - 1st Generation	3	13	17	46	34
Turkey - 2nd Generation	12	9	7	40	32

TABLE B-2D (Continued)

	Number of children (thousands)	Children with fathers who have 8 or fewer years of education (percent)	Children with mothers who have 8 or fewer years of education (percent)	Children whose fathers have four or more years of college education (percent)	Children whose mothers have four or more years of college education (percent)
Italy - 1st Generation	8	33	34	24	16
Italy - 2nd Generation	171	19	15	19	14
Portugal - 1st Generation	14	68	65	3	3
Portugal - 2nd Generation	64	38	34	8	5
United Kingdom - 1st Generation	31	1	3	56	27
United Kingdom - 2nd Generation	178	1	1	41	26
Canada - 1st Generation	33	4	3	58	31
Canada - 2nd Generation	230	3	2	38	26
South Africa - 1st Generation	5	1	1	63	35
South Africa - 2nd Generation	10	0	1	70	42
Netherlands - 1st Generation	2	0	3	60	34
Netherlands - 2nd Generation	36	2	1	40	26
India - 1st Generation	45	4	9	62	46
India - 2nd Generation	130	1	2	80	63
Philippines - 1st Generation	83	7	9	46	52
Philippines - 2nd Generation	316	3	6	37	45
Ireland - 1st Generation	4	12	7	36	13
Ireland - 2nd Generation	40	4	2	31	20

NOTE: Countries are listed from highest to lowest official poverty rate for first and second generations combined.

Source: Hernandez and Darke (1998).

TABLE B-2E   Language Use and Citizenship for First- and Second-
Generation Children by Country of Origin for First and Second Generations
Separately: 1990

	Number of children (thousands)	Children who do not speak English at home (percent)
All First-Generation Children	2,084	87
All Second-Generation Children	6,288	58
Third and Later Generations by Race and Ethnicity:		
White, Non-Hispanic	40,201	1
Black, Non-Hispanic	8,031	1
Asian, Non-Hispanic	329	3
American Indian	562	7
Hispanic	3,489	15
First- and Second-Generation Children by Country of Origin:		
Laos - 1st Generation	49	97
Laos - 2nd Generation	64	95
Cambodia - 1st Generation	30	97
Cambodia - 2nd Generation	34	87
Dominican Republic - 1st Generation	48	97
Dominican Republic - 2nd Generation	131	91
USSR - 1st Generation	38	96
USSR - 2nd Generation	24	57
Mexico - 1st Generation	643	97
Mexico - 2nd Generation	1,975	88
Thailand - 1st Generation	36	95
Thailand - 2nd Generation	33	32
Vietnam - 1st Generation	99	97
Vietnam - 2nd Generation	33	76
Guatemala - 1st Generation	35	98
Guatemala - 2nd Generation	66	83
Honduras - 1st Generation	17	93
Honduras - 2nd Generation	35	69
El Salvador - 1st Generation	77	98
El Salvador - 2nd Generation	126	90
Nicaragua - 1st Generation	39	97
Nicaragua - 2nd Generation	35	75

Children who do not speak English exclusively or very well (percent)	Children not U.S. citizens (percent)	Children who are not U.S. citizens, or who have at least 1 parent in the home who is not a citizen (percent)
45	84	87
19	N/A	59
N/A		N/A
N/A		N/A
N/A		N/A
N/A		N/A
N/A		N/A
57	89	91
65	N/A	88
62	89	92
54	N/A	80
55	85	89
31	N/A	68
61	83	84
12	N/A	29
59	86	89
32	N/A	74
65	93	94
9	N/A	56
52	78	81
34	N/A	51
56	89	91
26	N/A	76
48	88	92
18	N/A	64
53	89	91
35	N/A	79
58	96	97
22	N/A	69

continued on next page

TABLE B-2E   (Continued)

	Number of children (thousands)	Children who do not speak English at home (percent)
Haiti - 1st Generation	28	91
Haiti - 2nd Generation	77	67
Jordan - 1st Generation	2	98
Jordan - 2nd Generation	17	55
Belize - 1st Gen.	3	28
Belize - 2nd Gen.	12	14
Iraq - 1st Generation	4	90
Iraq - 2nd Generation	17	62
Ecuador - 1st Generation	12	98
Ecuador - 2nd Generation	52	80
Venezuela - 1st Generation	8	95
Venezuela - 2nd Generation	15	49
Israel - 1st Generation	13	91
Israel - 2nd Generation	46	54
Trinidad and Tobago - 1st Generation	12	7
Trinidad and Tobago - 2nd Generation	41	5
Colombia - 1st Generation	29	96
Colombia - 2nd Generation	88	78
Pakistan - 1st Generation	11	94
Pakistan - 2nd Generation	28	60
Costa Rica - 1st Generation	4	94
Costa Rica - 2nd Generation	19	61
Panama - 1st Generation	6	86
Panama - 2nd Generation	33	32
Brazil - 1st Generation	9	93
Brazil - 2nd Generation	21	50
Romania - 1st Generation	11	91
Romania - 2nd Generation	15	54
Spain -1st Generation	6	91
Spain - 2nd Generation	22	56
Lebanon - 1st Generation	8	92
Lebanon - 2nd Generation	28	62
Jamaica - 1st Generation	40	7
Jamaica - 2nd Generation	92	6
Guyana - 1st Generation	18	8
Guyana - 2nd Generation	28	7

Children who do not speak English exclusively or very well (percent)	Children not U.S. citizens (percent)	Children who are not U.S. citizens, or who have at least 1 parent in the home who is not a citizen (percent)
47	84	90
21	N/A	71
28	72	79
8	N/A	33
10	72	80
3	N/A	70
13	72	78
10	N/A	37
38	87	90
20	N/A	73
36	90	92
12	N/A	68
28	74	75
15	N/A	31
4	84	86
1	N/A	68
38	87	90
17	N/A	64
29	74	80
14	N/A	46
38	88	91
13	N/A	63
31	77	79
9	N/A	43
47	91	96
11	N/A	68
33	77	79
14	N/A	25
26	83	85
12	N/A	60
26	69	71
12	N/A	32
2	81	85
2	N/A	59
2	80	81
2	N/A	51

continued on next page

TABLE B-2E   (Continued)

	Number of children (thousands)	Children who do not speak English at home (percent)
Nigeria - 1st Generation	5	59
Nigeria - 2nd Generation	29	15
China - 1st Generation	34	97
China - 2nd Generation	97	74
Indonesia - 1st Generation	4	88
Indonesia - 2nd Generation	13	20
Iran - 1st Generation	24	93
Iran - 2nd Generation	52	49
Cuba - 1st Generation	27	98
Cuba - 2nd Generation	184	77
Peru - 1st Generation	18	98
Peru - 2nd Generation	43	69
Korea - 1st Generation	67	92
Korea - 2nd Generation	163	50
Syria - 1st Generation	2	93
Syria - 2nd Generation	13	52
Taiwan - 1st Generation	32	96
Taiwan - 2nd Generation	65	68
Argentina - 1st Generation	10	96
Argentina - 2nd Generation	26	55
Yugoslavia - 1st Generation	5	94
Yugoslavia - 2nd Generation	39	57
Hong Kong - 1st Generation	17	97
Hong Kong - 2nd Generation	39	66
Chile - 1st Generation	5	94
Chile - 2nd Generation	17	66
Australia - 1st Generation	3	27
Australia - 2nd Generation	14	8
Austria - 1st Generation	1	84
Austria - 2nd Generation	20	22
France - 1st Generation	7	91
France - 2nd Generation	34	35
Hungary - 1st Generation	3	99
Hungary - 2nd Generation	22	35
Egypt - 1st Generation	5	88
Egypt - 2nd Generation	25	48

Children who do not speak English exclusively or very well (percent)	Children not U.S. citizens (percent)	Children who are not U.S. citizens, or who have at least 1 parent in the home who is not a citizen (percent)
27	89	89
3	N/A	81
63	83	85
23	N/A	32
43	89	92
6	N/A	37
34	89	90
10	N/A	57
36	84	89
15	N/A	42
42	88	89
16	N/A	59
38	81	85
14	N/A	43
35	77	77
10	N/A	37
41	80	81
16	N/A	39
26	89	91
12	N/A	50
22	77	86
8	N/A	39
54	77	78
22	N/A	23
32	87	90
12	N/A	57
3	93	95
3	N/A	71
32	68	71
7	N/A	26
30	90	91
5	N/A	49
28	75	81
11	N/A	20
27	65	67
10	N/A	28

continued on next page

TABLE B-2E   (Continued)

	Number of children (thousands)	Children who do not speak English at home (percent)
Germany - 1st Generation	16	69
Germany - 2nd Generation	243	14
Greece - 1st Generation	3	87
Greece - 2nd Generation	65	69
Japan - 1st Generation	32	94
Japan - 2nd Generation	68	34
Barbados - 1st Generation	3	7
Barbados - 2nd Generation	11	2
Poland - 1st Generation	18	96
Poland - 2nd Generation	62	55
Turkey - 1st Generation	3	87
Turkey - 2nd Generation	12	45
Italy - 1st Generation	8	85
Italy - 2nd Generation	171	35
Portugal - 1st Generation	14	96
Portugal - 2nd Generation	64	69
United Kingdom - 1st Generation	31	19
United Kingdom - 2nd Generation	178	5
Canada - 1st Generation	33	30
Canada - 2nd Generation	230	7
South Africa - 1st Generation	5	18
South Africa - 2nd Generation	10	7
Netherlands - 1st Generation	2	77
Netherlands - 2nd Generation	36	9
India - 1st Generation	45	84
India - 2nd Generation	130	53
Philippines - 1st Generation	83	75
Philippines - 2nd Generation	316	21
Ireland - 1st Generation	4	17
Ireland - 2nd Generation	40	4

NOTE: Countries are listed from highest to lowest official poverty rate for first and second generations combined.

Source: Hernandez and Darke (1998).

Children who do not speak English exclusively or very well (percent)	Children not U.S. citizens (percent)	Children who are not U.S. citizens, or who have at least 1 parent in the home who is not a citizen (percent)
15	78	84
4	N/A	34
27	58	69
10	N/A	34
66	96	97
10	N/A	62
2	72	76
1	N/A	53
31	80	86
9	N/A	45
18	79	84
5	N/A	44
21	60	71
7	N/A	37
28	80	85
12	N/A	58
3	90	92
1	N/A	59
5	91	92
2	N/A	57
4	84	84
2	N/A	43
10	89	88
3	N/A	41
24	84	90
10	N/A	60
27	72	76
5	N/A	36
5	87	90
0	N/A	44

APPENDIX C

Glossary

acculturation: The process of adopting the culture of the receiving country.

acculturative stress: The psychological tensions that individuals and families experience as they acculturate to values and mores that may conflict with their own.

alien: Any person not a citizen or national of the United States.

assimilation: The process of immigrants' becoming part of American society. Assimilation is usually conceived as taking place not only within individuals, but also over generations.

assimilation, segmented: Refers to assimilation of immigrants who are racially or ethnically distinct in American terms, for example, Hispanic or black, who may potentially assimilate not to the mainstream (white, non-Hispanic) culture but to the segment associated with Hispanics or blacks.

biculturalism: The ability to identify with the cultures of both the country from which the child emigrated and the country to which the child immigrated.

citizen: Persons are citizens of the United States either by virtue of birth in this country or through the naturalization process.

children: Persons in the age range of 0 to 17 years.

deeming: Access of *legal permanent residents* to SSI, food stamps, and AFDC benefits has been conditioned by "deeming," that is, ascribing the incomes of their sponsors to the immigrants for three to five years following entry.   Under deeming, the income of an immigrant's sponsor is deemed to be available to the immigrant for purposes of qualifying for means-tested benefit programs.

diversity: Used in reference to the growing racial, ethnic, linguistic, and cultural variation of the U.S. population.

first-generation children: Children born in a foreign country who immigrate to the United States.

illegal immigrant: An immigrant who enters the United States illegally (i.e., without an invitation) or without inspection, or who enters legally (e.g., as a visitor, student, or temporary employee) but then fails to leave when his or her visa expires; also called an undocumented immigrant.

legal immigrant: An immigrant who enters the United States as a legal permanent resident and who, after five years of continuous residence, is eligible to apply for citizenship.

legal permanent resident: Aliens lawfully accorded the privilege of residing permanently in the United States.   They may be issued immigrant visas by the Department of State overseas or adjusted to permanent resident status by the Immigration and Naturalization Service in the United States.

minority children: Children belonging to any of the racial and ethnic groups in the United States other than non-Hispanic whites, that is, groups currently in the numerical minority, such as blacks, Asians, Hispanics, and American Indians.

naturalized citizen: Those upon whom citizenship was conferred after birth.

public benefits: Cash or non-cash benefits or services received from government programs such as Medicaid, Supplemental Security Income (SSI), the Food Stamps Program, the Special Supplemental Nutrition Program for Women, Infants and Children (WIC), and the Temporary Assistance to Needy Families Program (TANF, formerly Aid to Families with Dependent Children).

racial and ethnic stratification: Social stratification generally refers to the unequal ranking of groups defined in specific ways. Racial stratification distinguishes persons according to what different races "look" like, as this is defined in a particular culture. Ethnic stratification distinguishes persons according to cultural traits, such as similarity in foods, ways of dress, and language. Race and ethnicity are neither identical nor interchangeable, but as used here both can involve social hierarchies that have implications for a person's life chances. Systems of racial and ethnic stratification are long-lasting, but can change through time.

receiving country: Country to which an immigrant has migrated.

refugee: Any person outside his or her country of nationality who is unable or unwilling to return to that country because of persecution or a well-founded fear of persecution (persecution or fear of persecution may be based on the person's race, religion, nationality, membership in a particular social group, or political opinion).

second-generation children: Children born in the United States to at least one parent who was born in a foreign country and immigrated to the United States.

selective migration: The circumstance in which immigrants who choose to come to the United States are not representative of the full spectrum of citizens of their country of origin due to factors such as higher (or lower) education levels.

sending country: Country from which an immigrant has migrated.

sponsor: The person who signs an affidavit of support, pledging to support an immigrant who is being admitted to the United States for permanent residence.   Under the Illegal Immigration Reform and Immigrant Responsibility Act of 1996 the sponsor must be the person petitioning for admission of his/her relative, must have an income equal to at least 125 percent of the federal poverty line and be able to maintain the sponsored immigrant at that income level.

SSI: The Supplemental Security Income (SSI) Program is a means tested, federally administered income assistance program authorized by title XVI of the Social Security Act.   Established in 1972 and begun in 1974, SSI provides monthly cash payments in accordance with uniform, nationwide eligibility requirements to needy aged, blind, and disabled persons.

third- and later-generation children: Children born in the United States to parents who were born in the United States.

undocumented immigrant: See illegal immigrant.

WIC: The Special Supplemental Nutrition Program for Women, Infants and Children (the WIC Program) provides food assistance and nutritional screening to low-income pregnant and postpartum women and their infants, as well as to low-income children up to age 5.

youth: Children who are adolescents, that is, approximately in the age range of 12 to 17 years.

APPENDIX D
Biographical Sketches

EVAN CHARNEY (*Chair*) is professor and chair emeritus of the Department of Pediatrics at the University of Massachusetts Medical Center and director of the Generalist Physician Faculty Scholars Program supported by the Robert Wood Johnson Foundation. Previously he was professor of pediatrics at the Johns Hopkins University School of Medicine and pediatrician-in-chief at Sinai Hospital. He has held academic positions at Harvard University and at the School of Medicine and Dentistry at the University of Rochester. A member of the Institute of Medicine since 1989, he was elected in 1996 to its governing council. He is the recipient of awards from the Ambulatory Pediatric Association, including the George Armstrong award and the excellence in education award for programs at Sinai Hospital and the University of Massachusetts. His research and publications deal with pediatrics, medical education, neighborhood health centers, childhood obesity, and childhood lead poisoning. He has a B.S. degree from Cornell University and an M.D. from Albert Einstein College of Medicine.

KATHLEEN GAINOR ANDREOLI is the vice president for nursing affairs and the John L. and Helen Kellogg dean of the College of Nursing at Rush University and professor of nursing at Rush-Presbyterian-St. Luke's Medical Center in Chicago. She has been on the faculty of several university medical centers including Duke, Georgetown, Alabama, and Rush. Highlights of her career include participation in the development and implementation of the first coronary care unit and educational program at Duke University Medical Center in the 1960s; authorship of a major textbook on coronary care, now in its eighth edition; leadership of one of the early family nurse practitioner programs, at the University of Alabama in Birmingham in the 1970s; creation and implementation of the Office of Academic Affairs at the University of Texas Health Science Center in Houston in the 1980s; and, since 1987, leadership of the College of Nursing at Rush University and the Home Health Service at Rush-Presbyterian-St. Luke's Medical Center. She is a member of the Institute of Medicine and the American Academy of Nursing. She has a B.S.N. from Georgetown University, an M.S.N. from Vanderbilt University, and a D.S.N. from the University of Alabama, Birmingham.

E. RICHARD BROWN is founder and director of the Center for Health Policy Research at the University of California, Los Angeles, and professor of public health in the university's School of Public Health. He has served as president of the American Public Health Association and as a senior consultant to the President's Task Force on National Health Care Reform and has testified before numerous committees of Congress and the California legislature. He has written widely on public health issues; his recent research focuses on health insurance coverage, access to health services, and public policy, especially as it affects low-income populations and ethnic and racial minorities. He is a reviewer for numerous scientific and professional journals and was a member of the Institute of Medicine's Committee on the Prevention and Control of Sexually Transmitted Diseases and its Public Health Roundtable. He has M.A. and a Ph.D. degrees in the sociology of education from the University of California, Berkeley.

DONALD J. COHEN is director of the Child Study Center and Irving B. Harris professor of child psychiatry, pediatrics, and psychology at the Yale University School of Medicine. His clinical and research activities have focused on the serious neuropsychiatric disorders of childhood, including pervasive developmental disorders and stereotypic and tic disorders. He has published more than 300 articles, books, and monographs. He is president of the International Association of Child and Adolescent Psychiatry and Allied Professions and training and supervisory psychoanalyst at Western New England Institute of Psychoanalysis. He is a member of the Institute of Medicine and chairman of the publications committee of the Yale University Press. He has a B.A. from Brandeis University and an M.D. from the Yale University School of Medicine.

JANET CURRIE is professor of economics at the University of California, Los Angeles. Previously she taught at the Massachusetts Institute of Technology. She has conducted research and written extensively on welfare, the well-being of children, and labor-related issues and has served as coeditor or advisor to several journals. She was the recipient of an Alfred P. Sloan Foundation research fellowship. She has B.A. and M.A. degrees in economics from the University of Toronto and a Ph.D. in economics from Princeton University.

KATHERINE DARKE *(Research Assistant)* is research associate at the Urban Institute. Previously she served as research assistant for the Board on Children, Youth, and Families. She has a B.A. in government and an M.P.P. from the College of William and Mary.

DAVID L. FEATHERMAN is director and senior research scientist at the Institute for Social Research and professor of sociology and psychology in the College of Literature, Science and the Arts at the University of Michigan. Prior to 1994, he served as president of the Social Science Research Council in New York. Previously, for 21 years he was on the faculty of the University of Wisconsin, Madison, where he chaired several departments and institutes and was the John Bascom professor in sociology. His research has spanned the multidisciplinary fields of demography, social psychology, human development, and gerontology. He has written or coauthored five books and dozens of published papers about socioeconomic inequality and social mobility in Western industrial nations. In 1990 he received the distinguished career of research award of the American Sociological Association's Section on Aging and the Life Course. He is a fellow of the American Academy of Arts and Sciences, the American Association for the Advancement of Science, a 1978-1979 fellow of the Center for Advanced Study in the Behavioral Sciences, and a former Guggenheim fellow. He has Ph.D. and M.A. degrees from the University of Michigan in sociology and social psychology.

MICHAEL FIX is an attorney and principal research associate at the Urban Institute, where he directs the Immigrant Policy Program. He has served as a consultant to the Equal Opportunity Division of the Rockefeller Foundation. The substantive focus of his work has been on immigration and immigrant policy, civil rights, regulatory reform, and federalism. He has coauthored several books and articles on these subjects, including *Immigration and Immigrants: Setting the Record Straight* (with Jeffrey Passel) and *Clear and Convincing Evidence: Testing for Discrimination in America* (coeditor with Raymond Struyk). He has a B.A. from Princeton University and a J.D. from the University of Virginia.

NANCY GEYELIN *(Research Assistant)* is research assistant as well as assistant director of communications for the Board on Children, Youth, and Families. Prior to joining the staff of the board, she was a researcher and fundraiser for the Heartland Alliance for Human Needs and Human Rights in Chicago, a research assistant working on a history of the Fels family of Philadelphia, and a legal assistant for an immigration law firm in Philadelphia. She has a B.A. in history from Haverford College.

DONALD J. HERNANDEZ *(Study Director)* is chief of the Marriage and Family Statistics Branch of the U.S. Bureau of the Census. Previously he was a senior research scholar at the Center for Population Research at Georgetown University, a staff associate at the Center for Coordination of Research on Social Indicators of the Social Science Research Council, and an assistant professor in the Department of Sociology at the University of South Carolina. He will join the faculty of the State University of New York at Albany as professor of sociology in fall 1999. He has a Ph.D. in sociology from the University of California, Berkeley.

FERNANDO GUERRA is director of health at the San Antonio Metropolitan Health District and a practicing pediatrician. Previously he was clinical professor in the Department of Pediatrics at the University of Texas Health Science Center. He is a fellow of the American Academy of Pediatrics and a founding scholar of the Public Health Leadership Institute. He is active in a variety of forums on health issues, including improving access to health care for immigrant children and their families, reducing domestic and interpersonal violence, and community-based programs and services for HIV/AIDS efforts. He has a B.A. from the University of Texas, Austin, an M.D. from the University of Texas, Galveston, and an M.P.H. from the Harvard School of Public Health.

BILL ONG HING is visiting professor at the King Hall School of Law of the University of California, Davis; he also volunteers as executive director of the Immigrant Legal Resource Center in San Francisco. Previously, he was on the faculty of Stanford Law School and Golden Gate University Law School. He is the author of several books on immigration law, including *To Be An American: Cultural Pluralism and the Rhetoric of Assimilation, Handling Immigration Cases*, and *Making and Remaking Asian America Through Immigration Policy*. He has an A.B. in psychology from the University of California, Berkeley, and a J.D. from the University of San Francisco.

ARTHUR KLEINMAN is Maude and Lillian Presley professor of medical anthropology, professor of psychiatry, and chairman of the Department of Social Medicine at the Harvard Medical School, as well as professor of social anthropology in the Department of Anthropology, Harvard University. Previously he held faculty positions at the University of Washington. He directed the World Mental Health Report, was a member of the steering committee of the American Psychological Association and National Institute of Mental Health's Taskforce on Culture and Psychiatric Diagnosis, and was cochair of the Committee on Culture, Health and Human Development of the Social Science Research Council. He is the author of more than 150 articles and 5 books and editor or coeditor of 15 volumes. He has A.B. and M.D. degrees from

Stanford University and an M.A. in social anthropology from Harvard University.

ALAN M. KRAUT is professor in the Department of History at American University. He is the author of several books on immigration, including *Huddled Masses: The Immigrant in American Society, 1880-1921,* and the coauthor of *American Refugee Policy and European Jewry, 1933-1945* (with R. Breitman). He was awarded the Theodore Saloutos prize by the Immigration History Society and the 1994 Phi Alpha Theta book award by the International Honor Society in History for *Silent Travelers: Germs, Genes, and the "Immigrant Menace."* As a specialist in both immigration history and the history of medicine, he has published many articles on the health of immigrants and refugees in the United States. He has a B.A. in history from Hunter College and an M.A. and a Ph.D. degrees in American history from Cornell University.

NANCY S. LANDALE is professor of sociology at the Pennsylvania State University. Previously she was on the faculty of the Department of Sociology at the University of Chicago. She specializes in the area of family demography, with an emphasis on the demographic behavior of racial and ethnic minority groups. She is currently conducting a study of maternal and infant health among Puerto Ricans, focusing on the effects of migration and acculturation processes on infant health outcomes. She has authored or coauthored numerous articles dealing with immigration. She has M.A. and Ph.D. degrees in sociology from the University of Washington.

ANTONIO McDANIEL is associate professor of sociology and chair of the Graduate Group in Demography at the University of Pennsylvania. His research focuses on African and African American population dynamics. He is the author of a book on the colonization of Liberia in the nineteenth century; his recent work has appeared in numerous scholarly journals. He is currently conducting research in Africa and the Americas and completing a book on the demography of race in South Africa, Brazil, and the United States. He has a Ph.D. from the University of Chicago.

FERNANDO S. MENDOZA is chief of the Division of General Pediatrics and associate dean of student affairs at the Stanford University School of Medicine, as well as associate professor of pediatrics at the Lucile Salter Packard Children's Hospital. His research has focused on assessing the health and nutritional status of Hispanic-origin children in the United States. He has published extensively on the nutritional status of Mexican American and mainland Puerto Rican children, identifying the effects of poverty on the growth patterns of these children. He also has examined chronic illness and perceived health status among Hispanic children and the effects of poverty and acculturation on these health parameters. His current work is focused on differentiating the health and nutritional status of Mexican American children by generational status. He has received the Henry J. Kaiser award for outstanding and innovative contributions in medical education from the Stanford University School of Medicine and has been honored for his work with Hispanic children by the Latino Health Affairs Council and COSSMHO. He has a B.A. from San Jose State University, an M.D. from the Stanford University School of Medicine, and an M.P.H. from Harvard University.

VICTOR NEE is Goldwin Smith professor of sociology and chair at Cornell University. Previously he was director of the Comparative Societal Analysis Program at Cornell and a member of the faculty of the University of California, Santa Barbara. He was a visiting scholar at the Russell Sage Foundation, as well as a fellow at the Center for Advanced Studies in the Behavioral Sciences. The focus of his research has been on economic sociology, ethnicity and immigration, and political sociology; he has authored or coauthored more than 80 books and articles in these fields. He has a B.A. in history and biology from the University of California, Santa Cruz, and an M.A. in East Asian studies and sociology and a Ph.D. in sociology from Harvard University.

MARY L. de LEON SIANTZ is professor in the Department of Family and Child Nursing at the University of Washington School of Nursing. She has also been on the faculties of Indiana University, Georgetown University, the University of Michigan, and the University of California, Los Angeles. Her research has focused on factors that influence the successful outcomes of migrant pre-school children. She is a fellow of the American Academy of Nursing, a member of the National Advisory Council on Nursing Research, and the National Institute of Nursing Research and a founding and executive board member of the National Association of Hispanic Nurses. She is the author or coauthor of numerous publications in the field of the mental health and development of Hispanic children and their families. She has a B.S. in nursing from Mount Saint Mary's College, Los Angeles, an M.N. in child psychiatric nursing from the University of California, Los Angeles, and a Ph.D. in human development from the University of Maryland.

DAVID R. SMITH is president of the Texas Tech Health Sciences Center. Previously he was commissioner of the Texas Department of Health, professor in pediatrics at the School of Medicine at Texas Tech, medical director of the Brownsville Community Health Center, and deputy director of the Division of Special Populations and Program Development of the U.S. Department of Health and Human Services. He is a board-certified pediatrician who currently serves on the U.S. Department of Health and Human Services' National Vaccine Advisory Committee and on the U.S. Environmental Protection Agency's Good Neighbor Environmental Board. He has written more than 100 academic articles, chapters, and opinion pieces. He has an A.B. from Cornell University and an M.D. from the University of Cincinnati.

ALEX STEPICK is director of the Immigration and Ethnicity Institute and professor of anthropology and sociology at Florida International University. Previously he was a visiting scholar at the Russell Sage Foundation in New York and a visiting Fulbright professor in Oaxaca, Mexico. His coauthored book, *City on the Edge*, on how immigration has changed Miami, won the Robert Park award for the best book in urban sociology and the Anthony Leeds Award for the best book in urban anthropology. His most recent book is *Pride Against Prejudice: Haitians in the United States.* He received the Margaret Mead award from the American Anthropological Association and the Society for Applied Anthropology for his work with Haitian refugees. He has a Ph.D. in social sciences from the University of California, Irvine.

SYLVIA FERNANDEZ VILLARREAL is clinical professor of pediatrics at the University of California, San Francisco, pediatric inpatient director and director of the Kempe Clinic for teen mothers, high-risk children, and their families, and chief of staff at San Francisco General Hospital. Previously, she was assistant professor of pediatrics at the University of Colorado, Denver. Her current research focuses on Hispanic and African American teenage pregnancy, work on substance abused infants and children, and post-traumatic stress disorder in teenage pregnancy. She has a B.A. in biology and theology from St. Mary's University and an M.D. from the Stanford University School of Medicine.

Index

F

research recommendations, 165,
172, 177
see also Assimilation;
Discrimination; *specific racial/
ethnic groups and nationalities*
Reading
literacy, 47
test scores, 96, 98, 161
Refugee Act, 120
Refugees, 31, 37
defined, 274
employment, 8, 44
Medicaid eligibility, 10, 114, 118,
144
socioeconomic status, 8, 43-44, 52-
53
Southeast Asian, 9
state government role, 126
Supplemental Security Income,
114, 116, 118
violence and crime, 57-58
welfare, 4, 113(n.3), 114, 116-118,
120-121, 126, 134, 153
*see specific refugee nationalities (e.g.,
Cambodians)*
Religious factors, 33
Eastern European Jews, 123
Research methodology
African Americans, 2, 5, 12, 170,
171, 181
Asians, 1-2, 3, 170, 171
assimilation research, 24
blacks, 20, 26, 28, 38, 44, 181
Children's Bureau, 124
cohort studies, 35-36, 171
cost factors, 166, 178, 179
country of origin, general, 14,
164, 165, 168, 170, 176-181
linguistic/cultural factors, 64, 108
New Immigration Survey, 171-
172
report at hand, *xv-xvi*, 2, 12, 17-
19, 127-128, 136-137, 144
risk-protective factors, 32-33

U.S. born/immigrant
comparisons, 12, 17-18, 36-37
see also Ethnographic research;
Longitudinal studies;
Monitoring systems;
Sampling
Research recommendations, 2-3, 11-
15, 18, 22-23, 34-37, 164-181
Respiratory ailments, 64, 65, 66-67,
70, 107
asthma, 66, 69-70, 79, 80, 107, 138,
159
tuberculosis, 6, 42, 70, 71
Rhode Island, 21, 74
Risk factors, general, 3, 18, 31-34,
40-58, 156, 157-159
adolescents, 6, 35
defined, 32
report methodology, 2, 18
research recommendations, 11,
14, 22, 164-165, 166, 169
tabulated by country of origin
and duration of residence,
212-271
see also Behavioral risk factors;
Protective factors; *specific risk
factors*
Rubella, 68

S

Salvadorans, 8, 43-44, 77, 107
socioeconomic/demographic
status, tables, 212-213, 218-
219, 224, 227, 230-231, 238-
239, 246-247, 255, 260, 264-265
Sampling
country of origin sampling, 11,
14-15, 36, 40, 64, 97, 153, 164,
171-172, 174, 176-180 (passim)
health and welfare reform, 13-14
microdata, 14, 177
research recommendations, 11,
12-14, 15, 171, 174, 177, 179-
180

Other Reports from the Board on Children, Youth, and Families

New Findings on Poverty and Child Health and Nutrition: Summary of a Research Briefing (1998)

Educating Language-Minority Students (1998)

Violence in Families: Assessing Prevention and Treatment Programs (1998)

Welfare, the Family, and Reproductive Behavior: Report of a Meeting (with the NRC Committee on Population) (1998)

Improving Schooling for Language-Minority Students: A Research Agenda (1997)

New Findings on Welfare and Children's Development: Summary of a Research Briefing (1997)

Youth Development and Neighborhood Influences: Challenges and Opportunities: Summary of a Workshop (1996)

Paying Attention to Children in a Changing Health Care System: Summaries of Workshops (with the Board on Health Promotion and Disease Prevention of the Institute of Medicine) (1996)

Beyond the Blueprint: Directions for Research on Head Start's Families: Report of Three Roundtable Meetings (1996)

Child Care for Low-Income Families: Directions for Research: Summary of a Workshop (1996)

Service Provider Perspectives on Family Violence Interventions: Proceedings of a Workshop (1995)

"Immigrant Children and Their Families: Issues for Research and Policy" in *The Future of Children* (1995)

Integrating Federal Statistics on Children (with the Committee on National Statistics of the National Research Council) (1995)

Child Care for Low-Income Families: Summary of Two Workshops (1995)

New Findings on Children, Families, and Economic Self-Sufficiency: Summary of a Research Briefing (1995)

The Impact of War on Child Health in the Countries of the Former Yugoslavia: A Workshop Summary (with the Institute of Medicine and the Office of International Affairs of the National Research Council) (1995)

Cultural Diversity and Early Education: Report of a Workshop (1994)

Benefits and Systems of Care for Maternal and Child Health: Workshop Highlights (with the Board on Health Promotion and Disease Prevention of the Institute of Medicine) (1994)

Protecting and Improving the Quality of Children Under Health Care Reform: Workshop Highlights (with the Board on Health Promotion and Disease Prevention of the Institute of Medicine) (1994)

America's Fathers and Public Policy: Report of a Workshop (1994)

Violence and the American Family: Report of a Workshop (1994)